contents

WORKING WITH ELECTRICITY
4

BASICS
6 Understanding electricity
7 Working safely
8 Electricity in your home
10 Service panels
12 Grounding basics

CUTTING POWER
15 Cutting power at the panel

TESTING
16 Testing with a noncontact tester

TOOLS & MATERIALS
18

TOOLS
20 Hand tools
21 Power tools
22 Electrical testers

ELECTRICAL BOXES
23 Choosing electrical boxes
25 Installing new work boxes
26 Removing knockouts
27 Fixture boxes

CABLES & WIRES
28 Cable & conduit
30 Clamps
31 Securing cable to framing
32 Stripping NM cable sheathing with a cable ripper
33 Stripping cable with a utility knife
34 Choosing wire
35 Splicing wires

RECEPTACLES & SWITCHES
36

TOOLS & MATERIALS
38 Choosing receptacles & switches
41 Attaching wires to devices
42 Testing for power

WIRING RECEPTACLES
43 Wiring a duplex receptacle
45 Wiring a GFCI receptacle
47 Wiring a split-tab receptacle
48 Making receptacles flush
49 Getting box edges flush

WIRING SWITCHES
50 Wiring switches
50 Wiring a single-pole switch
52 Wiring a switch loop
54 Remodel wiring: Replacing a single-pole switch
56 Wiring a linear slide dimmer
58 Installing a wireless switch
59 Making up a three-way switch box
60 Wiring a three-way switch
61 Wiring a three-way switch loop
62 Wiring a four-way switch

WIRING SPECIALTY SWITCHES
63 Wiring specialty switches
64 Wiring a vacancy sensor
65 Wiring a timer switch

» » » »

LIGHTING
66

BASICS

68 Lighting basics
69 Bulb types and technologies
70 Halogen bulbs
70 Installing halogen bulbs
71 Compact fluorescents (CFLs)
72 LEDs (light-emitting diodes)
74 An LED retrofit: converting an incandescent fixture
75 Mounting light fixtures

WALL SCONCES

77 Removing an existing wall sconce
78 Connecting a new sconce

CHANDELIERS

79 Prepping & mounting a ceiling box
80 Disconnecting a ceiling fixture
81 Installing a chandelier

RECESSED LIGHTING

82 Retrofitting recessed lighting
83 Cutting a ceiling hole for recessed lighting
84 Wiring a recessed fixture
85 Securing the can

UNDERCABINET FLUORESCENTS

86 Undercabinet fluorescent fixtures

LOW-VOLTAGE FIXTURES

88 Low-voltage fixtures
89 Installing low-voltage cable lighting
89 Anchoring low-voltage standoffs
90 Running cable
91 Tensioning cables
92 Locating the canopy
93 Mounting the box & wiring the transformer
95 Installing the canopy
96 Attaching the feed rods & fixtures

MONORAIL TRACK LIGHTING

97 Installing low-voltage monorail track lighting
98 Locating the track & standoffs
99 Mounting & wiring the transformer
101 Hanging the track
103 Installing the light fixtures

REPAIRING LOW-VOLTAGE CONTROLS
104

DOORBELLS

106 Troubleshooting a doorbell
109 Replacing a doorbell switch
110 Installing a chime unit

THERMOSTATS

112 Replacing an old thermostat
113 Installing a programmable thermostat

MULTIMEDIA
114

TOOLS & MATERIALS

116 Multimedia cable & connectors
117 Stripping cable

ADDING PHONE JACKS

118 Extending a phone line
121 Mounting a new jack

DISTRIBUTION PANELS

122 Mounting a media distribution panel
125 Running cables to a media distribution panel
126 Connecting cables at the panel

INSTALLING A MULTIMEDIA OUTLET

127 Locating the multimedia outlet
128 Installing cable connectors
129 Connecting Panduit jacks
130 Installing Leviton jacks
131 Attaching jacks to an outlet plate

Taunton's

SECOND
EDITION

WIRING COMPLETE

EXPERT ADVICE FROM START TO FINISH

The Taunton Press

Text © 2013 by Michael W. Litchfield and Michael McAlister
Photographs © 2013 by The Taunton Press Inc., except as noted.
Illustrations © 2013 by The Taunton Press, Inc.
All rights reserved.

The Taunton Press
Inspiration for hands-on living®

The Taunton Press, Inc.
63 South Main Street, PO Box 5506
Newtown, CT 06470-5506
e-mail: tp@taunton.com

Editor: Christina Glennon
Technical editor: Clifford A. Popejoy
Copy editor: Seth Reichgott
Indexer: Jay Kreider
Jacket/Cover design: Kimberly Adis
Interior design: Kimberly Adis
Layout: Cathy Cassidy
Illustrator: Trevor Johnston
Photographer: Michael Litchfield, except where noted on p. 265

Library of Congress Cataloging-in-Publication Data in progress

ISBN 978-1-60085-846-8

Printed in the United States of America
10 9 8 7 6 5 4 3 2 1

The following manufacturers/names appearing in *Wiring Complete* are trademarks:
Adapt-Touch®, Aldes®, Broan®, COPALUM®, Decora®, Delta®, DeWalt®, DMF
Lighting®, Federal Pacific®, Fein®, Fluke®, GRAFIK Eye®, Greenlee® Nail Eater®,
Grip-Lok®, iPhone®, iPod®, Kevlar®, Kindle®, Kobe®, Leviton®, Lutron® Maestro
Wireless®, Milwaukee®, National Electrical Code®, NFPA 70E®, Nouvelle®, Nutone®,
Panasonic®, Panduit®, Phillips®, Pico®, RadioRA®, Radio Powr Savr™, Romex®,
Roto-Split®, Scandia®, Sivoia®, Snap-Tite®, Speed Square®, Tech Lighting®,
Universal E-Cut®, Wago®, WD-40®, Wire-Nut®, Zinsco®

In the seven years since the first edition of *Wiring Complete* was published, there have been many new product developments, especially in the domain of energy-saving lamps such as compact fluorescents (CFLs) and light-emitting diodes (LEDs); and in the realms of multimedia and whole-house control systems. Many of these systems start as niche products and soon become mainstream.

Gathering information from electricians in the field also unearths new ways of doing things with tried and true materials. Ingenuity springs from a problem to be solved, so it's not surprising that you find it so often in the field.

Dozens of people made this book possible. We are especially indebted to the electricians and builders who got us onto job sites and allowed us to photograph them at work. Thanks to Rafael Maldonado and the crew of Blue Electric in Berkeley, for sharing their craft. Thanks to Daniel Kealey of MRM Electrical, Berkeley. Likewise, Kevin McCarthy of McCarthy Electric. A million thanks to Mike Zelinka and colleagues at Laner Electric in Richmond, California, Mike Schuhriemen at Independent Electric Supply in San Francisco, and many thanks to Lutron Electronics Co., Inc. and their representatives at Associated Lighting Representatives for generously providing us with equipment to photograph.

Hats off to Jamie Carlen and Chris D'Andrea of Jamie Carlen & Co., Berkeley; and Chip Harley, Jesus Beltran, and Gelber Guzman of Holland-Harley. Thanks to architect Gary Earl Parsons of Berkeley and his associate Cecil Lee. And big thanks to James R. Davison III.

Thanks to Roger Robinson of the First Rate Property Inspection of Oakland, California, for letting us cherry-pick his photo archive of code violations.

Thanks to homeowners Catherine Moncrieff and Stuart Brotman, Martha and Dean Rutherford, Jean Revere, Judith and Stanley Lubman, Laurie Case, and Andy Baker.

Finally, high-fives to the Taunton Press family and friends, including Executive Editor Peter Chapman, Christina Glennon, Sharon Zagata, Fernando Pagés Ruiz, and most especially Clifford Popejoy, whose keen attention to details and deep knowledge of electrical wiring made this a much better book.

—Michael Litchfield and Michael McAlister

SPEAKERS

133 Retrofitting a speaker

USB CHARGER/ RECEPTACLE COMBOS

135 Retrofitting a USB charger/receptacle combo

WALL-HUNG TELEVISIONS

137 Installing a wall-hung television

WHOLE-HOUSE SYSTEMS

140 Whole-house control systems
142 Integrating whole-house systems
144 A typical installation
145 Multi-room audio systems
147 Setting up the whole-house system

FANS
148

WIRING TIPS

150 Before you begin

BATHROOM VENT FANS

151 Choosing a bathroom fan
152 Locating a bathroom fan
153 Installing the roof vent
155 Mounting the fan box
156 Retrofitting a bathroom fan
157 Wiring a bathroom fan

RANGE HOODS

159 Mounting & ducting a range hood
160 Wiring the range hood

CEILING FANS

162 Installing the ceiling fan box
164 Mounting the ceiling fan

PLANNING
166

BEFORE YOU BEGIN

168 Inspecting the fuse box or breaker panel
170 Assessing the condition of wiring
171 Is the system adequately sized?

ACCORDING TO CODE

173 General wiring guidelines
174 General-use circuit requirements
175 Requirements room by room

WORKING DRAWINGS

176 Developing a floor plan
178 Electrical notation
180 Wiring schematics

ROUGH-IN WIRING
186

GETTING STARTED

188 Rough-in basics
190 Tools for rough-in
192 Materials for rough-in
194 Laying out the job

OUTLET BOXES

196 Installing new work boxes
197 Installing ceiling boxes

RUNNING CABLE

198 Drilling for cable
199 Pulling cable
200 Feeding cable through corners
201 Fishing cable behind finish walls
202 Fishing cable to a ceiling fixture

RETROFIT WORK

204 Cutting a wall box into plaster
204 Cutting a wall box into drywall
205 Retrofitting a ceiling box
206 Creating a wiring trench
207 Pulling cable to retrofit boxes

>> >> >> >>

APPLIANCES
220

OUTDOOR WIRING
232

PANELS & SUBPANELS
246

MAKING UP BOXES

208 Making up an outlet box

209 Making up a can light

210 Making up a single-gang switch box

211 Making up a multigang switch box

METAL CABLE & CONDUIT

212 Flexible metal cable

213 Installing AC cable

214 Installing MC cable

215 Working with EMT steel conduit (interior)

216 Making bends with metal conduit (interior)

217 Fishing wire through conduit

218 Prepping receptacles for surface metal boxes

219 Wiring outlets

BASICS

222 A quick look at kitchen appliances

223 Preparing an unfinished appliance cord

GARBAGE DISPOSERS

224 Installing a garbage disposer

OVENS

226 Roughing in an oven outlet

227 Wiring a drop-in oven

HOUSEHOLD APPLIANCES

228 Wiring laundry setups

230 Installing baseboard heaters

231 Electric water heaters

BEFORE YOU BEGIN

234 Planning your outdoor system

235 Choosing outdoor lights

236 Tools & materials

OUTDOOR OUTLETS

238 Tapping into an existing outlet

240 Mounting & wiring an exterior outlet

OUTBUILDINGS

241 Running power to an outbuilding

OUTDOOR PATH LIGHTS

243 Installing low-voltage path lights

MOTION-SENSOR LIGHTS

245 Installing a motion-sensor light

UNDERSTANDING PANELS

248 Understanding service panels & subpanels

251 Power to the panel

252 Grounding the system

253 Sizing for the load

253 Organizing a panel box

ADDING A CIRCUIT

257 Adding a circuit

258 Wiring a standard one-pole breaker

259 Testing a new circuit for shorts

260 Installing a two-pole breaker

261 Installing an AFCI breaker

INSTALLING A SUBPANEL

262 Installing a subpanel

GLOSSARY
264

PHOTO CREDITS
265

INDEX
266

INTRODUCTION

Electrical wiring requires attention to detail, patience, and a little dexterity, but it's nothing the average homeowner can't tackle. Before you buckle on that tool belt, however, take a few moments to read the first section, which provides an overview of electrical systems and a handful of essential safety tips. Section Two walks you through the tools you'll need and various techniques you'll use again and again. The remainder of the book takes you through every step of the wiring process—from replacing an old light fixture to wiring an entire house.

Before you buy tools and materials, however, check with local building code authorities. Although most local building codes do not forbid an owners doing his or her own electrical work, most require a rough inspection—that is, before wires are connected to switches, receptacles, and so on—and a final inspection when everything is wired, trimmed, and tested. Besides, building inspectors are usually knowledgeable: They can tell you if local codes conform to the National Electrical Code® (NEC) or, if not, how they vary. Finally, check with your insurance agent to make sure that doing your own electrical work won't jeopardize your homeowner's insurance coverage.

WORKING WITH ELECTRICITY

BEFORE WORKING WITH ELECTRICITY, you should have a basic understanding of how it works. This chapter is designed to give you a quick overview of the electrical system in your home, including the major components. Since grounding is essential to keeping you safe, we cover that in detail. We'll also show you how to do a basic inspection of your home for wiring problems.

Respecting the power of electricity is essential to working safely. Always follow the instructions carefully, use appropriate safety equipment, and when in doubt consult a licensed electrician.

Before beginning work, check with local building authorities to make sure local regulations allow you to do your own work and that you are conforming to local code requirements.

BASICS
Understanding electricity, p. 6

Working safely, p. 7

Electricity in your home, p. 8

Service panels, p. 10

Grounding basics, p. 12

CUTTING POWER
Cutting power at the panel, p. 15

TESTING
Testing with a non-contact tester, p. 16

UNDERSTANDING ELECTRICITY

Electricity (flowing electrons called *current*) moves through a wire like water in a pipe. The flow of water is measured in gallons per minute; the flow of electrons is measured in amperes or *amps*. Water pressure is measured in pounds per square inch, and the force behind the electrons in a wire is measured in *volts*. The larger the pipe, the more water that can flow through it; likewise, larger wires allow a greater flow of electricity. A small-diameter pipe will limit the flow of water, compared to a larger pipe; similarly, wiring that is too small will resist the flow of current. If that resistance (measured in *ohms*) is too great, the wires will overheat and may cause a fire.

Think of alternating current (AC) electrical systems as a loop that runs from the generation point (or power source) through a *load* (something that uses electrical power, a lightbulb, for instance) and back to the generation point. In your home, the main loop, which is the service to your home, is split into smaller loops called *circuits*. Typically, a hot wire (usually black or red) carries current from the service panel to one of the various loads, and a neutral wire (typically white or light gray) carries current back to the service panel.

CIRCUIT BASICS

Electricity always flows in a circuit. The hot wire carries the current from the power source to the fixture and the neutral wire returns it to the power source.

Ground wire

Black "hot" wire

White "neutral" wire

Fixture

Key Terms

Watts
A measure of power consumed. In residential systems, watts are virtually the same as volt-amps.

Voltage
The pressure of the electrons in a system. Voltage is measured in volts (v).

Amperes (amps)
The measure of the number of electrons flowing through a system (current).

Current
The flow of electrons in a system. Current is measured in amperes (amps). There are two types of current: DC (direct current) and AC (alternating current). AC power is supplied by utility companies to homes.

Power (volt-amps or VA)
The potential in the system to create motion (motors), heat (heaters), light (fixtures or lamps), etc. Volt-amps = available volts × available amps (VA).

Ohms
The measure of resistance to the flow of electrons (current) in an electrical system. The higher the resistance, the lower the flow of electrons.

WORKING SAFELY

To work safely with electricity, you must respect its power. If you understand its nature and heed the safety warnings in this book—especially shutting off the power and testing with a voltage tester to make sure power is off—you can work on electrical systems safely. The cardinal rule of home-improvement projects, which goes double for electrical work, is this: Know your limitations.

Unless you have previous experience doing electrical work and feel confident about your skills, you should leave certain projects to a pro. Working inside a service panel or even removing its cover can be especially dangerous. In most panels, there is an area around the main breaker that remains hot (energized) even after the breaker is set to the off position. Also, some older panels don't have a main breaker, and it takes experience to understand the layout of a panel.

Never attempt to remove the cover of, or work in, an energized service panel or an energized subpanel. Call a licensed electrician rather than risk harm.

The safety alerts and safe working practices explained in this chapter will go far to protect you, but the best protection is knowledge. I strongly recommend that readers visit the OSHA/NIOSH website on electrical safety (www.cdc.gov/niosh/docs/2009-113) as well.

Always wear appropriate safety gear, including rubber-soled shoes, heavy gloves, safety glasses, and a respirator or dust mask when sawing or drilling overhead. Remember that 120 volts can kill or cause serious shock, so learn and use safe work practices; your life depends on it.

Turn off the power to the circuit at the main service panel before removing receptacle, switch, or fixture covers.

Test to make sure the power is off. Do this before **and** after removing the plate or cover on an electrical device. Never work on an energized circuit.

Wear gloves to protect your hands from the sharp edges of wires, cables, and metal boxes.

Wear safety glasses when sawing or drilling, especially when working overhead.

SAFETY ALERT

Test the tester first and last. No matter what kind of tester you're using, test it first on a circuit that you know is hot to make sure the tester is working properly, and do the same after you've done the testing. Most testers run on batteries, and those batteries could die after your pre-test check and before the voltage test. The post-test check will catch that.

ELECTRICITY IN YOUR HOME

Power from the utility service is commonly delivered through three large wires, or conductors, which may enter the house overhead or underground. Overhead service wires are called a *service drop*. The drop runs to a *weatherhead* atop a length of rigid conduit. When fed underground, service conductors are installed in buried conduit or run as underground service-entrance (USE) cable. Whether it arrives overhead or underground, three-wire service delivers 120 volts to ground and 240 volts between the energized conductors.

Service conductors are attached to a meter base and then to the *service panel*. Straddling the two sets of terminals on its base, the meter measures the wattage of electricity as it is consumed. The service panel also routes power to various circuits throughout the house.

The utility company will install the drop wires to the building and will install the meter. The homeowner is responsible for everything beyond that, including the meter base and breaker panel, which a licensed electrician should install.

Ground-fault circuit interrupter (GFCI) receptacles detect minuscule current leaks and shut off power almost instantaneously. All bathrooms and kitchens must be GFCI protected, as well as outdoor outlets and garage outlets. Local codes may require additional GFCI protection.

Modern three-prong outlets provide a low-impedance path to ground in case a fault occurs.

Some appliances require dedicated circuits. This is a 30-amp 125/250v dryer receptacle; the breaker for this circuit must also be rated for 30 amps.

WIRING INSIDE OUT

Cable for dining room receptacles

Water heater junction box

Bonding jumper

Rigid conduit

GFCI-protected receptacles in kitchen

Home-run cables from main (service) panel to loads (run through attic, ceiling, or basement)

Service panel

Grounding electrode conductor

Grounding electrode

Dedicated circuit for dryer receptacle

Bonding jumper

A typical three-wire service assembly has two insulated hot conductors and a bare neutral. The bare neutral has an internal steel "messenger" to support the assembly.

The meter provides a measure of the electrical power consumed. Positioned outside the house, it allows the power company to monitor consumption.

The service panel distributes power to circuits throughout the house. Breakers interrupt power if the circuits become overloaded. Some service panels only house the main breaker.

SERVICE PANELS

At the service panel, the two hot cables from the meter base attach to lugs or terminals on the main breaker. The incoming neutral cable attaches to the main lug of the neutral/ground bus. In the main panel, neutral/ground buses must be connected together, usually by a wire or metal bar called the *main bonding jumper*. In subpanels and all other locations downstream from the main service panel, ground and neutral components must be electrically isolated from each other.

In a main fuse box, the hot conductors from the meter attach to the main power lugs and the neutral cable to the main neutral lug. Whether the panel has breakers or fuses, metal buses run from the main breaker/main fuse. Running down the middle of the panel, buses distribute power to the various branch circuits either through fuses or through breakers. The neutral/ground buses are long aluminum bars containing many terminal screws, to which ground and neutral wires are attached.

Each fuse or breaker is rated at a specific number of amps (15-amp and 20-amp breakers or fuses take care of most household circuits). When a circuit becomes overloaded or a short circuit occurs, the breaker trips or a fuse strip melts, thereby cutting voltage to the hot wire. All current produces some heat, and as current increases, the heat generated increases. If there were no breakers or fuses, and if too much current continued to flow, the wires would overheat and could start a fire. Amperage ratings of breakers and fuses are matched to the size (cross-sectional area, measured as "gauge") of the circuit wires.

The main breaker

All electricity entering a house goes through the main breaker, which is usually located at the top of a main panel.

INSIDE A SERVICE PANEL

- Incoming ground
- Hot feeder lines (incoming power)
- Incoming neutral
- Main breaker
- Hot bus bar (behind breakers)
- Neutral bus bar
- Ground bus bar
- Individual circuits

Branch circuits

The service panel houses incoming cables from the meter as well as the breakers and wires that distribute electricity to individual circuits. At the service, neutral conductors (white wires), equipment-grounding conductors (bare copper or green insulated wires), the metal service panel, and the grounding electrode system (grounding rods) must be bonded together.

- Hot cables from meter attach to lug terminals
- Incoming ground
- Incoming neutral
- Neutral/ground cable attaches here.
- Main breaker
- Main bonding jumper
- Neutral buses
- Hot wire
- Neutral wire
- Ground wire
- Ground buses
- Hot buses
- Knockouts for circuit cables on all sides of panel
- Grounding electrode conductor

In an emergency, throw the main breaker to "off" to turn off all power to the house. The main breaker is also the primary over-current protection for the electrical system and is rated accordingly. (The rating is stamped on the breaker handle.) If the main breaker for a 200-amp panel senses current that exceeds its load rating, the breaker will automatically trip and shut off all power.

Meter-mains

Increasingly common are meter-mains, which house a meter base and a main breaker in a single box. Meter-mains allow a homeowner to put the main breaker outside the house, where it can be accessed in an emergency—if firefighters need to cut the power to the house before they go inside, for example. When meter-mains are used, electricians often locate a panel with the branch circuit breakers (called a subpanel) in the garage or another centralized location inside that is easy to access, such as a laundry room.

Fuse boxes

Many older homes still have fuse boxes. Fuses are the earliest overcurrent protection devices, and they come as either Edison-type (screw-in) fuses or cartridge (slide-in) fuses. Edison-style fuses are more common. They have little windows that let you see a filament. When the circuit has been overloaded and the fuse is blown, the filament will be separated. A blackened (from heat) interior could mean a short circuit—a potentially dangerous situation calling for the intervention of a licensed electrician. The less common cartridge fuses are used to control 240v circuits and are usually part of the main disconnect switch, or serve heavy-duty circuits for an electric range or a clothes dryer.

A meter-main combo, placed outside the house, provides easy access for service or emergencies.

Labeling breakers is required by code to identify the loads served.

Stay away from the area around the main breaker switch. The terminals above the breaker remain hot even when the main is off, presenting a serious hazard when the cover is off.

An older fuse box.

PLAY IT SAFE

Only a licensed electrician should work in a service panel—or even remove the cover. Even with the main fuse or breaker turned off, some of the parts inside a panel are always *hot* (carrying voltage) and could electrocute you. Don't mess with electric meters, either. Call the utility company to install meters or upgrade their service drop wires.

To work safely on existing circuits, *always* turn off electrical power at the service panel, and use a voltage tester (see the photos on p. 16) at the outlet to verify the power is off.

GROUNDING BASICS

Because electricity moves in a circuit, it will return to its source unless the path is interrupted. The return path is through the white neutral wires that bring current back to the main panel. Ground wires provide the current with an alternative low-resistance path.

Why is having a grounding path important? Before equipment-grounding conductors (popularly called *ground wires*) were widespread, people could be electrocuted when they came in contact with voltage that, due to a fault like a loose wire, unintentionally energized the metal casing of a tool or an electrical appliance. Ground wires bond all electrical devices and potentially current-carrying metal surfaces. This bonding creates a path with such low impedance (resistance)

that *fault currents* flow along it, quickly tripping breakers or fuses and interrupting power. Contrary to popular misconceptions, the human body usually has a relatively high impedance (compared with copper wire); if electricity is offered a path with very low resistance—the equipment grounding conductor—it will take the low-resistance path back to the panel, trip the breaker, and cut off the power.

➡ **See "Avoiding Electrical Shocks," below.**

Ground wires (equipment grounding conductors) connect to every part of the electrical system that could possibly become energized—metal boxes, receptacles, switches, fixtures—and, through three-pronged plugs, the metallic covers and frames of

Inside this service panel, the smaller copper wire (top) and the insulated white wire feed a subpanel in the house; the thicker copper wire runs to a ground rod.

AVOIDING ELECTRICAL SHOCKS

GROUND FAULTS CAN KILL!

Current flowing unintentionally to ground ("earth") is called a *ground fault*. The ground wire is intended to be a low-impedance path to ground, to safely carry the current of a ground fault until the circuit breaker trips. You, however, can also be a path to ground should you come in contact with an energized conductor. In this case, you would become part of the circuit, with current flowing through you. So be careful: Only a little current flowing through your heart can kill you.

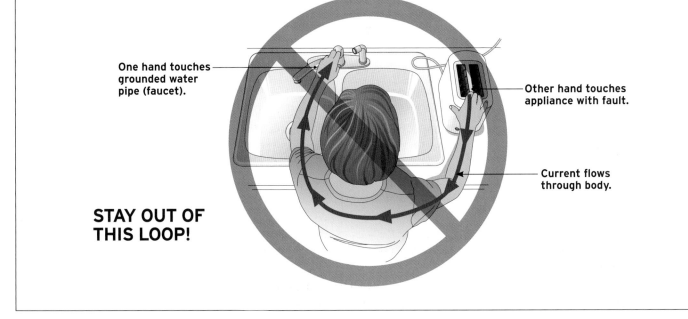

One hand touches grounded water pipe (faucet).

Other hand touches appliance with fault.

Current flows through body.

STAY OUT OF THIS LOOP!

Connections to cold-water pipes and gas lines prevent shocks should the pipes become inadvertently energized.

The main ground wire from the service panel clamps to an 8-ft. rod-grounding electrode (or ground rod) driven into the earth. It diverts outside voltage, such as lightning strikes.

tools and appliances. The conductors, usually bare copper or green insulated wire, create an effective path back to the main service panel in case the equipment becomes energized. That allows fault current to flow, tripping the breaker.

The neutral/ground bus

In the service panel, the ground wires attach to a neutral/ground bus bar, which is bonded to the metal panel housing via a *main bonding jumper*. If there's a ground fault in the house, the main bonding jumper ensures the current can be safely directed to the ground—away from the house and the people inside. It is probably the single most important connection in the entire electrical system.

MAKING SENSE OF GROUNDING

Grounding confuses a lot of people, including some electricians. Part of the problem is that the word *ground* has been used imprecisely for more than a century to describe electrical activity or components. The term *ground wire*, for example, may refer to one of three different things:

- The large, usually bare-copper wire clamped to a ground rod driven into the earth, or to rebar in a concrete footing. Because the rod or the rebar is technically a grounding electrode, this "ground wire" is correctly called a *grounding electrode conductor*.

- Short conductors (wires) that connect two pieces of electrical equipment to eliminate the possibility of a difference in potential (impedance) between them. These short wires should be called "bonding conductors" or "bonding jumpers."

- The bare copper or green insulated wires in all modern circuits, which ultimately connect electrical equipment, such as receptacles and fixtures, to the service panel neutral/ground bar. These connections create a low-impedance fault path back to the service panel. Why? In case the equipment becomes energized by a hot wire touching a metal cover or other part, this conductor allows current to flow safely and trip the breaker. In this book, the term *ground wire* or *grounding conductor* refers to this conductor. These wires are properly called *equipment-grounding conductors*.

Also attached to the neutral/ground bus in the service panel is a large, usually bare, copper ground wire—the grounding electrode conductor (GEC)—that clamps to a grounding electrode, usually either a *ground rod* driven into the earth, or a "Ufer grounding electrode," a 20-ft. length of steel rebar or heavy copper wire in the footing of the foundation. The grounding electrode's primary functions are to divert lightning and other outside high voltages to the earth before they can damage the building's electrical system, and to provide a

GROUNDING BASICS (CONTINUED)

MAJOR GROUNDING ELEMENTS

The equipment-grounding system acts as an expressway for stray current. By bonding conductors or potential conductors, the system provides a low-impedance path for fault currents. In a ground fault, the abnormally high amperage (current flow) that results trips a breaker or blows a fuse, disconnecting power to the circuit.

The NEC requires the interior metal water piping and interior metal gas piping be bonded so that if it becomes energized, the breaker will trip and cut power. An underground metal water pipe may be used as one of the grounding electrodes, and a grounding electrode conductor run from the pipe to the panel within 5 ft. of where the pipe enters the building. This reduces the chance that the grounding path will be interrupted if part of the piping should be replaced with plastic pipe. The other grounding electrode is typically either a Ufer (rebar in a concrete footing) or a driven rod.

ground reference. Although the grounding electrode system (GES) is connected to the equipment grounding system at the service panel, the GES has virtually nothing to do with reducing hazards from problems in the wiring inside the house. That's the role of the equipment grounding conductors.

The National Electrical Code (NEC) requires grounding electrode conductor size to be based on the sizes and types of conductors in the service. Typically, residential GECs are size 6 American wire gauge (6AWG) copper. Ground rods are typically $1/2$-in. or $5/8$-in. copper-clad steel rods at least 8 ft. long. The Ufer or concrete-encased electrode is the preferred grounding electrode and must be used if new concrete footings are poured.

GFCIs

Ground-fault circuit interrupters (GFCIs) are sensitive devices that can detect very small current leaks and shut off power almost instantaneously. The NEC now requires GFCI protection on all bathroom receptacles, receptacles within 6 ft. of a sink other than in kitchens, all receptacles serving kitchen counters, all outdoor receptacles, all unfinished basement receptacles, all garage receptacles, and all receptacles near pools, hot tubs, and the like. Wiring a GFCI receptacle is covered on p. 45.

CUTTING POWER AT THE PANEL

A In a normal breaker box, simply flip the relevant breaker to the off position.

B If you're working on a fuse panel, unscrew and remove the fuse that protects the circuit you're working on.

C If cartridge fuses are used, remove the cartridge or cartridge block.

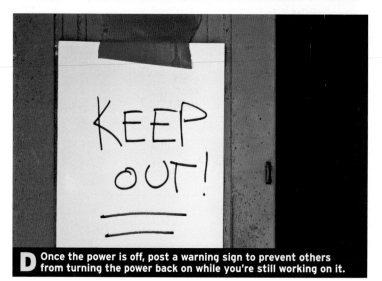

D Once the power is off, post a warning sign to prevent others from turning the power back on while you're still working on it.

Always shut off the power to an outlet before working on it—and then test with an electrical tester to be sure there's no voltage present. In rare instances, a circuit may be mistakenly fed by more than one breaker! Because individual devices such as receptacles, switches, and fixtures can give false readings if they are defective or incorrectly wired, the only safe way to shut off the electricity is by flipping a breaker in the service panel or subpanel.

Turning off the power at a breaker panel is usually straightforward. After identifying the breaker controlling the circuit, push the breaker's handle to the off position **A**. The breaker handle should click into position; if it doesn't, flip it again until you hear a click. (A breaker that won't snap into position may be worn out or defective and should be replaced by an electrician.)

If your home has a fuse panel instead, remove the fuse that controls the circuit **B**. Partially unscrewing a fuse is not a solution because the fuse body is still in contact with the socket and possibly could be jiggled or screwed in enough to reenergize the circuit.

Remove the fuse. Likewise, if circuits are controlled by cartridge fuses, pull the cartridge or cartridge block out of the panel **C**.

Once you've cut off the power, shut the panel cover and tape a sign to it, telling others to stay out **D**. Otherwise, someone not aware of the situation could flip the switch on, or screw the fuse in, energizing the circuit you're working on.

TESTING WITH A NONCONTACT TESTER

A noncontact tester is a popular battery-operated voltage tester that is reliable, inexpensive, and small enough to fit in a shirt pocket. Its plastic tip glows (and it may beep, depending on the model) when it is brought close to or touched to a hot (energized) screw terminal, receptacle slot, wire, or other item. Each time you use a non-contact tester—or any voltage tester—test that it's functioning properly first on a receptacle that you know is hot ❶, and test it afterward as well.

After shutting off power at the panel, insert the tester tip into the narrow (hot) slot of a receptacle ❷. If the tester tip does not glow, there is probably no voltage present. To be sure, insert the tester tip into the receptacle's wide (neutral) slot ❸ and into the grounding slot ❹. This should protect you in case the receptacle was incorrectly wired.

If you need to remove the receptacle—say, to replace it—remove the cover *and test one more time*. Being careful not to touch the sides of the receptacle, unscrew the two mounting screws holding the receptacle to the outlet box. (If the box is metal, avoid touching it, too.) Grasp the mounting straps, and gently pull the receptacle out of the box. First, touch the tip of the tester to the hot (black) wire ❺ and to the brass screw terminal, then touch the tip to the white (neutral) wire ❻ and to the silver screw terminal. Also test the green (grounding) terminal and wire. If the tester tip does not glow, it's safe to handle the receptacle and the wires feeding it.

A noncontact tester will often glow when its tip is merely near a hot wire—that is, it can "read" current through a wire's insulation or through a cover plate. Thus you can sometimes detect electrical current at a switch or fixture without removing the outlet cover.

➜ For more on testing switches and light fixtures, see Chapters 3 and 4.

TRADE SECRET
Using a non-contact tester is more reliable and far safer than using a two-prong neon tester: It's possible to get shocked by touching the bare probes of neon testers. Whatever voltage tester you use, always hold it by its insulated shaft.

1 Always test the voltage tester first, on an outlet that you know to be hot.

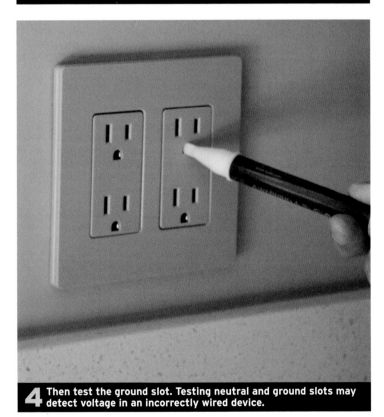

4 Then test the ground slot. Testing neutral and ground slots may detect voltage in an incorrectly wired device.

2 Turn off power to the circuit. To make sure power is off, test the hot slot first.

3 Next test the neutral slot.

5 Remove the cover and mounting screws. Without touching the sides of the receptacle, test all conductors with a voltage tester.

6 Then test the neutral conductor. If the tester tip does not glow after touching all conductors, it is safe to handle the device.

TOOLS & MATERIALS

YOU DON'T NEED A LOT OF EXPENSIVE tools to wire a house successfully. And there's little uniformity among the tools electricians prefer. Some pros carry a dozen different pliers and wire strippers in their tool belts, whereas others streamline their movements and save time by using the fewest tools possible. This chapter introduces the basic tools and materials you'll need and a few of the basic techniques you will perform repeatedly. All materials must be UL- or NRTL-listed, which indicates that they meet the safety standards of the electrical industry.

The first test of any tool is to fit your hand comfortably; the second, that it feels solid and well made. Better tools tend to be a bit heftier and cost more.

TOOLS
Hand tools, p. 20
Power tools, p. 21
Electrical testers, p. 22

ELECTRICAL BOXES
Choosing electrical boxes, p. 23
Installing new work boxes, p. 25
Removing knockouts, p. 26
Fixture boxes, p. 27

CABLES & WIRES
Cable & conduit, p. 28
Clamps, p. 30
Securing cable to framing, p. 31
Stripping NM cable sheathing
with a cable ripper, p. 32
Stripping cable with a utility knife, p. 33
Choosing wire, p. 34
Splicing wires, p. 35

Fish tape

Lineman's pliers

Cordless screwdriver

Screwdriver set

Utility knife

Plug-in circuit analyzer

Needle-nose pliers

Diagonal cutters

Combination wire stripper/crimper

Cable ripper

Wire stripper/cutter

Noncontact tester

HAND TOOLS

Phillips-head screwdriver

Drywall saw

Torpedo level

Retractable tape measure

Hammer

7-in-1 tool (useful to free device plates encased in paint)

A tool belt is especially helpful for wiring work. Assign each tool a specific place in the belt and you can easily retrieve it without searching.

A combination stripping tool **not only cuts and strips wire but also crimps connectors, cuts small machine screws, and more.**

All hand tools should have cushioned handles and fit your hand comfortably. Manufacturers now make tools in various sizes, so choose the ones that are right for you. Don't scrimp on quality.

Pliers and strippers

Lineman's pliers are the workhorse of an electrician's toolbox. They can cut wire, hold wires fast as you splice them, and twist out box knockouts. *Needle-nose* (long-nose) pliers can grasp and pull wire in tight spaces. These pliers can loop wire to fit around receptacle and switch screws. A large pair can also loosen and remove knockouts in metal outlet boxes. *Diagonal-cutting* and *end-cutting* pliers can cut wires close in tight spaces; *end cutters* (sometimes called nippers) also pull out staples easily. A multipurpose or *combination stripping tool* is used to strip individual wires of insulation, cut wire, crimp connections, and quickly loop wire around screw terminals.

A *cable ripper* (see p. 32) strips the plastic sheathing from Romex® cable without harming the insulation on the individual wires inside. Many pros use a utility knife to strip sheathing, but that takes practice and a light touch to avoid nicking the insulation of individual wires. To strip armored cable, use a Roto-Split® cable stripper (p. 212); it's vastly superior to the old method of using a hacksaw and diagonal cutters.

Other useful tools

No two electrician's tool belts look the same, but most contain a tape measure, flashlight, small level, hammer, Speed Square®, and a large felt-tipped marker. In the course of a wiring job, you may need several sizes of slot-head and Phillips-head screwdrivers or nut drivers. *Jab saws* (drywall saws) are also mighty handy in remodel wiring.

If you're wiring a whole house, rent a *wire reel* (p. 190), a rotating dispenser that enables you to pull cable easily to distant points. Reels hold 250 ft. of cable.

Adequate lighting is essential to both job safety and accuracy. If a site is too dark to see what color wires you're working with, your chances of making a wrong connection increase. LED headlamps are fantastic tools.

Sturdy stepladders are a must. In the electrical industry, only fiberglass stepladders are Occupational Safety and Health Administration (OSHA)-compliant because they're nonconductive. Wood ladders are usually nonconductive when dry, but if they get rained on, wood ladders can conduct electricity.

POWER TOOLS

Buy power tools that are appropriate to your strength and to the task at hand. More powerful tools tend to be heavier and harder to manage; and for wiring, they're often overkill. If possible, test-drive a friend's power tool before buying your own.

Drills

A 1/2-in. right-angle drill allows you to fit the drill head between studs or joists and drill perpendicular to the face of the lumber. The pros use drills with 1/2-in. chucks, such as the Milwaukee® Hole-Hawg, the DeWalt® stud and joist drill, and so on. They're very versatile tools. It's not necessary to get a drill with a clutch; such tools tend to be very heavy and expensive—overkill even for wiring a house. A right-angle, D-handle drill and a sharp bit are more than adequate.

➜ To see a right-angle drill in action, see p. 187.

Drill bits

Spade bits cut quickly but tend to snap in harder wood. For this reason, most pros prefer auger bits. Self-feeding chipper bits drill doggedly through hard, old wood but won't last long if they hit nails. A 7/8-in. Greenlee® Nail Eater® bit is a wise buy if your old lumber is nail infested; many companies offer similar nail-eater bits.

Reciprocating saw

A reciprocating saw with a demolition saw-blade (see p. 206) is indispensable for most remodeling jobs because it can handle the occasional nail without destroying the blade. You can use a recip saw to cut openings in plaster, but an oscillating tool with a Universal E-Cut® blade will cut plaster in a more controlled manner.

Oscillating multi-tools

Oscillating multi-tools, cordless or corded, are unequalled for cutting materials in place. Often called Fein® tools because that company has dominated the niche for decades, multi-tools have blades that vibrate rather than spin.

Thanks to precise (3.2 degrees) oscillations per minute (OPM), they can make fine-kerf, controlled cuts where it would be hard or impossible for most cutting tools to fit.

Multi-tools are so good for creating box openings in finish surfaces that they have largely supplanted *rotary cutters*, long a favorite of drywallers. Typically, drywallers installed panels over installed outlet boxes, then used a rotary cutter to trim around the outside of a box. But it took a seasoned hand, because rotary cutter bits tend to jump around and so can nick wire insulation. Oscillating multi-tools, in comparison, are easier to control.

Cordless power tools

Cordless drills and saws enable you to keep working when the power is off or not yet connected. They don't need an extension cord and so are much more convenient in places with limited access.

Gone fishin'

Spring-steel fish tapes or fiberglass fish rods are used to run cable behind finish surfaces. A fish tape is invoked in almost every old wiring how-to book on the market. Today's pros, however, swear by a *pulling grip*, also called a *swivel kellum grip* (see p. 202).

In many cases, however, it's simplest to use a *flex bit* (flexible bit) to drill through the framing. When the bit emerges, a helper can attach the new cable to a small "fish hole" near the bit's point. Then, using a swivel kellum to keep the new cable from getting twisted, put the drill in reverse and pull the bit (and cable) back through the holes it drilled. No fish tape required.

A 48-in. drill extension will increase the effective drilling length of a flex bit. Use an insulated steering guide to keep the flex bit from bowing excessively.

Auger bit

Spade bit

1/2-in. right-angle drill

Reciprocating saw

Oscillating multi-tool

ELECTRICAL TESTERS

Testing to see if a circuit or device is energized is crucial to safety and correct wiring. Remember: Always test a tester first to be sure it's working correctly. The first three items below are voltage testers, and some perform multiple functions.

Noncontact testers

Noncontact testers provide a reading without directly touching a conductor. They often allow you to detect voltage without having to remove cover plates and expose receptacles or switches. Touch the tool's tip to an outlet, a fixture screw, or an electrical cord. If the tip glows red, it means there's voltage present. Noncontact testers rely on battery power.

Plug-in circuit analyzers

Plug-in circuit analyzers or polarity testers can be used only with three-hole receptacles, but they quickly tell you if a circuit is correctly grounded and, if not, what the problem is. Different light combinations on the tester indicate various wiring problems, such as no ground and hot and neutral reversed. They're quite handy for quick home inspections.

Solenoid voltage testers

Solenoid voltage testers (often called *wiggies*) test polarity as well as AC voltage, and DC voltage from 100v to 600v. Most models vibrate and light a bulb when current is present. Solenoid testers don't use batteries, so readings can't be compromised by low battery power. However, because of their low impedance, solenoid testers will trip GFCIs.

In addition to voltage testers, get a *continuity tester* to test wire runs and connectors for short circuits or other wiring flaws prior to energizing the circuit.

Multimeters

Multimeters offer precise readings in multiple scales (in both AC and DC), which you select beforehand. Expensive and extremely sensitive, multimeters can detect minuscule amounts of voltage but, in truth, they offer more functionality than most do-it-yourselfers need.

Neon voltage testers

Neon testers are inexpensive and widely available, but limited in function. A neon voltage tester is better than nothing at all, but you'll rarely see one on a pro's tool belt. If you use one, take care not to touch its bare metal probes—you could get shocked.

Digital multimeters provide precise readings in multiple scales.

Popular electrical testers. Clockwise from left: Fluke® T-5 600 voltage and current tester; plug-in circuit analyzer; noncontact tester.

Solenoid voltage testers don't require batteries to give a reading.

CHOOSING ELECTRICAL BOXES

There is a huge selection of electrical boxes, varying by size, shape, mounting device, and composition. One of the first distinctions to note is that of *new work boxes* and *remodel* or *cut-in boxes*. New work boxes are designed to be attached to exposed framing, as is often the case in new construction and sometimes in renovations where walls and ceilings are gutted. Cut-in boxes are designed for attachment to existing finish surfaces—which frequently involves cutting into plaster or drywall.

But of all the variables to consider when choosing boxes, size (capacity) usually trumps the others. Correctly sized boxes are required by code and make your job easier because you don't have to struggle to fit wires and devices into a space that's too small.

Box capacity

The most common shape is a *single-gang box*. A single-gang box 3½ in. deep has a capacity of roughly 22½ cu. in.; enough space for a single *device* (receptacle or switch), three 12-2 w/grd cables, and two wire connectors. *Double-gang boxes* hold two devices; *triple-gang boxes* hold three devices. Remember: Everything that takes up space in a box must fit without cramping—devices, cable wires, wire connectors, and cable clamps—so follow NEC recommendations for the maximum number of conductors per box.

You can get the capacity you need in a number of ways. Some pros install shallow *4-squares* (4 in. by 4 in. by 1½ in. deep) throughout a system because such boxes are versatile and roomy. If a location requires a single device, pros simply add a *mud-ring* cover. Because of their shallow depth, these boxes can also be installed back to back within a standard 2×4 wall. This allows you to keep even back-to-back switch boxes at the same height from one room to the next. Shallow *pancake boxes* (4 in. in diameter by ½ in. deep) are commonly used to flush-mount light fixtures.

Where you're installing GFCI receptacles or need more room for connectors and devices, use a 4S deep box. Finally, cover 4-square boxes with a mud-ring cover.

Metal vs. plastic boxes

Metal boxes are sturdy and are available in more sizes than are plastic boxes. Some metal boxes can be inter-

>> >> >>

Single-gang plastic **Double-gang plastic** **Triple-gang plastic**

Single-gang adjustable with (orange) snap-on data ring **Double-gang adjustable** **Single-gang metal**

Single-gang boxes come in three sizes, 18 cu. in., 20.4 cu. in., and 22.5 cu. in. Bigger is better.

Throw a single- or double-gang mud-plaster ring on a 4-in. box and it's hard to overfill.

BOX-FILL WORKSHEET*

Item	Size (cu. in.)	Number	Total
#14 conductors exiting box	2.00		
#12 conductors exiting box	2.25		
#10 conductors exiting box	2.50		
#8 conductors exiting box	3.00		
#6 conductors exiting box	5.00		
Largest grounding conductor; count only one		1	
Devices; for each device, two times the largest connected conductor size			
Internal clamps; one for all clamps, based on largest wire present		1	
Fixture fittings; one for each type based on largest wire			

* Table based on NEC 2011 and adapted with permission from Redwood Kardon and Douglas Hansen, *Code Check: Electrical* (The Taunton Press, 2012).

CHOOSING ELECTRICAL BOXES (CONTINUED)

locked for larger capacity. Also, metal boxes are usually favored for mounting ceiling fixtures because steel is stronger than plastic. If code requires steel conduit, armored cable (BX), or MC cable, you *must* use steel boxes. All metal boxes must be grounded.

For most other residential installations, plastic is king. (Plastic boxes may be polyvinyl chloride [PVC], fiberglass, or thermoset.) Electricians use far more plastic boxes because they are less expensive. Also, because they are nonconductive, they're quicker to install because they don't need to be grounded. However, even if a box doesn't need to be grounded, all electrical devices inside must be grounded by a ground wire that doesn't depend on a device for continuity.

Cut-in boxes

The renovator's mainstay is the *cut-in box (remodel box)* because it mounts directly to finish surfaces. These boxes are indispensable when you want to add a device but don't want to destroy a large section of a ceiling or wall to attach the box to the framing. Most cut-in boxes have metal or plastic flanges that keep them from falling into the wall cavity. Where they vary is with the tabs or mechanisms that hold them snugly to the back side of the wall: screw-adjustable ears, metal-spring ears, swivel ears, or bendable metal tabs also called "battleships" (Grip-Lok® is one brand).

➤ **For information on installing remodel boxes, see p. 204.**

The screw on the side of an adjustable box enables you to raise or lower the face of the box to make it flush to the finish wall.

A remodel box (cut-in box) mounts to a wall surface such as drywall or plaster—rather than mounting to a stud. Typically, "ears" on the box flip out at the turn of a screw, and as they are tightened they draw the box tight to the wall.

SAFETY ALERT

All cut-in boxes, whether plastic or metal, must contain cable clamps inside that fasten cables securely. That is, it's impossible to staple cable to studs and joists when they are covered by finish surfaces, so you need clamps to keep the cables from getting tugged or chafed.

CUT-IN REMODEL BOXES

Single-gang box with Grip-Lok tab, aka Madison strap or cut-in strap (should be used only for switches)

Single-gang box with swivel ears

Goof ring (used when a box is set too deep)

Single-gang box with adjustable ears

Double-gang box with swivel ears

Round box with metal spring ears

INSTALLING NEW WORK BOXES

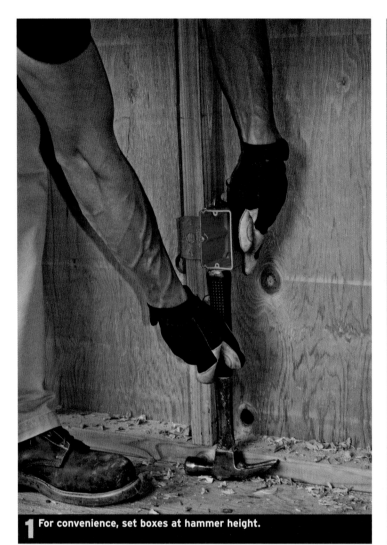

1 For convenience, set boxes at hammer height.

2 Screw an adjustable box to the framing.

In residences, 18-cu.-in. single-gang PVC plastic boxes are by far the most common. They're large enough for a single outlet or a single switch and two cables.

Set each box to the correct height, as summarized on p. 194. Boxes for general-use receptacles are typically set 12 in. above the subfloor—which you can approximate by resting a box atop a hammer held on end **1**. As important, set box depth so that its edge will be flush to the finish surface. If you use adjustable boxes, simply screw them to a stud **2**, then turn the depth-adjusting screw.

Side-nailing boxes typically have scales (gradated depth gauges) on the side. If not, use a scrap of finish material (such as 1/2-in. drywall) as a depth gauge. Metal boxes frequently have brackets that mount the box flush to a stud edge; after the box is wired, add a mud ring (plaster ring) to bring the box flush to the finish surface.

Multiple-gang boxes mount to studs in essentially the same way, although they may require the additional support of blocking or brackets (p. 196).

ACCORDING TO CODE

Before positioning outlet boxes, check to see if local building codes require them to be set at a certain height.

REMOVING KNOCKOUTS

Once you've mounted boxes, you'll need to remove the appropriate number of box knockouts and install cable connectors (clamps). Single-gang, new construction plastic boxes don't need clamps: Simply strike a screwdriver handle with the heel of your hand to drive out the knockout. To remove a metal-box knockout, jab it with the nose of a needle-nose pliers to loosen it **A**, then use the pliers' jaws to twist it free **B**.

Use a screwdriver to remove a plastic-box knockout.

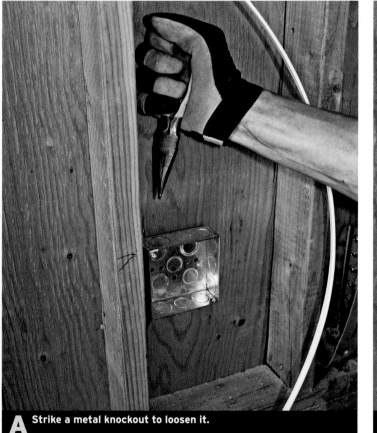

A Strike a metal knockout to loosen it.

B Once the knockout is loose, remove it using pliers.

FIXTURE BOXES

Heavyweight bar for new work where there is access to framing.

Heavyweight, fan-rated remodel bar is passed through an opening in the ceiling and adjusted in place.

Lightweight bars should be used only for a lightweight fixture such as a wall sconce.

The type of mounting bracket, bar, or tab you use depends on whether you're mounting a box to finish surfaces or structural members. When you're attaching a box to an exposed stud or joist, you're engaged in "new work," even if the house is old. New-work boxes are usually side-nailed or face-nailed through a bracket; nail-on boxes have integral nail holders.

The mounting bracket for adjustable boxes is particularly ingenious. Once attached to framing, the box depth can be screw-adjusted until it's flush to the finish surface.

Adjustable bar hangers enable you to mount boxes between joists and studs; typically, hangers adjust from 14 in. to 22 in. Boxes mount to hangers via threaded posts or, more simply, by being screwed to the hangers. Bar hangers vary in thickness and strength, with heavier strap types (rated for ceiling fans) required to support ceiling fans and heavier fixtures.

A mounting bar **is screwed into the ceiling joists.**

CABLE & CONDUIT

NONMETALLIC SHEATHED CABLE

Neutral

Ground

12/3

Black or red (hot)

12/2

Neutral

The number of wires and their gauges are marked on the jacket.

Some old houses still have knob-and-tube wiring, which doesn't necessarily need to be replaced. Have it tested to make sure it's still in good shape.

M ost modern house wiring is plastic-sheathed cable (Romex is one brand), but you may find any—or all—of the wiring types described here in older houses. Inside cables or conduits are individual wires, or conductors, that vary in thickness (gauge) according to the current (amps) they carry. More about that in a bit.

Nonmetallic sheathed cable

Nonmetallic sheathed cable (NM or Romex) is by far the most common type of cable. Covered with a flexible thermoplastic sheathing, Romex is easy to route, cut, and attach. Cable designations printed on the sheathing and the sheathing color indicate the gauge and the number of individual wires inside.

Typically, Romex cable has two insulated wires inside and a ground—which may be insulated or, more often, bare wire. Thus, the Romex used for a standard 15-amp lights-and-outlets circuit will be stamped

14/2 w/grd. For a 20-amp circuit, *12/2 w/grd* is required. Three-way switches are wired with 14/3 or 12/3 cable, which has an additional insulated wire. Again, wire gauge is rated for the current it can carry, so although you can wire 15-amp circuits with 12-gauge wire, you can't use 14-gauge wire anywhere in a 20-amp circuit.

Knob-and-tube

Knob-and-tube wiring is no longer installed, but there's still plenty of it in older houses. If its insulation is intact and not cracked, it may still be serviceable. You may even be able to extend it, but have an electrician do the work.

MC or AC cable

Metal-clad (MC) cable or armored cable (AC) is often specified where wiring is exposed and could be damaged. In AC cable, the metal covering of the cable acts as the ground; in

MC cable, there is a separate insulated green wire that serves as a ground. To strip either type of metal cable, use a Roto-Split cable stripper; it's vastly superior to the old method of using a hacksaw and diagonal cutters.

Conduit

Conduit may be specified to protect exposed wiring indoors or outdoors. It is commonly thin-wall steel (electrical metallic tubing, or EMT), or PVC plastic. Metal conduit serves as its own ground. Apart from service entrances, conduit is seldom used in home wiring. When connected with weathertight fittings, conduit can be installed outdoors—and PVC conduit even underground.

CABLE AND CONDUIT FOR SERVICE PANELS

Type-SER is used between panels and subpanels in dry, protected areas.

Flexible conduit is used in areas that are dry, but need hard-shell protection.

Schedule-40 PVC conduit is for damp crawlspaces or underground.

READING A CABLE

Cables provide a lot of information in the abbreviations stamped into the sheathing. For example, *NM* indicates nonmetallic sheathing, and *UF*, underground feeder which can be buried. The size and number of individual conductors inside a cable are also noted: *12/2 w/grd* or *12-2 W/G*, for example, indicates two insulated 12AWG wires plus a ground wire. Cable stamped *14/3 W/G* has three 14AWG wires plus a ground wire. (The higher the number, the smaller the wire diameter.) The maximum voltage, as in *600V*, may also be indicated.

Individual wires within cable have codes, too. *T* (thermoplastic) wire is intended for dry, indoor use, and *W* means wet; thus *TW* wire can be used in dry and wet locations. *H* stands for heat resistant. *N*, for nylon jacketed, indicates a tough wire that can be drawn through conduit without being damaged.

Finally, make sure the cable is marked *NM-B*. Cable without the final "-B" has an old-style insulation that is not as heat resistant as NM-B cable.

ELECTRICAL CABLE

12-2G NON-METALLIC SHEATHED CABLE TYPE NM-B 600V E1

Type-NM (Romex)

ESSEX 10-2 WITH GROUND TYPE UF-B 600 V SUNLIGHT RE

Type-UF (underground)

Armor clad (AC)

Metal clad (MC).

The silver wire in the AC cable is a bonding wire, not a ground. In the MC cable, the green wire is ground, the white is neutral, and the red and black are hot.

CLAMPS

Romex cable connectors. From bottom to top: plastic push-in connector, two-cable hit-lock connector, ³/₈-in. NM clamp with locknut, metal box with internal clamps. Cable connectors are set in box knockouts to prevent wires from wearing against sharp edges and to protect electrical connections in the box, should a cable get yanked.

Every wiring system—whether nonmetallic, MC, or AC—has clamps (connectors) specific to that system. Clamps solidly secure cable to boxes to protect connections inside the box, so wire splices or connections to devices cannot get yanked apart or compromised. Cable clamps in metal boxes also keep wires from being nicked by burrs created when metal box knockouts are removed (see p. 26).

The exception to this rule is single-gang plastic boxes. If framing is exposed and cable can be stapled within 8 in. of the box, code doesn't require cable clamps in a single-gang plastic box. However, two-gang plastic boxes must have cable clamps—typically, a plastic tension clip that keeps cables from being pulled out. And, as noted earlier, all cut-in boxes must contain cable clamps.

Two-piece locknut connectors **A** are still the most common type of clamp, but professional electricians racing the clock swear by *plastic snap-in* cable connectors **B**, which seat instantly and grip NM cable tightly.

SAFETY ALERT

Cordless drills and screwdrivers reduce the tedium of screwing wires to terminals, attaching devices to boxes, putting on cover plates, and connecting myriad other items. But always tighten cable clamps by hand to avoid overtightening them and damaging the incoming wires.

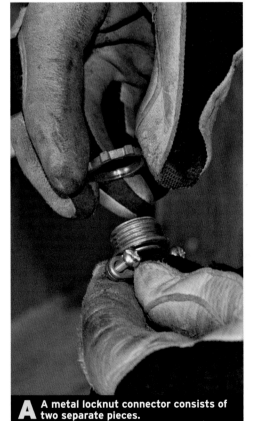

A A metal locknut connector consists of two separate pieces.

B Plastic snap-in connectors snap easily into place to secure cable.

SECURING CABLE TO FRAMING

Drilling and pulling cable between outlets is described on pp. 198-199; here we'll take a quick look at securing it to framing. The quickest way to secure cable is to staple it. The trick is to staple it correctly—staples should be snug but not too tight. Code requires staples at least every 54 in., within 12 in. of boxes, and within 8 in. of single-gang plastic boxes. Use particular care when stapling cable overhead ❶. Avoid making a sharp bend immediately after a staple.

Staple cable along stud centers to prevent nail or screw punctures. It's acceptable to stack two cables under one staple, but use standoffs ❷ to fasten three or more cables traveling along the same path. (Multi-gang boxes ❸ are fed by multiple cables, for example.) Standoffs and ties bundle cables loosely to prevent heat buildup. As you secure cable, install nail plates (p. 199) where needed.

ACCORDING TO CODE

Cables should be fastened to framing at least every 54 in. Cables must also be fastened within 12 in. of a box, or within 8 in. of a single-gang plastic box.

SAFETY ALERT

Cables should not be stacked tightly under single staples—it's called bundling—for a distance of more than 2 ft. Bundling may cause wires to overheat, thus reducing the amperage they can carry safely. Instead, use a cable standoff to hold cables loosely apart in the middle of the stud so they can't get pierced by drywall screws.

1 Staple snugly but not tightly enough to squeeze the sheathing.

2 Nail cable clips within 12 in. of the box the cables will enter.

3 Neatly feed the cable into the clip.

Another style of cable clip. It holds the cable near enough to the box but out of harm's way.

STRIPPING NM CABLE SHEATHING WITH A CABLE RIPPER

Most professional electricians favor utility knives for removing plastic sheathing. But DIYers should use a cable ripper to avoid nicking wire insulation. Because the ripper's tooth is intentionally dull (so it won't nick wire insulation), it usually takes several pulls to slit the sheathing completely ❶. Once that's done, pull back the sheathing and the kraft paper and snip off both, using diagonal cutters ❷.

Because cable clamps grip sheathing—not individual wires—there must be at least ¼ in. of sheathing still peeking out from under cable clamps when you're done. If you leave more than ½ in., you make working with the wires more difficult.

If there is only one cable entering a box, just cut the individual wires to length—typically, 8 in. If the box is metal, first bond the cable's ground wire to the box, using a grounding clip or a green grounding screw ❸. Once the wires are stripped and the box is grounded, fold the rest of the wires back into the box until you're ready to wire devices ❹ during the trim-out phase.

1 Pull a cable ripper along the length of the last few inches of cable.

2 Snip both the sheathing and the paper.

3 Attach the ground wire to the metal box.

4 Tuck wires into the box until you're ready to wire the device.

STRIPPING CABLE WITH A UTILITY KNIFE

1 Lightly score the front and back of the sheathing. Be careful not to cut into the insulation of individual wires inside.

2 Slide the sheathing off of the cable.

3 Remove the kraft paper covering the ground wires, and you're ready to make connections.

Many electricians use a utility knife to slit and remove NM cable sheathing, but it requires a light touch that takes a lot of practice. Using a cable ripper is a safer method for amateur electricians.

Typically, pros hold the blade at a low angle to the cable and lightly run the blade tip down the middle of the cable and over the bare ground wire inside. Alternatively, you can score the front and back face of the sheathing with diagonal slits **1** and then yank the sheathing and slide it off **2**.

Once the sheathing is off, cut off the kraft paper covering the bare ground wires **3**. You can also use cable strippers for the task; they are easy to use and reasonably priced.

Cable strippers remove the wire's jacket without damaging the conductor insulation.

CHOOSING WIRE

**WIRES
AND WIRE
CONNECTORS**

6-gauge stranded

**60 amps: central
air-conditioners
and furnaces**

10-gauge stranded

**30 amps: ranges and
central air-conditioners**

12 gauge

**20 amps: lights,
20-amp receptacles**

**14-gauge bare
copper ground wire**

14 gauge

**15 amps: lights, average
duty receptacles**

C ircuit components must be matched according to their load ratings. For example, a 20-amp receptacle must be fed by 12AWG cable, which is also rated at 20 amps, and protected by a 20-amp breaker or fuse. Thus, wire comes in several gauges meant for different loads. The higher the gauge number, the smaller the wire. Larger wires can carry greater amperage, just as a larger pipe can carry greater water volume. If you use too small a wire, the resistance (measured in ohms) is too great and the wire can melt, causing a house fire. That's why it's important to use the right gauge wire for the load. Calculating loads and sizing a system is described at length in "Planning" (p. 166).

Wire connectors

Wire connectors, sometimes called by the popular brand name Wire-Nut®, twist onto a group of like-colored wires to splice them together and ensure a solid mechanical connection. The importance of solid connections between spliced wires (or between wires and devices) can't be overstated. If wires work loose, electricity can arc (leap the gaps) between them and cause a house fire. Wire connectors are sized according to the number of wires and/or wire gauge they can accommodate; each size is color coded.

A divided pouch transforms a 5-gal. bucket into a portable hardware store of wire connectors, cable clamps, screws, staples, and other small items.

Twist-on wire connectors are color coded to fit wires of different sizes. Green connectors, used to splice ground wires, have a hole in the cap that facilitates running a bare ground wire to a device or a metal box.

SPLICING WIRES

After removing sheathing from cables, rough-cut individual wires about 8 in. long, group like wires, and, to save time later, splice all wire groups. This step, called "making up a box" (p. 208) is the last step of rough wiring.

Typically, electricians start by splicing the ground wires, which are usually bare copper. (If they're green insulated wires, first strip 3/4 in. of insulation off the ends.) If you use standard wire connectors, trim the ground wires and butt their ends together, along with a 6-in. pigtail, which you'll connect later to the green ground screw of a receptacle.

However, many pros prefer to twist the ground wires together, leave one ground long, and thread it through the hole in the end of a special wire connector ❶. If the box is metal, first bond the ground wire to the box, using a grounding screw or clip.

Splicing hot wire groups and neutral wire groups is essentially the same. Trim wires to the same length ❷. Strip 3/4 in. of insulation off the cable wires ❸, and use lineman's pliers to twist the wires together ❹. Then twist on a wire connector ❺. If a box has more than one circuit in it, all the grounds must be spliced together, but the neutrals of the different circuits must be kept separate.

Once wire groups are spliced, gently accordion-fold the wires back into the box ❻ until you're ready to wire switches and receptacles.

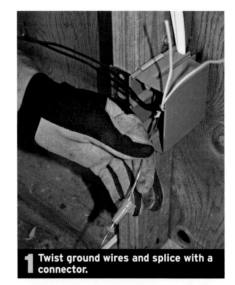

1 Twist ground wires and splice with a connector.

2 Trim hot wires, leaving enough length to work around the device.

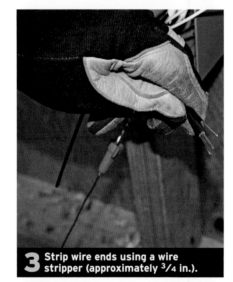

3 Strip wire ends using a wire stripper (approximately 3/4 in.).

4 Twist the wires together with lineman's pliers.

5 Twist on a wire connector until it's tight.

6 Carefully fold the wires into the box.

RECEPTACLES & SWITCHES

RECEPTACLES AND SWITCHES ARE the most-used electrical devices in a house. They're generally reliable and durable, but they are often replaced when they become outdated or cease to work. Replacing them is straightforward and safe if you first shut off the power to the circuits that feed them—and test with a voltage tester to be sure that power is off. *All work in this section must be done with the power off.*

Wiring an electrical device is considered part of finish wiring—also called the *trim-out stage*—when finish walls are in place and painted. At the trim-out, everything should be ready so that the electrician needs only a pair of strippers and a screwdriver or screw gun.

TOOLS & MATERIALS

Choosing receptacles & switches, p. 38

Attaching wires to devices, p. 41

Testing for power, p. 42

WIRING RECEPTACLES

Wiring a duplex receptacle, p. 43

Wiring a GFCI receptacle, p. 45

Wiring a split-tab receptacle, p. 47

Making receptacles flush, p. 48

Getting box edges flush, p. 49

WIRING SWITCHES

Wiring switches, p. 50

Wiring a single-pole switch, p. 50

Wiring a switch loop, p. 52

Remodel wiring: Replacing a single-pole switch, p. 54

Wiring a linear slide dimmer, p. 56

Installing a wireless switch, p. 58

Making up a three-way switch box, p. 59

Wiring a three-way switch, p. 60

Wiring a three-way switch loop, p. 61

Wiring a four-way switch, p. 62

WIRING SPECIALTY SWITCHES

Wiring specialty switches, p. 63

Wiring a vacancy sensor, p. 64

Wiring a timer switch, p. 65

CHOOSING RECEPTACLES & SWITCHES

Receptacles and switches now come in a wide range of quality, functionality, and colors—with matching cover plates.

Better quality receptacles and switches are usually heftier and more reliable. The quality receptacle on the right has a nylon face and its back is reinforced with a brass yoke.

Tamper-resistant (TR) receptacles have internal shutters (the milky plastic visible in the slots) held shut by tension springs. Shutters will not slide open unless both plug prongs are inserted at the same time, and with the necessary pressure.

Receptacles and switches can differ greatly in quality. Over the life of the device, the difference in price is trivial, but the difference in performance can be substantial. For this reason, buy quality. As you can see in the top photo at right, cheap receptacles are pretty much all plastic, their thin metal mounting tabs will distort easily, and they tend to crack if subjected to heavy use.

High-quality receptacles and switches tend to have heavier nylon faces and may have metal support yokes that reinforce the back of the devices.

Another telling detail is how wires are attached—whether they're (1) screwed to terminals on the side of the device, (2) stabbed into holes in the receptacle back (*backstab* or *push-wire* devices) and held by small spring bronze strips, or (3) inserted into the back of the device and held by internal clamps tightened by the side screws (*clamp back-wired*). Screw-terminals or internal clamps tightened by side screws are the best.

➡ For more about attaching wires to devices, see p. 41.

Most general-use household receptacles are rated for 15-amp circuits and can be wired with either 14AWG or 12AWG wire. It's much easier to work with 14-gauge wire, so general illumination circuits (to which general-use receptacles are wired) commonly are wired with 14-gauge cable. The NEC specifies 20-amp circuit protection for small appliance branch circuits, which are required for kitchen countertop receptacles and dining room receptacles and also for other circuits.

Polarized receptacles
Receptacles, plugs, and fixtures are *polarized* so they can fit together only one way. A receptacle's brass screw terminal connects to hot wires and, internally, to the hot (narrow) prong of a polarized plug. The receptacle's silver screw terminal connects to neutral wires and, internally, to the neutral (wide) prong of a polarized plug. Finally, the green ground screw connects to the ground wire and the grounding prong of the plug.

POLARIZED RECEPTACLES

The 20-amp receptacle (at right) has a T-shaped neutral slot so it can receive a special 20-amp plug in addition to standard 15-amp plugs. But 15-amp receptacles cannot receive 20-amp plugs. Both receptacles are also polarized, so that only the large blade of a plug can fit into the large slot of the receptacle.

The only case in which a 20-amp receptacle is required by the code is when there is a single receptacle on a 20-amp circuit. If a standard duplex receptacle is installed on a 20-amp circuit, it may be a 15-amp receptacle. There's no good reason to use a 20-amp receptacle in residential wiring. It is a good idea to use "specification-grade" or higher quality 15-amp receptacles. It used to be that to get a good quality receptacle you had to use a 20-amp version. Not any more. GFCI receptacles come in both 15-amp and 20-amp versions, and a 15-amp GFCI receptacle is the best choice for residential wiring.

The 2011 NEC requires that receptacles (including GFCI receptacles) be *tamper-resistant*, except for those more than 5½ ft. above the floor, those behind a not-easily moved appliance, those that are part of a light fixture, and nongrounding receptacles used for replacements in nongrounding wiring.

You can also buy various specialty 15-amp receptacles, such as weather-resistant (WR) receptacles for damp locations, recessed receptacles that allow plugs to sit flush, and covered floor receptacles. In addition, there are receptacles specifically matched to the plugs of 30-amp, 40-amp, and 50-amp appliances. Your electrical supplier can help you find the right receptacle for your needs.

>> >> >>

ACCORDING TO CODE

The NEC now requires GFCI protection on all bathroom receptacles, receptacles within 6 ft. of a sink other than in kitchens, all receptacles serving kitchen counters, all outdoor receptacles, all unfinished basement receptacles, all garage receptacles, and all receptacles near pools, hot tubs, and the like.

CHOOSING RECEPTACLES & SWITCHES (CONTINUED)

RECEPTACLES FOR DIFFERENT LOADS

Clockwise, from upper left: 30-amp dryer (125/250v), 50-amp range (125/250v), 20-amp duplex, 15-amp duplex, 15-amp tamper-resistant duplex, 15-amp GFCI.

Switches are also increasingly specialized. An exciting new entry to the switch family is the *wireless switch*, a great boon to renovators because wireless switches can be installed without tearing up walls and ceilings. See "Installing a Wireless Switch," on p. 58.

Matching load ratings

Circuit components must be matched according to their ampacity ratings. That is, a 20-amp receptacle must be fed by 12AWG cable, which is also rated at 20 amps, and protected by a 20-amp breaker or fuse. A 15-amp receptacle or switch is typically fed by 14AWG cable, which is rated for 15 amps, and protected by a 15-amp breaker or fuse.

There is no harm in using "oversize" components on a circuit, however, and there may be a positive benefit in some cases: for example, using 12AWG cable on a 15-amp circuit if the length of the cable from the breaker to the load is over 75 ft. and if the expected load is close to the 15-amp rating

of the circuit. In that situation, there would be an unacceptable voltage drop due to the impedance of the wire if 14AWG cable were used. In that situation, using a larger gauge cable (12AWG) is recommended because it will reduce voltage drop.

NM cable manufacturers have voluntarily chosen to color-code the cable sheathing for commonly used gauges to help correctly match wire size to breakers: White sheathing denotes 14-gauge; yellow sheathing, 12-gauge; and orange sheathing, 10-gauge.

ATTACHING WIRES TO DEVICES

There are several mechanisms for attaching wires to devices, which trade off time, ease of installation, and cost.

Screw terminals

The most common and most secure way to attach wires to receptacles or switches is to strip and loop wire ends and tighten them beneath side screw-terminals. This method takes a bit more time and technique, but can be mastered quickly.

Most wire strippers have a small *looping hole* on the tool face. After stripping a wire end, simply insert it into the looping hole and twist your wrist 180 degrees to create a perfect loop, ready to slip onto a screw. Stripping and looping with one tool also saves time. If you bend the loop correctly—so its opening is just large enough to fit onto a screw shaft—you shouldn't need pliers to squeeze the loop smaller.

Three tips: As screws tighten clockwise, insert loops in that direction. Second, exert a slight pull on the wire you're attaching and it will be less likely to slip off as the screw head compresses it. Third, never cross a wire end over itself, which will create a high spot and prevent the screw head from making contact with the whole loop.

Backstab or push-in devices

Backstab devices, also called *spring backwire* devices, have holes in the back into which you insert stripped wire ends, which are grabbed by strips of spring metal. They're quicker to wire than screw terminals, but the internal spring clamps of cheaper backstab devices can weaken, leading to loose wires, flickering lights, and arcing.

Backstab *receptacles* can be problematic: Each time you insert and remove plugs, the receptacles move slightly, which increases the likelihood of clamp failure. Manufacturers have stopped making backstab 20-amp receptacles.

Back-wired *switches*, on the other hand, rarely fail because switches aren't subject to the stresses of inserting and removing plugs. Nonetheless, many pros don't like backstab switches either because their spring clamps can fatigue and loosen.

High-quality hybrids

Quality devices such as the GFCI receptacle shown on p. 45 allow you to loop wires around its screw terminals or insert wires into holes on the back of the device. Here, back-wiring is acceptable because you must tighten screws on either side to engage internal clamps that grip the wire and ensure a solid connection.

Solid connections are the key to reliable wiring, and looped wire ends tightened beneath screw terminals are very solid. Screws tighten clockwise, so orient wire loops in the same direction.

To speed the task of looping wires, insert stripped wire ends into the small hole on the face of the wire stripper. Flip your wrist 180 degrees and—voilà—a perfect loop.

Back-wired switches are acceptable, but side-wired ones are better. Use the stripping gauge on the back of the device to determine how much insulation to strip from the wire end.

After stripping the wire end, insert it into the push-wire slot until the wire bottoms out, then pull gently to make sure that the device's internal clamp has gripped the wire securely.

TESTING FOR POWER

To identify the circuit that serves a particular receptacle, insert tester prongs into the receptacle and have a helper at the service panel flip breakers until the tester light goes out. To identify the circuit that serves a particular switch, turn on the fixture it controls and flip breakers until the light goes out.

If that test is inconclusive or you aren't sure if the receptacle or switch is operable, remove the cover plate and, using a noncontact tester, touch each screw terminal.

Once you've identified and turned off the breaker (or removed the fuse) controlling the switch, lock the breaker panel or fuse box until your repairs are complete.

SAFETY ALERT

In some old houses, the neutral wires—rather than the hot wires—may be attached (incorrectly) to receptacles or switches, in violation of code. So when testing existing receptacles, switches, or fixtures, test *all* wires for voltage.

Before touching an existing receptacle, switch, or fixture, use a noncontact tester to see if power is present.

WIRING A DUPLEX RECEPTACLE

1 Connect the ground wire first.

2 Next connect the neutral-wire pigtail to a silver screw terminal.

3 Finally, tighten the hot-wire pigtail to a brass screw-terminal.

4 Carefully fold wires into the box so the face of the device will be parallel to the wall.

5 Secure the device to the box.

The duplex receptacle is the workhorse of house wiring, because it enables you to plug in a variety of energy users at locations around the house. Receptacles are so indispensable to modern life that code dictates that no space along a wall in a habitable room should be more than 6 ft. from a receptacle and any wall at least 2 ft. wide must have a receptacle.

➡ **For detailed drawings of receptacle wiring, see pp. 180-181.**

Wiring a duplex receptacle in mid-circuit

When a duplex receptacle is in the middle of a circuit, there will be two 12/2 or 14/2 cables entering the box—one from the power source and the other running downstream to the next outlet.

To ensure continuity downstream, all wire groups will have been spliced with wire connectors during the rough-in stage. A pigtail from each splice will need to be connected to a screw terminal on the receptacle. Unless the small tab between screw pairs has been removed, you need attach only one conductor to each side of the receptacle.

Loop and install the ground wire to the receptacle's green grounding screw first **1**. Place the loop clockwise on the screw shaft so that when the screw is tightened down the screw head will grip—rather than dislodge—the wire.

Next, loop and attach a neutral conductor to a silver screw terminal **2**. (Some electricians also tighten down the screw that isn't used as a matter of good practice.) Then flip the receptacle over to access the brass screw terminals on the other side. If a looped wire end is too wide, use needle-nose pliers to close it.

Screw down the brass screw so that it grips the hot wire **3**. Pros frequently use screw guns for this operation, but weekend electricians should tighten the screw by hand to ensure a solid connection.

Push the wired receptacle into the box by hand, keeping the receptacle face parallel to the wall **4**. You can hand-screw the device to the box **5**, but if you take it slow and use

>> >> >>

WIRING A DUPLEX RECEPTACLE (CONTINUED)

a fresh bit, a cordless drill/driver is much easier. Finally, install a cover plate to protect the electrical connections in the box and to prevent someone from inadvertently touching a bare wire end or the end of a screw terminal.

Wiring a duplex receptacle at circuit end

When a receptacle is at the end of a circuit—where only one cable feeds an outlet—there's no need for pigtails. Just attach incoming wires directly to the receptacle as shown in the photo at far right. As with pigtail wiring, connect the ground wire first, then the neutral, then the hot wire.

The preferred way to wire a midcircuit receptacle.

At the end of a circuit, wires from the cable attach directly to the receptacle.

Wiring in an orderly way
Any habit that increases your safety is worth adopting. When connecting wires to devices, most electricians connect the ground wire first, then the neutral wire, and then the hot wire. When disconnecting wires, they reverse the order: Disconnect the hot first, then the neutral, then the ground wire. Because the ground wire offers the lowest impedance path to ground, it makes sense to leave it connected as long as possible. Even if you're working on circuits that are disconnected, as veteran electricians say, "Treat every conductor as if it were live and you'll stay alive."

TWO-SLOT RECEPTACLES (NONGROUNDING)

Receptacles with only two slots are ungrounded. Because they are fed by 2-wire cable without a ground wire, they are inherently less safe than three-slot receptacles fed with a cable that has a ground wire. If existing cables and receptacles are correctly wired and in good condition, most codes allow you to keep using them. Should you add circuits, however, code requires that they be upgraded—that is, wired with grounded cable (12/2 w/grd or 14/2 w/grd) and three-slot receptacles.

Replacing a two-slot receptacle with a GFCI receptacle can be a cost-effective way to add protection to that outlet. There will still not be a ground wire on the circuit, but the GFCI will trip and cut the power if it detects a ground fault.

> For more on wiring GFCI receptacles, see the facing page.

Note: If one slot of a two-slot receptacle is longer, the receptacle will be polarized. That is, a receptacle's brass screw terminal will connect to a hot wire and, internally, to the hot (narrow) prong of a polarized two-prong plug. The receptacle's silver screw terminal connects to neutral wires and, internally, to the neutral (wide) prong of a polarized plug.

> For more about polarity, see p. 38.

Receptacles with two slots (instead of three) are nongrounded types. If the two slots are the same height, the receptacle is also nonpolarized and should be replaced with a polarized nongrounding receptacle.

WIRING A GFCI RECEPTACLE

When wiring a GFCI receptacle, it's important to connect incoming wires (from the power source) to the terminals marked "line" on the back of the receptacle. Attach outgoing wires (to outlets downstream) to terminals marked "load." To distinguish line and load wires during rough-in, write each term on small pieces of the cable sheathing and slip them over the appropriate wires before folding them into the box.

> **See p. 181 for a drawing of GFCI wiring.**

If the GFCI is going to protect users at a single outlet, attach wires to only the "line" set of screw terminals **1** (see p. 46). The yellow tape across one set of screws indicates that they are load terminals. If you are hooking up the device to protect only a single point of use, leave the tape in place and connect wires only to the screw terminals marked "line." After attaching the ground pigtail, screw down the silver screw to secure the neutral pigtail **2** (see p. 46).

Connect the hot pigtail to the brass screw last, then push the device into the box carefully, hand screw it to the box, and install a cover plate.

Feeding the circuit through a GFCI receptacle

If you want to use a single GFCI receptacle to protect downstream outlets, connect the outgoing cable to the "load" terminals of the GFCI receptacle. That is, connect incoming and outgoing cable wires directly to the device, rather than using pigtails. Again, it's important to connect incoming wires to the terminals marked "line" and outgoing wires to terminals marked "load."

>> >> >>

Quality GFCI receptacles can be reliably wired by inserting stripped wire ends into terminal holes in the back where screws tighten pressure plates to hold the wires, or by attaching wires to screw terminals on the side. Note the "LOAD" and "LINE" descriptors; they are important.

WIRING A GFCI RECEPTACLE (CONTINUED)

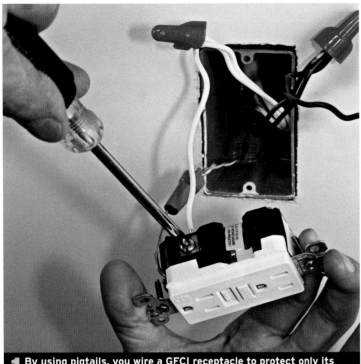

1 By using pigtails, you wire a GFCI receptacle to protect only its outlet and not outlets downstream.

2 A GFCI receptacle wired to protect a single outlet has just three wires attached. Attach hot and neutral wires to LINE terminals.

A GFCI receptacle wired to protect outlets downstream does not use pigtails for hot and neutral wires. Incoming wires from the power source attach to terminals marked "LINE"; outgoing wires attach to terminals marked "LOAD."

⚠ ACCORDING TO CODE

A GFCI will operate properly and provide GFCI protection in a box without an equipment ground. If you install GFCI receptacles on an ungrounded circuit, however, the NEC requires that you label those receptacles as having "no equipment ground."

A GFCI protecting an ungrounded box must be labeled.

WIRING A SPLIT-TAB RECEPTACLE

Standard duplex receptacles have a small metal tab between the brass screw terminals. The tab conducts power to both terminals, even if you connect a hot wire to just one terminal. However, if you break off and remove the tab, you isolate the two terminals and create, in effect, two single receptacles—each of which requires a hot lead wire to supply power.

This technique, known as split-tab wiring, is often used to provide separate circuits from a single outlet, a configuration commonly used when connecting a disposal and a dishwasher. The disposal receptacle is almost always controlled by a switch, which allows you to turn off the disposal at another location. To supply two hot leads to a split-tab receptacle, electricians usually run a 12/3 or 14/3 cable.

To create a split-tab receptacle, use needle-nose pliers to twist off the small metal tab between the brass screws ❶. Next, connect the bare ground wire to the green grounding screw on the device and connect the white neutral wire to a silver screw. If you keep a slight tension on the wires as you tighten each screw, they'll be less likely to slip off ❷.

Flip the receptacle over to expose the brass screws on the other side, and connect a hot lead to each brass screw. If you're running 12/3 or 14/3 cable, one hot wire will typically be red and the other black ❸. Finally, push the receptacle into the box, install the mounting screws, and apply the cover plate ❹.

Although this 15-amp split-tab receptacle is fed with 12/3 cable (rated for 20 amps), there's no danger of the load exceeding the rating of the receptacle.

Because of the configuration of the slots, the receptacle can receive only a 15-amp plug.

1 Twist off the tab to convert a standard duplex receptacle into two single receptacles.

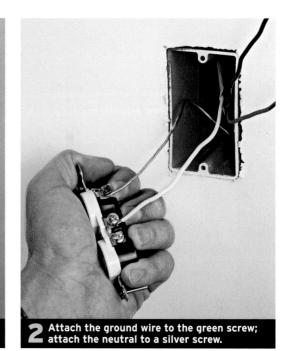

2 Attach the ground wire to the green screw; attach the neutral to a silver screw.

3 Attach the two hot wires last, to the two brass screws.

4 Correctly wired split-tab receptacle. Typically, one wire is controlled by a switch.

MAKING RECEPTACLES FLUSH

Before starting this repair, turn off the power to the outlet and test to be sure it's off.

Outlet boxes installed below finish surfaces are a common problem in older homes. In some cases, box edges were installed flush but remodelers later drywalled over existing walls in bad shape. Code allows a maximum box setback of ¼ in. from noncombustible surfaces. If a box edges are deeper than that, you must add a *goof ring* (box extender) to make box edges flush, as explained in the following section.

If an outlet box is only slightly below the surface, however (¼ in. or less), you should still bring the *device* flush to the drywall to mount it securely. If you're using adjustable boxes in new work, that's not a problem because you can turn a screw to raise the box until it's flush. But a nail-on box below a drywall or a plaster wall calls for a different solution: plastic spacers ❶.

Sometimes called *caterpillars*, plastic spacers build up the level of the receptacle or switch so its mounting tabs are flush to the drywall. These spacers take up the space between the mounting plate on the box and the device. Break off the pieces from the strip; the style shown in the photos fold. Insert the spacer behind the screw tabs, tighten the mounting screws, and the box will be snug ❷.

Avoid the temptation to use the plastic cover to pull a device up to the surface. After a plug is inserted into the receptacle a few times, the receptacle moves and the cover plate cracks, which is both unsightly and unsafe. In time, wire connections to a device can loosen and the resultant arcing may cause a house fire.

1 If nail-on boxes are set too low, use plastic spacers to build up the level of the receptacle or switch so its mounting tab is flush to the drywall.

2 After inserting the spacers between the device's mounting tab and the edge of the box, screw the device solidly to the box.

PRO TIP

If a box is recessed more than ¼ in. from a noncombustible surface, you must use a box extender, also known as a goof ring, to make it flush to the surface.

GETTING BOX EDGES FLUSH

1 If you suspect faulty wiring, check the circuit with a plug-in analyzer.

2 Cut the power, then test to be sure. This noncontact tester shows no voltage.

3 Unscrew and pull out the receptacle, then slide a goof ring over it.

4 Goof rings have integral spacers. Screwed to the box, the ring should raise the device flush.

5 If needed, install additional spacers to raise the device flush to finish surfaces.

If an outlet box is more than ¼ in. below a noncombustible surface, use an add-a-depth ring (aka a goof ring or a box extender) to make box edges flush. Plastic goof rings, being nonconductive, are best.

Before starting this repair, turn off the power to the outlet and test to be sure it's off. If this condition has existed for some time, it's also wise to plug in a circuit analyzer **1** to see if the circuit is correctly wired. Remove the plastic cover plate to expose

the conductors in the box and test again **2**. Once you've again verified that the power is off, unscrew the device and pull it out from the box.

Slide the plastic goof ring over the receptacle and fit both back into the outlet box **3**. As most goof rings have integral spacers **4**, you may not need to use plastic spacers to make the device flush. In the example shown, the cabinet back was not parallel to the wall (and to the outlet box behind it) so the elec-

trician added plastic spacers behind the top mounting tab of the receptacle **5**. When the cover plate was reinstalled, it now sat flush and the receptacle was solidly mounted.

Note: The cabinet back was particleboard, so the goof ring also corrected another code violation: Outlet boxes must be completely flush with combustible surfaces such as wood paneling or wood composites, with no gaps around the box.

WIRING SWITCHES

Before connecting or disconnecting wires to a switch, use a voltage tester to make sure that the power to the switch box is off. Test with the switch both on and off to be sure. And never assume an existing switch is correctly wired: Test all wires.

Switch wiring can be quite complex, especially three-way and four-way switches and switches with electronic components. And the electronic switch arrays shown on p. 64 are just the tip of the iceberg of what's available. So follow the manufacturer's instructions carefully.

Switches (from left): single-pole, three-way, four-way. Modest these switches may be, but even simple switches have a top and bottom, so wire them correctly.

WIRING A SINGLE-POLE SWITCH

The most commonly installed switch, a single-pole, is straightforward to wire. Spliced together during the rough-in stage, the neutral wires stay tucked in the outlet box ❶. Pull ground and hot-wire groups out of the roughed-in box. Use the hole in the handle of your wire strippers or use needle-nose pliers to loop the conductor ends so they can be wrapped around the screw terminals.

First, attach the ground wire to the green grounding screw on the switch. Orient the wire loop in a clockwise direction—the same direction the screw tightens. When the loop faces the other way, it can be dislodged as the screw head is tightened.

Next, connect the hot wires to the switch terminals ❷, again orienting wire loops clockwise. One black wire is hot (power coming in), and the other is the switch leg (power going out to the fixture). With a single-pole switch, however, it doesn't matter which wire you attach to which screw. Generally, pros attach the hot wire last, much as they attach the hot wire on a receptacle last.

Once the ground and hot wires are connected, the switch can be tucked into the box ❸. Always push the device into the box by hand until it's flush to the wall ❹. Don't use screws to draw a device to a box because the device may not lie flat and it's easy to strip the screw holes in a plastic box. Using a cordless drill/driver is a lot faster than using a screwdriver, but use a light trigger finger or the torque clutch on the driver to avoid stripping the screw head or snapping off the screw.

WIRING A SINGLE-POLE SWITCH

This switch controls a fixture at the end of a cable run. See p. 182 for the complete picture.

Ground

To fixture

Neutral

Incoming power

Hot

1 When wiring switches, leave neutral wires tucked in the box. Switches interrupt the current flowing through hot wires only.

2 Attach hot wires to terminals. One wire is hot (from the power source). The other is the switch leg running to the fixture.

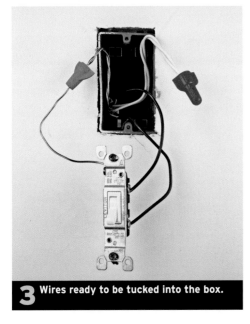

3 Wires ready to be tucked into the box.

4 Straighten switches in the box, and tighten the screws carefully so you don't strip the box's threads. Using a drill-driver will speed the task.

ACCORDING TO CODE

The 2011 NEC requires that there be a neutral wire in every switch box because some electronic timer switches and other energy-saving controls need a neutral to operate. If your switch doesn't need a neutral to operate, cap the neutral and tuck it into the box.

WIRING A SWITCH LOOP

HISTORICAL METHOD

1 In this historical method, tape the white wire black to show it is a hot wire.

2 As is customary, connect the ground wire first.

3 Connect the switch leg (black wire).

4 Connect the hot lead wire to the fixture last.

5 When all connections are tight, tuck in wires and screw the switch to the box.

This section shows two ways of wiring a switch when an outlet or fixture box is closer to the power source than to the switch box—commonly called a *switch loop*. The first way to wire a switch loop, shown in the drawing at right, can probably be found in 90 percent of homes but has been superseded by changes in the electrical code. The second way to wire a switch loop, shown in the drawing on the facing page, conforms to the 2011 NEC and should be used for new installations.

The historical method

Before the code changed it was common to run a single length of 12/2 or 14/2 cable as a switch loop. This means bringing the power down from the fixture to and through the switch and then back up to the fixture. As such, the white wire taped black in the 12/2 or 14/2 switch loop functions as the incoming hot wire, and the black wire acts as a switch leg to return the power to the fixture. Here, the white wire is actually a hot wire and is taped black to identify it as such.

At the outlet or fixture box, splice all the grounds together. Attach the source neutral wire to the fixture neutral wire. Attach the source hot wire to the white wire (taped black) of the switch loop. Last, connect the switch loop black wire to the black fixture wire.

Note: Here, for convenience, we bend the rule of using a white wire only as a neutral wire and instead wind black tape on each end of the white wire to show that—in this case—the white wire is being used as a hot wire.

At the switch, start by stripping and looping the wire ends. Next, tape the white wire with black electrician's tape to indicate that it is serving as a hot wire to the back-fed switch **1**. The NEC dictates that the white wire in back-fed wiring is always the hot lead (power coming in). The black wire, on the other hand, is the switch leg that runs back to the fixture.

First, connect the ground wire to the green ground screw **2** on the back-fed

---

WIRING A "SWITCH LOOP": THE HISTORICAL METHOD

In the "old school" way of wiring a switch loop, a single length of 2-wire cable serves as a switch loop. The white wire in the cable is taped black to show that it is being used as a hot wire. This method was a good solution because it conserved copper and was quick to wire, but it has been superseded by the method shown on the facing page.

A single length of 2-wire cable serves as a switch loop.

Ground

Switch loop

Hot white wire taped black

MODERN METHOD

1 With power off, strip sheathing from the 3-wire cable that runs from fixture box.

2 If the switch does not need a neutral wire, cap it and fold it into box.

3 First attach the ground wire to the switch.

4 Attach the switch leg (red wire), then the hot lead (black).

5 Fold the wired device into the box and secure it with mounting screws. Replace the cover plate.

switch. Next, connect the switch-leg wire (black) **3** (see the facing page), then the hot wire (white taped black) to the switch terminals **4** (see the facing page). To keep looped wire ends snug against the screw shaft as you tighten down the screw, pull gently on wires, as shown. Not fumbling with wire ends saves time.

Finally, tuck the wires into the box **5** (see the facing page), screw the switch to the box, and install the cover plate.

The modern method

This method of wiring a switch loop reflects recent code changes. Specifically, the 2011 NEC requires that there be a neutral in every switch box because some electronic timer switches and other energy-saving controls need a neutral. So if you want to use a switch-loop approach, you must use three-conductor (3-wire) cable. The neutral of the 3-wire cable must be connected to the neutral of the circuit, even if the neutral is not going to be used.

This installation sequence is done with the power off. From the power source at the fixture, run a length of three-wire cable to the switch box. Remove cable sheathing **1** and strip ³⁄₄ in. of insulation from the ends of insulated wires. If the switch doesn't need a neutral wire, cap the neutral wire **2** and fold it into the switch box.

If you are attaching switch wires to screw terminals, loop the wire ends. Connect the ground wire to the green ground screw **3** on the switch. Next, connect the switch-leg wire (red) **4**, then connect the hot lead (black), which runs back to the fixture. Keep looped wire ends snug against the screws as you tighten them down. When all wires are secured, gently fold them into the box **5**, screw the switch to the box, and install the cover plate.

WIRING A "SWITCH LOOP": THE MODERN METHOD

WIRING A "SWITCH LOOP": THE MODERN METHOD

The 2011 NEC requires that there be a neutral in every switch box because some electronic timer switches and other energy-saving controls need a neutral. Thus, if you want to use a switch-loop approach, you must use three-conductor (3-wire) cable, connect the neutral at the power source, and then cap off the neutral in the switch box. Because 3-wire cable has both a black and red conductor, there is no need to re-identify the white conductor as hot, as was done in the old method, because the white wire is a neutral.

Ground

Neutral available for electronic switch

REMODEL WIRING: REPLACING A SINGLE-POLE SWITCH

The old saw in remodeling, "You never know what you'll find till you open the wall," is especially true to remodeled wiring. Be prepared for anything, form a plan based on what's there, and follow the code and common sense as you proceed.

Testing is the essential first in wiring

First test the tester (p. 16). If the switch is working, turn the light on and have a helper at the service panel flip breakers till you find the one controlling the switch's circuit. Turn that breaker off and lock the panel; if it's a fuse box, remove the fuse. If the switch isn't working, remove the cover plate and touch the tester to both wires attached to the switch ❶. Flip the switch toggle to off and on positions. Have your helper at the panel turn off power to the circuit, as above. Continue testing, however.

Being careful not to touch the sides of the switch, unscrew its mounting screws and gently pull it out from the box. Then test again, touching the tester to every wire—white, black, and ground—and to spliced wire groups inside the box. If your noncontact tester indicates no voltage, it's safe to handle the wires.

Disconnect switch wires and note their condition

If the wire insulation is intact (not brittle, cracked, or falling off), the wires are probably safe to attach to the replacement switch. But first scrutinize the inside of the box. In the sequence shown, we found several things that needed attention ❷ before we could wire a replacement switch: (a) the metal box was ungrounded, (b) though wire groups were twisted together and taped with electrical tape, they lacked a solid mechanical connector, (c) the white wire attached to the switch, though being used as a hot lead to the fixture, was not identified as a hot wire, and (d) the box was full of dust and debris.

Cover all connections

All electrical connections not ending at a switch, fixture, or receptacle must be housed inside a covered junction box so they can't be disturbed. All switches, fixtures and receptacles must have a box in which the connections are made. Some kinds of fixtures (like can lights) have an integral junction box. Often, electricians will use an existing fixture box as a junction box in which to splice a cable feeding a new fixture. When there's not enough room in an existing box, use a separate junction box to house the splices.

1 Test for power with the cover plate on, then remove it and test again.

2 When you are sure power is off, unscrew and pull the switch out from the box. Assess its condition.

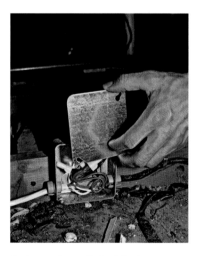

Code requires all electrical connections to be housed in a junction box.

3 If the metal box is ungrounded, screw a ground pigtail to the box.

4 Splice the box-bonding pigtail to the ground-wire group.

5 If a white wire is being used as a hot wire, tape it black.

6 Attach the grounding wire to the new switch's ground screw.

7 Attach the switch leg (black wire), then the hot lead (white wire taped black) that runs to the fixture.

Attend to any code violations

We started by vacuuming the box, which also gave us a better view of its contents. After unwinding tape from each wire group, we looped a bare ground lead wire around a ground screw **3**, screwed it into a threaded hole in the back of the box, and spliced that new lead wire to the ground-wire group, using a special grounding connector **4**. This grounded the metal box. We next secured wire connectors to the other wire groups, using lineman's pliers. Then we taped the white wire **5** that had been attached to the switch to identify that it was a hot wire.

Connect the wires to the new switch

First attach the ground wire to the green ground screw on the switch **6**. If there's no ground wire feeding the box, code doesn't require grounding a switch. Connect the switch-leg wire (black) **7**, then the hot lead (white wire taped black), which runs to the fixture. Once the wires are connected to the replacement switch, fold them into the box, tighten the mounting screws that hold the switch to the box, and replace the cover plate.

WIRING A LINEAR SLIDE DIMMER

Slide dimmers have a slide bar that allows you to set the light level and a separate on-off switch so you can turn the light on and off without changing the light level. You set earlier. Slide dimmers have largely replaced the old rotary type that combined both functions. Newer slide dimmers offer additional functions, so their wiring has become more complicated and many sport wire leads rather than screw terminal connections.

For standard single-pole dimmers, it may matter which wire you attach to dimmer leads, so always read the manufacturer's directions **1**. The slide dimmer shown in the photo can be wired as a single-pole or three-way switch, depending on which wires you connect. It has a bare-wire ground, red and black hot wires, and a yellow wire that is used to wire the dimmer as a three-way device **2**.

If the convertible device will be used as a single-pole dimmer, you won't need the yellow wire. So cap it with a wire connector **3**.

Splice the ground pigtail to the device's bare ground lead. Then splice the switch leg from the box to the red lead on the device. On devices with wire leads, typically a red lead attaches to the switch leg **4**.

Finally, attach the incoming hot wire to the other hot lead (black) on the device **5**. Carefully fold the wires into the box and push the wired dimmer into the box. Screw the device to the box, and install the cover plate.

Slide dimmers. From left: Skylark contour, Lumea, Illumatech, Diva, Maestro IR (infrared) with remote control. All have a slide bar to preset light levels and a separate on-off switch. The bare-metal flanges around the dimmers are heat sinks.

1 Dimmer specifics can differ from one manufacturer to the next. Read the directions before installation. It's critical which circuit wires you attach to dimmer leads.

2 Prepare the stranded dimmer leads by twisting them to compact them. This switch has pretinned wires, so there's nothing to twist.

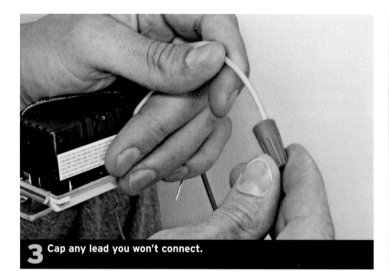

3 Cap any lead you won't connect.

4 Attach the ground wire, then connect the red lead to the switch.

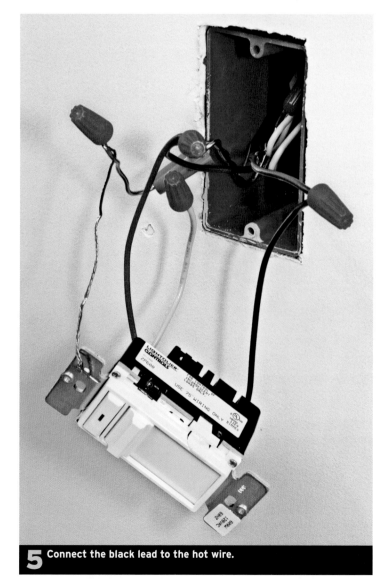

5 Connect the black lead to the hot wire.

Dimmable receptacle with matched plug
Receptacles are usually not controlled by dimmers because reduced voltage could harm appliance motors. If the outlet will be used only by a light fixture, however, you can install a dimmable receptacle which accepts only a matched plug.

Match the dimmer to the load
A dimmer must match the type of fixture it controls, whether incandescent, halogen, fluorescent, or LED. Typically, the dimmer rating is stamped on its face.

INSTALLING A WIRELESS SWITCH

All you need to retrofit wireless switches. *From left*, a wireless controller, a visor clip, a wall-mounting plate for the controller, an electronic master switch.

Turn the power off, remove the cover plate of an existing switch, and test to be sure the power's off.

Electronic switches are expensive, so read installation directions carefully. Here, existing hot and switch-leg wires are attached to the electronic dimmer's terminals. The green switch lead is connected to a bare copper ground.

Tuck in wires, screw the electronic switch to the box, then install the cover plate. After testing the switch, program the wireless controller. The controller will *talk* to the dimmer, telling it to raise or lower the lights—in effect, it is a three-way switch.

Down the hall, a small mounting plate is screwed to or stuck on the wall. The controller slides into the plate. No cutting, drilling, or wire-fishing required! Cover plates will make it look like any other switch.

Traditionally, adding a light fixture that could be controlled from several locations meant retrofitting three-way or four-way switches—and fishing the wires that serve them behind finish walls—which can turn into a nightmare. Fortunately, today's electricians have another, almost effortless option—installing wireless switches.

Installing three-way wireless capability can be as simple as replacing a mechanical switch (a single-pole toggle, for example) with an electronic master switch and locating a wireless controller at some distant point. In the photo sequence at right, we installed a Lutron® Maestro Wireless® dimmer and a companion Pico® Wireless control.

Start by turning off power to the existing (mechanical) switch, and use a voltage tester to be sure it's off. Remove the switch cover plate. To be doubly sure the power is off, apply the voltage tester to the switch's terminals and wires. Unscrew the switch from the outlet box, then pull out the switch and disconnect its wires.

Electronic switches are sensitive (and expensive), so follow the manufacturer's installation instructions exactly. As most do, the Lutron electronic dimmer looks like a standard back-wired switch, with a green grounding lead coming off it. Attach the wires per instructions, screw the device to the box, install the cover plate, turn the

power back on to the switch, and program the Pico Wireless control via buttons on its face.

Mounting the wireless control—say, at the far end of a hall—is as simple as sticking an adhesive-backed mounting plate to a finish surface. If you want a more permanent mounting, use the screws provided (and expansion anchors if the wall is drywall). The wireless control slips into the mounting plate and is in turn covered by a snap-on plate. The controller needs no wires because it has a tiny battery that's typically good

for 10 years. It needs only enough power to "talk" to the master switch.

Even modest wireless devices have a lot of useful functionality. The Pico control also can be clipped to a car visor so that as you approach home, you can turn on the porch light. Inside the house, you can program lights to turn off and on. In a baby's room, for example, you could program a light to dim slowly over a 10-minute period so the baby isn't startled by sudden darkness as he or she drifts off to sleep.

MAKING UP A THREE-WAY SWITCHBOX

1 Score the 12/3 cable along its length.

2 Pull the sheathing free.

3 Twist the ground wires before splicing them.

4 Splice and cap the neutrals.

5 Wrap the switch-leg wires around the travelers.

Three-way switches allow you to operate a light from two locations. They're often used at the top and bottom of a set of stairs or at two entrances to a room. If you get confused about which wire goes where, refer to the wiring schematics on pp. 183–184 or make a drawing of your own.

In new wiring, wires are roughed in when the framing is still exposed. Here, 12/2 and 12/3 cables were fished in to feed a three-way switch that was added after the drywall was up.

> ➡ **For more on fishing cables, see p. 201.**

After stripping sheathing from the 12/2 cable, strip the 12/3 cable. Removing 12/3 sheathing is a little different: Start by lightly scoring the 12/3 cable along its length, up into the box **1**. Then, when you reach the end of the cable, cut through the sheathing. Because you'll soon be stripping the ends of individual wires, cutting through the sheathing end won't compromise wire insulation.

> ➡ **For more on stripping cable, see p. 32–33.**

Starting at the cut-through sheathing at the end of cable, pull the sheathing free of the wires within **2**. The sheathing will separate easily along the scored line. At the cable's upper end in the box, carefully cut free the sheathing.

Twist together the ground wires before splicing them with a wire connector **3**. To use a green wire connector, cut one of the leads shorter than the other so that it sticks out of the hole in the end of the wire connector. Then connect that ground lead to the switch's green ground screw. Next, strip wire insulation from the neutrals, splice them, cap them with a wire connector, and push them into the box **4**. (Neutrals don't connect to standard switches.)

After professional electricians strip cable sheathing, many wrap individual wires in a distinct fashion so any other electrician will know which wires are travelers and which are switch-leg wires. Group and twist traveler wires clockwise, then wrap the switch-leg wire counterclockwise about the travelers. This way there's no need to put tape or labels on the wires to identify them or to pull out all the cables and figure out which wire is what **5**.

WIRING A THREE-WAY SWITCH

To wire a three-way switch, pull the conductors out of the outlet box. Unwrap the switch-leg wire from around the travelers and separate the wires so the travelers are on one side and the switch leg on the other ❶. To strip wire ends, give the strippers a quick twist, use your thumb as a fulcrum to push the wire insulation off, and loop the wire ends ❷.

After attaching the bare ground wire to the green grounding screw on the device, attach the first traveler wire ❸. Loop wires clockwise around the screw shafts, and they'll be less likely to slip off when the screws are tightened. Flip the switch over and connect the second (red) traveler ❹. (Note: It doesn't matter which traveler wire goes where—you'll still be able to turn lights off and on. The only critical connection is the common terminal.)

If you connect traveler wires in the same position on two three-way switches—say, you attach the red traveler to the first terminal, as just described—the lights will be off when switch toggles are both up or both down. This is a fine point and most people needn't agonize about it: The three-way switches will still work as long as you attach traveler wires to traveler terminals.

After attaching the second traveler, connect the hot conductor (switch leg or hot wire) to the common screw terminal, which is color coded black ❺. Push the device into the box by hand, screw the device to the box, and install a cover plate.

Photo ❻ is a frontal view of the switch we just wired; it's typical for a three-way that's located between the power source and the light fixture it controls.

Traveler wires attach to brass screws

Common (COM) terminal

PRO TIP

When replacing a defective or outdated three- or four-way switch, use a felt-tipped marker to note which wires connect to which switch terminal before disconnecting the wires. Of course, turn off power to the switch before you begin.

1 Separate the traveler and switch-leg wires.

4 Connect the second traveler.

WIRING A THREE-WAY SWITCH LOOP

When an outlet or fixture box is closer to the power source than to the switch box, the wiring leg to the switch box is called a *switch loop*. When the switch is a three-way switch, a single 3-wire cable runs to it. In other words, the white wire taped black serves as a hot wire and runs from a splice in the fixture box, and the red and black wires are travelers. The white wire here is not a neutral; thus it is taped black to indicate that it is the hot conductor connected to the common terminal.

➤ For more on wiring switch loops, see the drawings on pp. 52 and 53.

2 Strip the ends of the wires and loop them.

3 Attach the ground, then a traveler.

5 Connect the hot conductor last.

6 Typical connections for a three-way switch.

This is a typical **three-way switch** with existing back-fed wiring.

WIRING A FOUR-WAY SWITCH

Four-way switches have two travelers incoming (from the power source) and two travelers outgoing (to a second four-way switch) and they have a neutral in and a neutral out. Thus there will be two three-wire cables entering the box.

Twist and splice the neutral wires with a wire connector and push them out of the way, into the back of the box. Then strip and loop the ends of the ground wire and the hot conductors and twist them so they turn clockwise around the screw shaft. Next, connect the ground to the four-way switch, as you do for all devices ❶.

On each side of a four-way switch, there is a dark terminal and a brass terminal. The red and black travelers from one cable attach either to the brass terminals or to the black terminals ❷, and the red and black travelers from the second cable attach to the other (like colored) set of terminals ❸. Note how the electrician exerts a slight tension on the wires to keep them from slipping off as he tightens the screw terminals.

When you've got this many wires in a box, it's helpful if you partially accordion-fold the wires before you push them into the box. Screw the switch to the outlet box, then install the cover plate.

1 Connect the ground wire first.

2 Attach the travelers from one cable to the brass or black terminals.

3 Attach the second set of travelers to the other set of terminals.

NEW DEVICES, OLD BOXES

Flexible tubing

Backer plate

Box extension

GFCI receptacle

Steel box

Older shallow-back boxes might need an extension to accommodate a GFCI.

GFCIs, dimmers, and electronic switches are often larger than the older devices they replace and so they may be a tight fit in an old outlet box. Any upgrade must satisfy code requirements about box fill (see the chart on p. 23); there must be enough room so that device conductors do not come in contact with the box.

Some pros wrap electrical tape around the sides of switches or receptacles to prevent contact with steel box sides—not a bad idea—but correctly sizing the device is a better solution. You can buy "slim" versions of GFCIs and other devices, or you can add a wall box extender.

WIRING SPECIALTY SWITCHES

Push-in nuts

Splicing with twist-on wire nuts can be problematic in space-starved boxes or if an old box has very short leads. Wago® Wall-Nuts can ease the task: Strip wire ends about 1/2 in. and then push them into nut ports that hold the wires fast. The clear plastic housing also allows you to see if the wires are connected.

Top left: With the power off, first attach the ground wire to the green ground wire of this electronic switch.

Top right: If the electronic switch requires a neutral wire to operate, connect the neutral next.

Bottom: Attach the two hot wires, as specified in the manufacturer's installation instructions.

It's easy to be intimidated by the sophistication of electronic switches. So here are a few parting tips: **First**, always shut off the power and test to be sure it's off before installing or replacing a switch. **Second**, whatever bells and whistles a switch may have, its primary function is to interrupt the flow of current through hot wires: that's what switches do. **Third**, read manufacturers' instructions and follow them religiously to protect yourself and your equipment; many companies offer extensive support materials online, so use them. **Fourth**, be methodical: No matter how many wire leads a fancy switch may have, connect wires in the same order: ground, neutral (if any), and hot wires.

The switch above is a 3-wire version of the wireless switch shown on p. 58. Employing radio-frequency (RF) signals, it can speak to distant switches that require no hard-wiring. Yet you install the wires of this electronic master switch in the same order as the wires of simpler switches: ground, neutral (if any), switch leg, switch lead.

WIRING A VACANCY SENSOR

Vacancy and occupancy sensors frequently offer additional functions, including dimming, night lights, and multi-location infrared controls.

Vacancy sensors, occupancy sensors, and motion detectors are specialized switches that sense motion, typically by infrared or ultrasonic sensors. Their technology is similar, so each is distinguished more by where and how it's used. *Vacancy sensors* require an individual to turn the light on but will turn the light off automatically when motion is no longer detected. *Occupancy sensors* turn lights on automatically and off after an interval in which they sense no movement. *Motion detectors* turn lights on and off automatically like occupancy sensors, but motion detectors are typically installed outdoors and mounted in a light base. We'll use "vacancy sensor" as our default term.

Because manufacturing details vary widely, it's difficult to generalize about wiring vacancy sensors; the switch's location in the circuit—midcircuit or switch loop—will also dictate the type of cables feeding it and how they're connected to switch leads. Many newer vacancy sensors combine functions (wireless, multi-location control, and dimming or timer functions), so they require neutral wires.

The vacancy sensor shown above also has a dimming function. So its energy-conserving vacancy sensor could make a bathroom code-compliant and its dimmer could create a nice ambience for a soak in the tub. Despite its dual functionality, it does

1 This vacancy sensor also has a dimming function, yet needs no neutral.

2 Connect the ground wire first, then the two hot wires.

not need a neutral wire (it uses a tiny amount of "trickle current" to operate the sensor). Thus it can be easily retrofit to replace a standard single-pole switch. To wire it, cut power to the outlet and test to be sure, connect the ground wire to the switch's ground screw **1**, and then attach the two hot wires to switch screw terminals **2**.

By the way, the sensor is the bowed smaller section on the face of the device.

PRO TIP
When splicing stranded wire leads to solid conductors, place the tip of the stranded wire slightly beyond the solid conductors so that when you twist on the wire connector, its threads will fully engage the stranded wire and ensure a solid splice.

WIRING A TIMER SWITCH

This timer switch allows you to select time in 5-minute increments, as displayed by tiny LEDs along the left side. When the time expires, the switch shuts off the fan or light.

Timer switches do a great job of saving energy, exhausting stale air, and removing excess moisture to forestall mildew and worse. Use it to control a bath fan or light, set it for 10 or 15 minutes, and . . . forget about it. It will shut off automatically. Timer switches are especially useful in out-of-the-way places such as attics, basements, closets, and garages, where a light might remain on a long time unnoticed.

As with other switch types, the more functions a timer switch combines, the more likely it is to be electronic, feature control screens and programming buttons, and require a neutral wire to operate. The countdown timer shown uses little LEDs to show how much time is left before the switch will turn off. Happily, this timer doesn't need a neutral and so is an easy retrofit for a standard single-pole switch.

LIGHTING

BASICS

Lighting basics, p. 68
Bulb types and technologies, p. 69
Halogen bulbs, p. 70
Installing halogen bulbs, p. 70
Compact fluorescents (CFLs), p. 71
LEDs (light-emitting diodes), p. 72
An LED retrofit: Converting an incandescent fixture, p. 74
Mounting light fixtures, p. 75

WALL SCONCES

Removing an existing wall sconce, p. 77
Connecting a new sconce, p. 78

CHANDELIERS

Prepping & mounting a ceiling box, p. 79
Disconnecting a ceiling fixture, p. 80
Installing a chandelier, p. 81

RECESSED LIGHTING

Retrofitting recessed lighting, p. 82
Cutting a ceiling hole for recessed lighting, p. 83
Wiring a recessed fixture, p. 84
Securing the can, p. 85

UNDER-CABINET FLUORES-CENTS

Undercabinet fluorescent fixtures, p. 86

LOW-VOLTAGE FIXTURES

Low-voltage fixtures, p. 88
Installing low-voltage cable lighting, p. 89
Anchoring low-voltage standoffs, p. 89
Running cable, p. 90
Tensioning cables, p. 91
Locating the canopy, p. 92
Mounting the box & wiring the transformer, p. 93
Installing the canopy, p. 95
Attaching the feed rods & fixtures, p. 96

MONORAIL TRACK LIGHTING

Installing low-voltage monorail track lighting, p. 97
Locating the track & standoffs, p. 98
Mounting & wiring the transformer, p. 99
Hanging the track, p. 101
Installing the light fixtures, p. 103

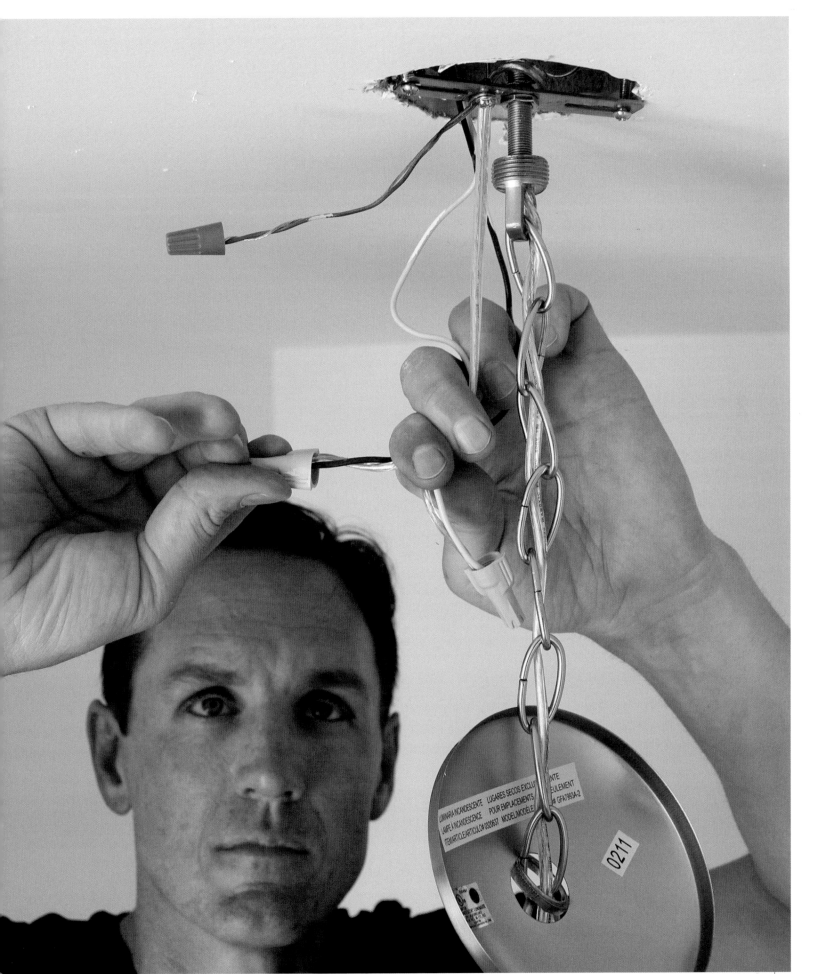

LIGHTING BASICS

The right lighting can transform a room and cut your energy bills big-time. In this chapter, you'll get a crash course in choosing bulbs and systems based on the quality of light you need for task, accent, and ambient lighting; different lighting systems, including halogen, compact fluorescent, and LED—and the advantages of each; mounting options for securing fixtures to walls and ceilings; and a host of how-to sequences that show you how to install (or replace) fixtures such as wall sconces, chandeliers, recessed lighting, undercabinet lighting, and two types of stylish low-voltage lighting systems.

Take heed: Before disconnecting or installing a light fixture, always turn the power off—and test (p. 16) to be sure it's off. Connect fixture wires in this order: ground, neutral, hot. Disconnect them in the reverse order: hot, neutral, and then ground. In this manner, the grounding system stays connected as long as possible to protect you. Remember to ground metal boxes, mounting plates, and fixtures. Good working habits can help keep you safe. As the pros say, "Treat every wire as if it were live and you'll stay alive."

Wiring and Lighting Terms

CFL
Compact fluorescent

IC-Rated
Applied to recessed lighting fixtures whose housing can safely come in contact with insulation (IC = insulation contact) without danger of overheating or causing a fire.

Lamp
For most of us, a light fixture that sits on a table or floor. To an electrician, lamp is the preferred term for a light bulb: A standard incandescent bulb is thus a "type A lamp."

Leads
Wires preattached to a fixture. Leads are spliced to supply wires to energize the fixture. Typically, a fixture has ground, neutral, and hot leads. Fixture leads are often stranded wire.

LED
Light-emitting diode

Light Box
An outlet box that serves a light fixture.

Line Voltage
The standard current in most house circuits: 120v.

Lo Vo or LV
Low voltage. These systems are typically 12v but sometimes 24v.

Lumens
A measure of light on the surface of a bulb; the amount of light produced per watt.

Nipple
Short section of hollow threaded rod.

Primary Wires
In a lo-vo system, wires running from a 120v power source to the transformer.

Secondary Wires
Wires running from a transformer to lo-vo tracks, cables, or fixtures.

Source or Supply Wires
Wires from the power source, typically 120v.

Transformer
An electrical device that reduces line voltage to low voltage. All lo-vo lighting systems require a transformer.

BULB TYPES AND TECHNOLOGIES

T-4 Biax Compact Fluorescent (13W) with GX23 base

T-4 Double Biax Compact Fluorescent (26W) with G24q-3 base

T-4 Triple Biax Compact Fluorescent (32W) with G42q-3 base

T-4 Triple Biax Compact Fluorescent (42W) with G42q-3 base

MR-16 Halogen (50W, 12v) with 2 pin GX5.3 base

A-19 Incandescent (clear) (75W) with Medium E-26 base

G-25 Incandescent (60W) with Medium E-26 base

Flame-tip candelabra (15W) with small base

ED-17 Ceramic Metal Halide (HID)(70W) with Medium E-26 base

T-8 U-line Fluorescent (32W) with Medium bi-pin G13 base

A-21 Incandescent (150W) with Medium E-26 base

T-8 Linear Fluorescent (32W) with Medium bi-pin G13 base

PAR30 Halogen (50W) with Medium NP E-26 base

T-5 Linear Fluorescent (17W) with Miniature bi-pin G5 base

Incandescent lighting has had a good run. The lighting found in most houses today is little changed from the technology Edison invented more than 100 years ago. A bulb screws into a threaded fixture socket and completes the circuit by making contact with the metal shell (neutral) and a *contact tab* (hot) in the bottom of the socket. Typically, that socket is energized with house current (120v), which heats a tungsten filament in the bulb, which gives off heat and light. A *lot more* heat than light, however.

Although they produce a pleasant light that approximates the hue of sunlight (see p. 70), incandescent bulbs guzzle energy. Only 10% of the energy they consume becomes light: the other 90% is wasted as heat. Consequently, as energy costs soared, environmental impacts emerged, energy codes reflected these changes, and the lighting industry invested massively in energy-saving technologies—such as halogen, compact fluorescent, and LED lighting.

Phasing out incandescent lighting will take time, but each new spike in energy prices hastens the end. So it's past time for homeowners to weigh their options by balancing the cost and ease of replacing existing fixtures, the quality of light each technology offers, the availability and variety of fixtures, durability, and, of course, the long-term cost of keeping the lights on. At this writing, the smart money is on LED and CFL lighting. Here's a quick look at the principal alternatives to incandescents.

HALOGEN BULBS

Halogen bulbs also produce light by heating a tungsten filament, but because halogen bulbs contain a different gas, they last longer (2,000 to 6,000 hours), burn hotter, and are roughly 20% more efficient than incandescent bulbs. Halogen lighting can be installed in both standard and low-voltage (lo-vo) systems. But even on reduced current, they burn bright—and hot. Thus they must be installed with requisite clearances—typically 6 in. from combustible materials—and placed where bulbs can't be accidentally touched.

For a time, halogen bulbs were the rising star of lighting. They offered greater efficiency, and standard halogen bulbs (such as "A" lamp shapes) were an easy swap with standard incandescents. Their real niche, however, seems to be in directional type lamps (MR, R, PAR) used as accent lighting in homes, retail environments, and museums. In these shapes you can direct (aim) a lot of light with a good natural daylight color and a decent color rendering index (CRI).

Halogens keep evolving. Halogen Infrared Reflective (HIR) lights have reduced excess heat and are roughly 30% more efficient than incandescents. They'll continue to be used where a focused light source is needed. But compact fluorescent and LED lighting, which are far more efficient, seem likely to dominate residential use in the years ahead.

INSTALLING HALOGEN BULBS

Before inserting any bulb into a fixture socket, check its rating. If the halogen bulb pins don't fit the socket, don't force them—you may have the wrong bulb. Grip the protective plastic wrapping—not the bulb—as you insert the halogen bulb into the socket. As you remove the bulb from its packaging, gently pinch the end of the bulb—a little like squeezing a fast-food packet of ketchup—until its pins stick out through the plastic. Once you've pressed the bulb into the socket, you can easily slide the plastic off.

Lo-vo bulb pins are so tiny that if they become oxidized, carbon can build up in the socket, causing the bulb to flicker or not shine at all. To avoid replacing a socket (which means rewiring the lamp), electricians routinely apply an antioxidant paste to the lo-vo pins before inserting them into a socket.

Touching a halogen bulb with bare fingers shortens the bulb's life. Instead, slit the plastic bag the bulb is shipped in and grip the bag as you insert the bulb.

The quality of light

White light is comprised of many colors; when the proportions of those colors change, so does the quality (hue) of light. Light's hue is assigned a correlated color temperature (CCT) measured in degrees Kelvin (K), which ranges from the 10,000°K of a blue sky to the 1,000°K of a fireplace ember. Humans tend to favor warm whites with the slightly amber hue of sunrise (2,700°K to 3,000°K), which tungsten-filament incandescent bulb-makers have successfully mimicked over the years.

The cooler white (4,100°K) of standard fluorescents is acceptable in workplaces, but it's not something that you'd want to illuminate a romantic dinner or a vanity mirror. Point being, pay attention to the CCT ratings of the halogen, CFL, or LED lamps you choose to replace incandescents. A 2,700°K to 3,000°K range will be most pleasing, and all lamp types now offer this range—but lamp quality varies greatly.

You may also see a CRI rating (color-rendering index), which refers to how "true" various colors look under a light source. CRI ratings range from 0 to 100, with ratings of 80 and above being most desirable.

COMPACT FLUORESCENTS (CFLS)

Fluorescent bulbs have been around for decades and have long been cooler and more energy efficient than incandescents—75% more efficient, on average. Because their flickering bluish light was not flattering to skin tones and their long tubes required ballasts (which hummed), early fluorescents were usually relegated to basement workshops and garages.

That's changed. Compact fluorescents are now available in a range of sizes and shapes and many have onboard electronic ballasts. Screw-in bases are also readily available, allowing CFLs to easily replace bulbs in existing fixtures. (Other CFLs have the familiar bi-pin bases that fit fluorescent-only fixtures.) The big news, though, is that CFLs now produce the warm hues associated with incandescents. Because they give off lots of bright, diffuse light, CFLs are good for ambi-ent and task lighting. They are not a good choice where you need an instantly bright light, because they need a little time to ramp up.

CFLs continue to shine as energy codes specify that a certain percentage of house lighting be high efficacy CFLs. Typically good for 10,000 hours, they last about ten times as long as incandescents. (CFLs cost much more but the payback time is short.) The knock on CFLs is that they contain 4 mg to 5 mg of mercury—very toxic—so you must be careful cleaning up a broken bulb and diligent about recycling them.

PRO TIP

If you want to dim your lights, read CFL and LED bulb specifications carefully. Some types are dimmable, but only with certain dimmers.

LEDS (LIGHT-EMITTING DIODES)

LEDs are specialized semi-conductors (about 1 mm square) whose convex covers focus the light they emit. LEDs have been around for years, but they were colored (red, green, blue) and not practical for general lighting use. In time, LED makers figured out how to produce a warm white light from those colors (phosphorous coating is one way) and how to create bulbs with enough output to satisfy almost any lighting requirement.

Individual LEDs are cool to the touch, but as manufacturers boosted LED output, they also increased heat. Consequently, most white-light LED bulbs have *heat sinks*, aluminum fins near the base, which dissipate excess heat and prolong bulb life. How long an LED bulb lasts depends on many factors—especially the quality of the bulb—but 25,000 to 50,000 hours is fairly common. (Based on average bulb use, that's 20 to 40 *years*.)

LEDs are pricey: A 23W Phillips® LED bulb that is the equivalent of a 100W incandescent costs $40 to $50. A screw-in LED replacement (p. 74) for a recessed light is about $125. Certainly, an LED's longevity will offset its purchase price. But the real story is LEDs' meager power consumption—a fraction of incandescents—and industry experts predict that LEDs will become even more energy efficient. Plus, LED prices will probably plummet as manufacturing efficiencies increase.

Throwing a highly focused beam, LEDs are superb for task and accent lighting. Even more intriguing, they are so small that they can be incorporated into light sources of almost any shape. As the photo on the facing page shows, they are already available as replacement bulbs for many common screw-in and bi-pin lamps. And LED strips are naturals for undercabinet or underdeck-railing applications. Outdoor applications will be big: Solid-state LEDs are impervious to cold, vibration, and, when properly encased, weather.

LED strips contain a series of light-emitting diodes 1 mm square. The upper strip yields white light; the lower strip has red, green, and blue LEDs and can be programmed to produce any color—including white.

LED LAMP TYPES

This array is a small sample of the LED lamps available. The descriptions below list the size and wattage of each, the equivalent wattage (EQ) of the lamp they replace, and why each LED type is a wise choice. (Note: Lamp size is often expressed in parabola size—PAR. Different PAR sizes may fit the same socket.)

1, 2: Par 38 - 20.3W (75W halogen EQ). Used in exterior floodlights, where halogen and incandescent lamps are energy hogs with a short lifespan. Not dimmable.

3, 4: Par 30 - 13W (60W halogen EQ). Typically used in 5-in. and 6-in. incandescent recessed cans, these LED versions can dramatically improve the efficiency of older cans. Screw them in and you are done. Dimmable.

5, 6: A Lamp - 8W (40W incandescent EQ). "A" lamps are the most common and recognizable lamp type in home use. These LED versions have attractive "tulip" heat sinks at the lamp base, so they look good exposed in lamps, chandeliers, etc. Dimmable.

7, 8: A Lamp - 5W (20W incandescent EQ). Can be used anywhere a traditional bulb is used. Not dimmable, but that's offset by the low price ($5.00), the least expensive LED.

9, 10: CB (candelabra) - 4.3W (20W incandescent EQ). Pretty "tulip" version looks great in wall sconces and chandeliers and is dimmable.

11, 12: MR-16 - 3.5W (20W halogen EQ). A great way to reduce cost in 4-in. low-voltage recessed cans. Dimmable. This style has limited options, maxes out at 20W EQ.

13: Par 20 - 5.5 W (40W incandescent EQ).

AN LED RETROFIT: CONVERTING AN INCANDESCENT FIXTURE

Lock the two cast pieces (trim and light source) together, connect the quick-disconnect, and push the whole assembly into the housing till the trim sits flush.

Similar retrofit kits fit either 3-in. or 4-in. cans. Although all come with some means of dissipating excess heat, the model shown, from DMF Lighting®, features an integral heat sink. But the beauty is in the eyes of the beholder: The 650-lumen lamp is dimmable to 5%, and though of comparable brightness to a 50-watt incandescent, it consumes less than 12 watts.

This simple kit can convert an incandescent ceiling fixture into an energy-saving LED fixture. Clockwise from lower right: a screw-in adapter, cast-aluminum trim plate, light source with heat sink.

After turning off the power to the fixture and testing to be sure, remove the trim plate and screw out the incandescent bulb. The recessed can stays put.

Snap the housing and trim plate together, screw in the adaptor, connect the (orange) quick-disconnect connector, and slide the assembly into the recessed can. Final mounting details will vary, but clips or universal mounting screws will hold the assembly to the can.

MOUNTING LIGHT FIXTURES

As shown on p. 27, there are many mounting options for boxes. The main choice is whether you nail or screw the box directly to a stud or ceiling joist or use an extendable mounting bar to which the box is attached. Either method works fine, but a box that slides along a mounting bar means you can more easily position the light fixture just where you want it.

Mounting fixtures to boxes

If mounting screws on all light fixtures were exactly the same diameter and spacing as the screw holes on all boxes, life would be simple and you'd screw the fixture directly to the box. But there are many different box sizes and configurations, and light fixtures vary considerably.

>> >> >>

In this basic setup, the ceiling box mounts to an adjustable bar, which is screwed to ceiling joists. The bracket is attached to the box and the fixture, is screwed to the mounting bracket. All metal boxes and brackets must be grounded to be safe. Many electricians use grounding screws in both the box and the bracket, but one ground is sufficient. The metal mounting screws provide grounding continuity to box and bracket.

If the fixture has a ground wire, it must be attached to either the ground wire in the box or to the grounding screw on the mounting bracket. It's best to leave the ground wire in the box long enough to attach to the ground screw in the box, and extend out the box for attaching to the fixture ground wire.

CEILING FIXTURE ELEMENTS

- Ceiling box
- Supply cable
- Adjustable bar
- Grounding screw
- Bare copper ground wire
- Hot supply wire
- Wire nut
- Neutral supply wire
- Mounting bracket
- Bracket/Mounting screw
- Grounding screw
- Hot fixture lead
- Neutral fixture lead
- Fixture base
- Globe-style bulb

MOUNTING BRACKETS

- 3/8-in. bar
- Pivoting offset bar
- European hanger (sconce hangs on it, rather than being screwed to it)
- Ring plate
- 1/8-in. bar
- 1/2-in. bar
- Trombone bar (sliding, adjustable)
- 1/2-in. offset bar

MOUNTING LIGHT FIXTURES (CONTINUED)

Consequently, there are many mounting brackets to reconcile these differences.

Always examine existing outlet boxes before buying new fixtures and make sure that fixture hardware can be mounted. Otherwise, a routine installation could turn into a long, drawn-out affair with a lot of trips to the hardware store.

Here's an overview of how various fixtures mount to outlet boxes. All metal brackets, boxes, and lamp fixtures must be grounded to be safe. There are special grounding screws (10-32 machine screws, colored green) that ensure a positive connection to metal boxes or plates when installed in a threaded hole. Do not use a wood screw or the like to attach the ground wire to the box; it doesn't provide a good enough connection.

Screwing a mounting bracket with a threaded nipple to a ceiling box.

This wall sconce requires a special flanged ring bracket to mount it.

SAFETY ALERT

Most bar and box assemblies are rated for 50 lb.; if your light fixture weighs more than that, install a fan box instead.

➡ **For more on mounting ceiling boxes, see p. 79.**

An IC-rated incandescent fixture can be covered with insulation.

Flat-mounting brackets

Typically, a mounting bracket is screwed to a fixture box, and the fixture is attached to the bracket, either by machine screws or, as is more common for chandeliers, by a threaded post that screws into a threaded hole in the center of the mounting bracket. Brackets can be as simple as a flat bar with screw slots, but some adjust by sliding, whereas others are offset slightly to provide a little more room for electrical connections—and fingers. Ring brackets can be rotated so the slots line up perfectly with outlet-box and fixture screw holes.

No brackets

Some fixtures, such as the recessed lighting fixture shown on p. 82, don't require a mounting bracket. The fixture has its own junction box; once inserted into a hole cut in the ceiling, the fixture is supported by the ceiling. Integral clips and trim pieces pull the fixture tightly to the plaster or drywall ceiling. Recessed cans can be *IC-rated* (they may be covered with insulation) or may be *non-IC-rated* (cannot be covered with insulation).

Play it safe! Electrical codes require that all fixtures and devices—everything that gets installed—must be "listed" and must be recognized by the authority having jurisdiction (AHJ), usually the local inspector checking your installation. Typically, light fixtures will have an Underwriters Laboratories (UL) listing or an NRTL listing. If an inspector doesn't see a UL or NRTL sticker, he or she could ask you to remove the fixture.

Pay attention to a fixture's wattage rating, usually specified on a sticker on the fixture's base. Substituting a bulb with a higher wattage can overheat and damage the fixture and, in some cases, ignite nearby combustible surfaces.

REMOVING AN EXISTING WALL SCONCE

1 Support the shades as you unscrew their holding screws.

2 Test to make sure the power is off.

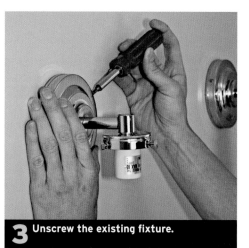

3 Unscrew the existing fixture.

4 Remove the fixture to expose the wires.

5 Disconnect the wires and remove the old bracket.

When removing an existing sconce, save all the old screws and incidental hardware—you never know what you might need when you attach the new one. Because the sconce shown on the next page is a low-voltage unit, it also requires a transformer, which fits under the fixture base.

First remove the glass shade from the existing fixture; most are held on by small setscrews. Always support the shade—especially if it's inverted—to prevent it from falling out and breaking **1**. Turn off power to the outlet, then use a noncontact tester to make sure the power is off **2**. If the tester doesn't light, it's safe to disassemble the fixture and handle its wires.

Remove the fixture's mounting screws; in this case, they're on the side of the fixture base **3**. Pull the fixture away from the wall to reveal its mounting brackets and the wire connectors that splice the supply and fixture wires **4**. (The green-and-yellow-striped wire is the fixture's ground lead.)

After disconnecting the splices to the fixture leads, remove the special mounting bracket because it won't be needed to mount the new fixture **5**. (Its holes won't line up with the new fixture's mounting screws.) Save this bracket in case you want to reinstall the old sconce elsewhere.

SAFETY ALERT
It's always best to turn off the circuit breaker or remove the fuse fixture rather than relying on a light switch to disconnect power.

CONNECTING A NEW SCONCE

Once the old sconce has been removed, you're ready to connect the new one. Install the new sconce's mounting bracket ❶. In this case, the new bracket has tabs on each side rather than a continuous flange, like the old one.

If you hold the fixture one-handed as shown, it frees your other hand to make connections ❷. Here, the fixture takes a 12v, bi-pin halogen bulb, so it requires a transformer (the black box) to reduce the house's 120v power. (The transformer here is an electronic, solid-state device—essentially, a circuit board—with no moving parts.)

Splice the ground wires, then the neutral wires, and then the hot wires ❸. After you finish splicing the wire groups, push the excess wire and the wire connectors into the outlet box behind the mounting bracket so there will be room for the transformer under the fixture base ❹.

Line up the holes in the fixture base to the holes in the mounting bracket, and screw the base to the bracket ❺. Don't tighten one screw all the way down until you've at least started the screw on the other side.

1 Install the new mounting bracket.

2 Prepare the wires before you place the fixture on the wall.

3 Use wire connectors to splice wires.

4 The transformer fits under the base.

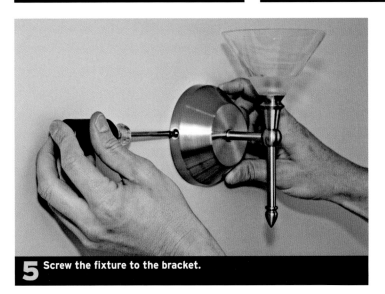

5 Screw the fixture to the bracket.

PREPPING & MOUNTING A CEILING BOX

1 Remove the center knockout.

2 Insert the bar fitting into the knockout.

3 Screw the box bracket onto the bar fitting.

Standard ceiling box and bar assemblies are rated for 50 lb. If your light fixture weighs more than that, install a fan box instead.

➡ **For more on mounting fan boxes, see p. 162.**

Start by using a sturdy pair of needle-nose pliers or lineman's pliers to knock loose and twist out the center knockout in the box **❶**. To attach the box to the bar, line up the threaded fitting on the bar to the knockout in the center of the box **❷**.

Most bar or bar assemblies come with a center screw and washer designed to attach the box to the bar. Fasten the screw and washer to the threaded fitting on the bar **❸**. Mounted together, the box and bar are rated to support a 50-lb. light fixture.

In new construction, this bar and box assembly would be installed before the ceilings are covered, from below. Thus the bar's tabs face down. In a retrofit, however, you'll often be screwing or nailing the tabs to joists from above (if there's access). So when retrofitting a ceiling box, bend up the tabs and they'll be easier to secure **❹**.

4 Bend bar tabs upward for retrofit applications.

5 Extend the bars and screw them to joists.

Extend the bar until both ends are snug against the joists. Measure the thickness of the ceiling, adjust the height of the mounting bar so the box will be flush to the ceiling below, and screw the bar tabs to the joists **❺**.

DISCONNECTING A CEILING FIXTURE

*T*urn off the power at the breaker panel or fuse box and test to be sure the power is off (p. 42) before disconnecting a ceiling fixture. *Warning:* Just turning off a wall switch is not safe, because there may be live wires in the ceiling box. Wear work gloves to protect against sharp metal edges, and safety glasses—many connections will be at eye level.

In the sequence shown here, the electrician swapped a modern fixture resembling a silver-plated manzanita bush ❶ with a more traditional chandelier with a fabric shade.

As quirky as the existing fixture looked, however, removing it was fairly straightforward. That is not always the case with older fixtures, which may have nonstandard mounting hardware and be attached to undersized ceiling boxes. A shallow "pancake box," for example, may not have enough room for electrical connections and would need to be replaced with a deeper 4×4 box. Or if the replacement fixture is especially heavy, you may need to install a mounting-bar assembly (p. 79) to support it. (Installation instructions typically specify mounting requirements.)

It's a good idea to have a helper support a ceiling fixture underneath while you unscrew its mounting screws. Otherwise, the fixture could come crashing down. So have a plan before you start, especially if you are working from a ladder. The fixture in our sequence wasn't terribly heavy, so the electrician's biggest challenge was snaking his forearm through the bush so he could unscrew the fixture canopy (base) from its bracket ❷.

As you lower the canopy, you will pull spliced wires out from the ceiling box ❸. If there's any question whether the power is off, avoid touching bare wire ends and test with a noncontact tester. Once you're sure the power is off, twist off the wire connectors and separate the wires. Cap any bare wire ends sticking out of the box. Lower and remove the fixture. Then examine the mounting bracket screwed to the ceiling box. If it is identical to the bracket of the replacement fixture, you may be able to leave it in place and reuse it. More likely, you'll need to unscrew it ❹ and install the new mounting device.

1 Turn off the power. Develop a plan for disconnecting the fixture safely.

2 Unscrew the canopy from the mounting bracket.

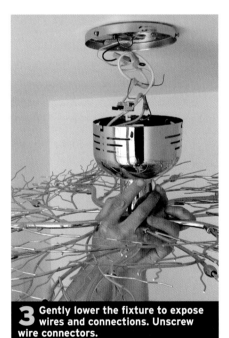

3 Gently lower the fixture to expose wires and connections. Unscrew wire connectors.

4 Unscrew and remove the existing mounting bracket from the ceiling box.

INSTALLING A CHANDELIER

This installation is done with the *power off*. Test to be sure. Wear work gloves to protect against sharp metal edges, and safety glasses—many connections will be at eye level.

Before you start: Review installation instructions, as each fixture is a little different. Check parts against the packing list and develop an installation plan. Often, you'll want to preassemble certain sections on the ground so you can hoist them into place and install them quickly. In our sequence, the electrician preassembled the threaded nipple to the mounting strip and then screwed that to the ceiling box.

He first attached the bare ground wire to the green grounding screw on the mounting strip ❶. On the ground, he assembled the fixture body, shortened the chain to put the fixture at the right height, slid the canopy over the chain, attached the collar loop to the last link, and wove the insulated fixture wire (and a separate bare ground) through the chain.

Holding the chain (and fixture) with one hand, he fed fixture wires through the threaded nipple ❷ attached to the ceiling box. Feed wires slowly so you don't crimp or nick their insulation. When the wires are fully through the nipple, screw the collar loop to the bottom of the threaded nipple ❸. (The collar loop is, in fact, a nut, with threads inside.) When the collar loop is snug, the fixture will be fully supported and you will have both hands free to make electrical connections.

Using wire connectors, the electrician spliced source and fixture ground wires, then neutral wires, then hot wires ❹. He carefully folded those spliced wires into the ceiling box, slid the canopy up to cover the spliced wires and the ceiling box, and then screwed on the nut that held the canopy in place ❺. A few minor tasks remained, including screwing the decorative finial onto the bottom of the fixture ❻, attaching socket sleeves, inserting bulbs, turning the power back on, and testing to see that everything worked.

PRO TIP

If a chandelier canopy is on the small side, make sure the ceiling box is large enough to house wires and wire connectors. Conversely, if the box is on the small side, a large canopy can hide the connections.

1 Screw the mounting strip to the box, then attach the ground wire.

2 Carefully feed fixture wires through the threaded nipple.

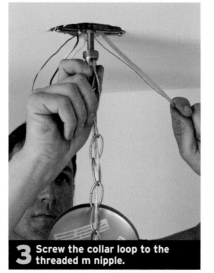

3 Screw the collar loop to the threaded m nipple.

4 Use wire connectors to splice source wires to fixture leads.

5 Cover spliced wires in the box with the canopy.

6 Attach remaining parts, such as the final nut on the bottom.

RETROFITTING RECESSED LIGHTING

As the name implies, recessed lighting fixtures fit into the space above the ceiling. Recessed fixtures create a strong cone of light and are frequently used to illuminate work areas or tight spaces. If desired, installing recessed fixtures spaced closely together (half the ceiling height for a 6-in. can with standard baffle and trim) will create even lighting, rather than "pools" of light.

In retrofit installations, the supply cable to the recessed lighting unit typically comes from an existing ceiling box or nearby switch box. The supply cable feeds to an integral junction box on the fixture. Finding the nearest power source and fishing the wires to the fixture is always an adventure if there's not accessible space above. If the recessed fixture is a low-voltage unit, it will come with a transformer, which reduces the 120v current of the supply cable.

RECESSED LIGHT FIXTURE

Recessed light fixtures vary. The low-voltage model in the photo sequence on the facing page has a transformer at the end of its assembly to reduce line voltage. This drawing shows a model that runs on line voltage (120v), so it has no transformer. If the unit is watertight, it will have additional trim or lens elements. Closely follow the installation instructions provided with your fixture.

Frame or armature
Supply cable
Armored cable
Junction box
Housing or can
Mounting clips extend, rest on ceiling
Finish ceiling
Can lip
Baffle or trim piece

Retrofitting recessed lighting In retrofit installations, the supply cable to the recessed lighting unit typically comes from an existing ceiling box or nearby switch box. The supply cable feeds to an integral junction box on the fixture. Finding the nearest power source and fishing the wires often means thinking spatially: The nearest power source may be in another room or on another floor. If the recessed fixture is a low-voltage unit, such as the one shown on the facing page, it will come with a transformer, which reduces the 120v current of the supply cable.

CUTTING A CEILING HOLE FOR RECESSED LIGHTING

1 Measure to center the light fixture. A single recessed fixture centered in one direction or another usually looks good.

2 Drill a pilot hole.

3 Keep the drill bit aligned vertically.

4 If the can is too snug—or doesn't fit at all—enlarge the hole as needed.

5 Test-fit the fixture. Wires are housed in the (gray) junction box.

SAFETY ALERT

To minimize hitting pipes or cables when drilling into a ceiling, use a bit that's 1 in. long—just long enough to drill through the plaster or drywall. Use a cordless drill to further reduce the chances of shocks.

There's no absolute rule on where to place a recessed light, but in a small space, such as a shower alcove, a fixture centered in one direction or another will look best **1**. In addition, you may want to use a stud finder to avoid hitting ceiling joists above.

Drill a pilot hole to see what's above **2** and to make sure there's room for the can. Make the hole small because if there's an obstruction above it, you'll need to patch it. After drilling the hole, you can insert a 4-in.

piece of bent wire and rotate it to see if it hits a ceiling joist.

Also, use the small pilot hole to keep the point of a hole-saw blade from drifting. Keep the drill vertical, and the circle of the sawblade parallel to the ceiling **3**. There are special carbide hole saws for drilling through plaster. A bimetal hole saw will also cut through drywall, but plaster will quickly dull the blade. Wear goggles.

If the hole saw is the right size for the can, you won't need to enlarge it. But for

the light shown here, the saw was a shade too small, so the installer used a jab saw to enlarge the hole slightly **4**. In a pinch, you can also use just a jab saw to cut the hole.

Test-fit the unit **5**. Although you want the can to fit snugly, the unit's junction box and transformer also need to fit through. The black box about to enter the hole is the transformer.

WIRING A RECESSED FIXTURE

To wire a recessed fixture, remove a Romex knockout from the unit's integral junction box ❶. Inside the knockout, there is a spring-loaded strain-relief clamp that will grip the incoming cable, so you don't need to insert a Romex connector. Run a length of (unconnected) Romex cable from the nearest power source and feed it into the knockout just removed. Of course, the cable must *not* be energized when you are working on it. (To wire the box with AC or MC cable, remove one of the circular ½-in. knockouts and insert an appropriate connector.)

➡ **For more on connectors, see p. 30.**

Inside the fixture's junction box will be two sets of wires that were spliced at the factory. They connect the secondary wires that run from the transformer to the socket. (At the transformer, the current is reduced from 120v to 12v, so polarity is no longer an issue.) There are also three unconnected fixture leads in the box, to which you'll splice the supply wires ❷.

Using wire connectors, connect the incoming ground wire to the green fixture lead, the incoming neutral to the white lead, and the hot wire to the black fixture lead ❸.

Tuck the spliced wire groups into the fixture junction box ❹. At the right of the junction box is a piece of threaded rod that can be adjusted to support the transformer at the correct height. Snap the junction box cover ❺ closed. As with other outlet boxes, code determines the number of wires you can splice in a fixture junction box, based on the cubic inches in the box.

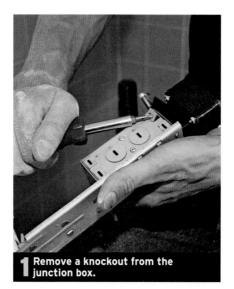

1 Remove a knockout from the junction box.

2 Remove the cable sheathing, then splice fixture leads to supply wires.

3 Always connect the ground wires first.

4 Tuck the spliced wires into the box.

5 Close the junction box cover, being careful not to pinch wires.

SECURING THE CAN

1 Feed the cable and the now-wired fixture into the hole.

2 If the fit is tight, use your fist to seat the lip of the fixture flush to the ceiling.

3 Use a screwdriver to engage the spring-loaded clips that secure the fixture.

4 Insert the bulb with steady pressure till all pins seat.

5 Install the trim assembly. The black ring is a moisture-proof gasket.

PRO TIP

If you have access to the space above a ceiling fixture, staple the Romex to a joist, leaving at least 12 in. of free cable so you can push the fixture components into the hole. A cable that's too short may prevent this.

O nce the recessed lighting fixture has been wired, push the fixture into the hole, being careful not to bind the Romex cable as you do so **1**. If the fit is snug, use the side of your fist to seat the lip of the fixture flush to the ceiling **2**.

Use a screwdriver to push up the spring-loaded clips that pivot and press against the back face of the drywall to hold the fixture snugly in place **3**. To remove the fixture later, pop out the clips.

Insert the bulb (the fixture here uses an MR-16 bi-pin halogen bulb) into the fixture

socket **4**. Here, the installer is gripping the lamp's rim, to keep the sides of the lamp clean. Skin oils can cause hot spots on the very hot-running lamps, shortening the life of the bulb. The lamp pins should seat securely. Install the trim piece—this one has a gasket. Snap in the lamp and socket, and push the assembly up into the can. The three arms on the side of the assembly will grip the inside of the can **5**.

PRO TIP

The pros apply a tiny dab of antioxidant paste to the lamp pins before seating them in a fixture socket to prevent oxidation. A good practice, but not imperative.

UNDERCABINET FLUORESCENT FIXTURES

Position undercabinet fluorescent fixtures to give you the countertop light coverage you want in each area. If you're running Romex cable to the fixture, you must protect it, either by placing the fixture flush against the back of the cabinet or by covering the Romex with a piece of trim. If you prefer to place the fixture out from the wall, you can also run MC cable, which can be left exposed.

For more on MC cable, see p. 28.

Run the supply cable to the fixture location. Allow at least 12 in. of cable inside the fixture to facilitate wire splices. Remove the sheathing and then feed the supply wires through a knockout in back of the housing shell. Clamp the cable, then screw the housing to the underside of the cabinet ❶. Hold up the housing with one hand and use a cordless screw gun in the other.

Snap on the wiring compartment ❷, which contains numerous prewired connections and the ballast (the white rectangle seen at the right in the photos). Use wire connectors to splice the fixture leads to the supply wires ❸. (Extend the stranded wire ends beyond the ends of the solid wires so that the wire connectors engage the stranded wires first.)

For more on splicing stranded wire, see p. 35 or the Pro Tip on p. 64.

As you shut the wiring compartment, do your best to keep the wires neat and compact ❹. Messy wires are more likely to get pinched by the cover and short out—which means taking the unit apart and starting all over. Also, avoid locating the wire connectors too near the ballast, which may keep the cover from shutting. Screw in the cover screws that secure the wiring compartment.

As with most fluorescent tubes, insert their end pins into the slots in each keystone, then rotate the bulb clockwise to seat the pins in the sockets ❺. When turning fluorescent bulbs, grab them close to their ends and never force the lamps into place—they should seat easily. Finally, snap the plastic diffuser (lens) of the fixture into place. Be gentle because the diffusers break easily ❻.

UNDERCABINET FLUORESCENT FIXTURE

- Ballast
- Ground wire
- Ground screw
- Supply wires
- Lens/Diffuser
- Prewired connections
- Tube pins
- Housing
- Keystone-style socket
- Fluorescent tube
- Socket
- Switch
- Wiring compartment

1 Feed in the wires, then screw the housing to the cabinet.

2 Snap on the wiring compartment.

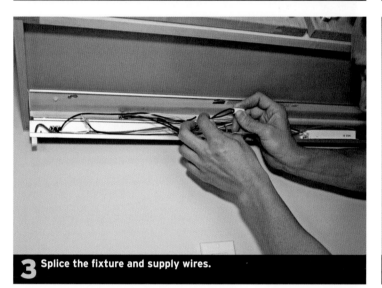

3 Splice the fixture and supply wires.

4 Close the wiring compartment.

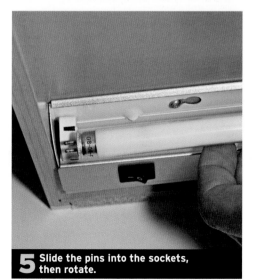

5 Slide the pins into the sockets, then rotate.

6 Snap the lens or diffuser into place.

LED hot spots?

Some electricians prefer not to use LED strips under cabinets because the individual lamps are visible as "train tracks" when installed over a dark shiny countertop. For uniform illumination without such hot spots, go with fluorescents.

LOW-VOLTAGE FIXTURES

Low-voltage tracks are safe to touch, but you should shut off power to the circuit before working on them.

Safety and low-voltage systems

Experienced electricians often handle low-voltage tracks while those parts are energized—with 12v of current—downstream from the transformer. If you install your lo-vo system correctly, and are careful never to touch the supply wires that run to the transformer, you can touch energized lo-vo tracks and install light fixtures without getting shocked. But if you have any confusion about which wires are 120v and which are 12v, shut the power off before doing any work on your lo-vo system. Best to be too cautious . . . and stay safe.

Low-voltage lighting systems are installed inside and outside houses and typically operate on 12v current, so they require a transformer to reduce standard house voltage from 120v. Transformers vary—some are coil-wound magnets, whereas others are electronic—so follow the installation instructions provided with your unit.

→ **For more on low-voltage systems, see p. 104.**

Lo-vo systems have become extremely popular because, with voltage roughly the same as a car battery, there is little risk of shock or electrocution. However, the large currents used in some instances can create a fire hazard if connections are poor. Systems can also be creatively constructed from a variety of different lighting materials. Lo-vo bulbs come in a greater range of options than incandescent bulbs; and, in general, lo-vo bulbs offer a better quality of light. Lo-vo systems can be controlled by standard switches or dimmers, but you should check the literature that comes with your system.

Though it's safe to touch the tracks of a lo-vo system, you should turn off the power when working on the system. The upstream part of the system (between the transformer and the power source) has 120v power, which could deliver a fatal shock. On the low-voltage side, there is a potential to short the system and damage the transformer.

After installing all the parts and doing a preliminary check of the system, it's safe to energize the system. (Note: Because any high-intensity bulb can get very hot, do not install any cable fixtures within 4 in. of a combustible surface.) Track-lighting systems are inherently complex, so read the instructions carefully before you begin the installation.

INSTALLING LOW-VOLTAGE CABLE LIGHTING

Track lighting systems may have a remote transformer or a surface-mounted transformer. There is also a range of cable standoff supports, both rigid and adjustable, mounting to walls and ceilings; they must be mounted solidly to framing if they are to keep posi-

tion when the cable is tensioned. Cables are typically spaced 4½ in. or 8 in. apart. The illustration has been adapted from installation instructions for a product from Alfa Lighting Systems; your instructions may vary.

ANCHORING LOW-VOLTAGE STANDOFFS

The key to a good-looking, correctly functioning cable system is getting the cables taut and level. Thus your first task in installing a lo-vo system is finding solid locations in which to anchor the cables. In this installation, the principal anchors were standoffs in each corner so the cable could be stretched around the perimeter of the room. Alternatively, you can anchor standoffs in a ceiling to support cables and bulbs. Standoffs are also called *re-routers* because cables often change direction as they emerge.

Use a laser level to establish level anchoring points around the room. Predrill holes in the plaster for anchor screws ❶. Plaster is harder than drywall and there may be lath nails in the way, so wear goggles and have extra drill bits on hand.

Because cables will be stretched taut, standoff anchors must be screwed to wood framing—in this case, into doubled studs in the corner ❷. Use screws at least

>> >> >>

1 Predrill all anchor holes.

2 Sink the anchors into the framing.

ANCHORING LOW-VOLTAGE STANDOFFS (CONTINUED)

2 in. long to attach the anchors. After sliding a chrome base plate (washer) over the anchor, screw the standoff socket to the exterior threading of the anchor ❸. Insert the ball end of the fiberglass rod into the standoff socket ❹. This ball-and-socket assembly allows the standoff to swivel freely so you can fine-tune the cable positions. The cables will be spaced 4½ in. apart.

3 Screw on the standoff socket.

4 Insert the standoff into the socket.

RUNNING CABLE

The next step in installing this system is to run the cable. Note the standoff at the top of photo ❶. Because the walls in this room were only 12 ft. apart, both cables could be run through a single angled standoff with two slotted posts, located in each corner. If the walls are farther apart, you may need a cable support in the middle of the run.

Measure the cable length you need and cut it 3 in. to 4 in. longer than your measurement so you can insert the ends into turnbuckles without having to struggle. Once you tighten the turnbuckles and tension the cable you can snip off any excess cable. On the other hand, if you cut a cable too short, you'll have to discard it and start again with a new piece.

Place each cable into a slotted post, rather than pulling it through the slot, whose sharp edges can cut into stranded cable ❷. (This is a quirk of the particular system shown here; other standoff types allow you to pull cable more freely.)

After placing the cable into a slotted post, screw on the post cap to keep it from popping out when the cable is tensioned ❸. As you place the cable into the subsequent standoffs, loosely tension it to take up the slack ❹. With this system, the second cable will be about 4½ in. from the first.

1 Cut the cable a bit long.

2 Place the cables carefully into the slots.

3 Screw on the post cap.

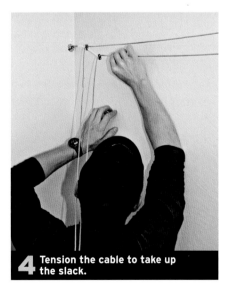

4 Tension the cable to take up the slack.

TENSIONING CABLES

Correctly installed, the cables of a low-voltage system should be more or less horizontal and equally spaced (parallel along their length). As with most systems, this installation uses turnbuckles to tighten the cables after they have been placed in the standoffs. The cables' Kevlar® core prevents stretching or sagging once the lightweight fixtures have been installed.

Once you've loosely run the cable, insert an end into a turnbuckle ❶. The cable end feeds in the end of the turnbuckle and exits in a slot in the middle. Tighten the setscrew(s) on the assembled turnbuckle to keep the cable from pulling out, then trim the excess cable sticking out ❷. Don't rush trimming the cable: Wait until you've made final adjustments to the whole layout before trimming.

A turnbuckle's center post has a thumbscrew with threads on both ends. As you turn the thumbscrew in one direction, it draws tight both ends of a cable; turn in the opposite direction to slacken cable tension ❸. With cable attached to both sides of a turnbuckle, the installer may struggle to draw the cable tight enough to join them ❹. This is a good reason not to trim the cable until the turnbuckle starts tightening both ends.

A certain amount of adjustment is necessary after both cables are taut. Here, the installer adjusts the cables so that the standoff comes out of the corner at a 45-degree angle, thus ensuring that the wires will be equidistant ❺.

1 Insert the cable into the turnbuckle.

2 Trim and discard excess cable.

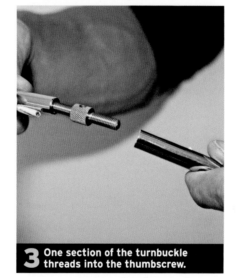
3 One section of the turnbuckle threads into the thumbscrew.

4 Draw the cable ends together.

5 Fine-tune cable angles and spacing.

PRO TIP
When working with stranded cable, tape the cable ends and then cut in the middle of the tape to keep the strands from unraveling.

LOCATING THE CANOPY

Once the tensioned cable has been installed, you'll need to locate the canopy. The canopy (also called a canopy feed) receives low-voltage current from the transformer and delivers it to the cables. The canopy mounts to a junction box on the ceiling or wall.

Before installing the canopy, make its holes—or those of its mounting bracket—line up to the holes of the junction box you'll be installing in the wall or ceiling ❶. The slotted mounting bar on the back of this 2-wire canopy can fit several box widths.

If the canopy will be ceiling mounted, drill a hole for it. To minimize the mess, use a hole-cutting tool with a dust cover ❷. Note: A screw gun with a ½-in. chuck will accept large-shank tools such as the one shown here. Set the hole-cutting tool's blade to the diameter of the junction box ❸. For large holes, this tool has a counterweight that attaches to the right side of the cutting bar to balance the torque of the blade.

Hold the cover of the tool snug against the ceiling so it can contain the dust ❹. Wait a few seconds for the dust to settle inside the cover before lowering the tool.

PRO TIP

Fixture canopies are often polished chrome, which is easy to cloud with fingerprints. Wearing lightweight plastic gloves solves the problem; nitrile plastic gloves are especially flexible.

1 Make sure the screw holes line up.

2 Use a dust cover to minimize the mess.

3 Set the cutter to the diameter of the box.

4 Hold the cover snug against the ceiling as you drill.

MOUNTING THE BOX & WIRING THE TRANSFORMER

1 Mount the ceiling box.

2 Place the transformer above the attic insulation.

3 Insert the lo-vo cable into the ceiling box.

4 Insert the cable into the transformer.

5 Run the supply cable to the transformer. All supply cable is de-energized: The power is *off*.

After the canopy has been located, it's time to mount the box and wire the transformer. The transformer shown here permits 12v or 24v wiring. Your installation may vary, so follow the instructions provided. Note: All wiring is done with the power *off*.

When retrofitting a ceiling box, bend up the bar tabs to make them easier to nail or screw. Extend the support bar until its tabs are snug against joists, adjust the height of the bar so the box is flush to the ceiling, and then screw the tabs to joists **1**.

➡ **For more on installing ceiling boxes, see p. 79.**

Install the transformer above the insulation so that its vents work properly and the unit can be accessed easily **2**. Run the secondary (lo-vo) cable between the transformer and the ceiling box, stapling it within 12 in. of a box and every 4 ft. along its run **3**. Feed the other end of the lo-vo cable into the transformer **4**. The gray cable connectors are one-way clamps: easy to insert but difficult to pull out.

Run the supply cable (120v) from an existing switch to the transformer **5**. Protect the cable by stapling it to the side of a joist or to a runner added for the purpose.

>> >> >>

MOUNTING THE BOX & WIRING THE TRANSFORMER (CONTINUED)

6 Splice the secondary wires.

7 Connect the primary wires.

8 Close the cover on the transformer.

After stripping 1/2 in. of insulation off the wire ends, use wire connectors to splice the secondary wires, which run from the transformer to the ceiling box **6**. Next, splice the primary ground wires, using a wire connector. Then connect the primary neutral to the common (neutral) terminal, as shown, and the primary hot wire to one of the tap terminals. Tighten the terminal screws to grip the wires **7**.

Close the transformer cover to protect the connections inside **8**.

INSTALLING THE CANOPY

The canopy is installed after the transformer has been wired. Install the mounting bracket to the new ceiling box; it will support the canopy that supplies lo-vo power to the cables ❶. The wire hanging from the box is the secondary (lo-vo) cable from the transformer.

Separate and strip the two wires in the lo-vo cable and solder their ends. Soldering fine-strand wire makes it solid and unlikely to smash flat as you tighten down the set screws on the canopy terminals. Soldered wire is also less likely to arc and overheat ❷. (Note the tiny Allen wrench inserted into the setscrew on the right of the photo.)

Use mounting screws that are long enough to extend beyond the canopy face ❸; they're faster to install than short screws because they give you room to maneuver.

Slide the canopy over the mounting screws and turn the canopy cap nuts onto the mounting screws ❹. When the nuts bottom out on the screws, continue turning the cap nuts, which will turn the extra-long screws back up into the box. This will make the canopy nice and snug.

1 Attach the mounting bracket to the ceiling box.

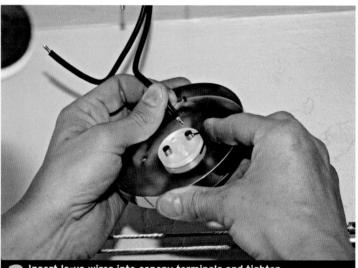

2 Insert lo-vo wires into canopy terminals and tighten.

3 Using extra-long mounting screws eases the installation.

4 Install the cap nuts on the mounting screws.

ATTACHING THE FEED RODS & FIXTURES

1 Bend the feed rods into position.

2 Test-fit and plumb each rod.

3 One rod has already been attached; the other has not.

4 Attach the fixture crossbars to cables.

5 Once everything is installed, turn on the power.

The final task for installing a low-voltage system is adding the feed rods and fixtures. The feed rods transfer low-voltage current from the canopy terminals to the cables. Setscrews on the terminals secure the rods.

Because the canopy is centered over the two cables, you may need to bend the feed rods to bring them to the cables **1**. Secure the rods in a vise between two wood scraps (to minimize marring the finish) and bend them at the point equal to the distance from the canopy to the cables. Some systems will provide horizontal connectors for this purpose, eliminating the need for bending.

Bend the first rod and test-fit it, using a torpedo level to ensure that the rod is plumb and the cable is still level **2**. If the first rod fits well, use it as a template for the second. Repeat the process with the second feed rod. Note that rod ends are slotted like the standoff posts that anchor the cables in the corners of the room. A cap nut screws on to the slotted rod end to capture the cable **3**.

Insert the bulbs into the fixtures before you attach fixtures to the cables. If your system uses halogen bulbs, don't touch them with your bare hands because the oil in your skin will shorten the bulb life. In general, fixtures need to connect both cables to become energized, so each fixture has a crossbar that spans the cables. Hand-tighten the fixture connectors so they're snug **4**. After you've installed all the fixtures and surveyed the system, turn on the power **5**.

INSTALLING LOW-VOLTAGE MONORAIL TRACK LIGHTING

Before installing lo-vo monorail track lighting, turn off the power at the breaker panel or fuse box. As with any low-voltage system, a transformer will reduce the 120v current to 12v or 24v. Because monorail track systems have a lot of small parts that are easily lost, don't open the packages until you're ready to use the parts.

In cross-section, the monorail track is two square pieces of chrome-plated copper conductor sandwiched together with a clear (insulating) plastic piece. Although the track is sturdy, it can be bent freehand or shaped against a curved piece of plywood.

LOW-VOLTAGE MONORAIL SYSTEM

In the installation shown, the transformer is surface-mounted in a circular housing. Although the transformer housing must be mounted to a ceiling box to be adequately supported, individual standoff supports can be anchored in drywall or plaster alone

because the track and fixtures are lightweight. The illustrations have been adapted from installation instructions from a product by Tech Lighting®; your instructions may be different.

Surface-mounted transformer

Housing nipple

Track housing

Auger anchor
Threaded washer
Screw
Standoff base
Standoff
Housing nipple

Housing nipple

Track housing

Lamp

Monorail track

Track housing

Housing nipple

Braided cable conductor

Pendant fixture

Track housing

LOCATING THE TRACK & STANDOFFS

If possible, before working overhead shape the track sections of your monorail system and preassemble them on the floor, then use a plumb bob or laser level to plumb up to the ceiling. First determine where you'll place the transformer box for the system, then mark off the standoffs that will mount the track to the ceiling.

With a helper holding one end, hold sections of the track against the ceiling and mark off standoff points at the track ends, where sections meet, and at intervals suggested by the fixture maker–usually, every 3 ft. **❶**. Standoffs have multiple parts, which anchor them to the ceiling and support the track (see "Standoff Parts" below).

Fortunately, because the track weighs little you can mount standoffs almost anywhere on a drywall or plaster ceiling, using auger anchors with wide threads. (That is, you don't need to mount standoffs to framing.) Sink the anchors flush, then screw a threaded washer to each anchor **❷**. Then, using a setscrew, screw the standoff base to that threaded washer **❸**.

Mount all the standoffs so that when you raise the monorail again you can attach it quickly to the standoffs and to the bottom of the transformer housing. If you need to reposition a standoff or two, it's easy to patch the small holes left by misplaced standoff anchors.

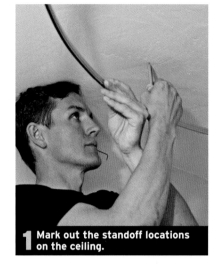

1 Mark out the standoff locations on the ceiling.

2 Screw threaded washers onto the anchors.

3 Screw the standoff base to the threaded washers.

STANDOFF PARTS

Standoff supports for monorail track systems consist of many small parts.

Auger anchor · Threaded washer · Screw · Standoff base · Allen wrench · Track housing · Standoff post · Housing nipple

MOUNTING & WIRING THE TRANSFORMER

1 Attach the mounting bracket.

2 Feed the supply wires into the housing.

3 Secure the transformer housing.

Once the standoffs are installed, mount the ceiling box to a ceiling joist and attach the bracket that will support the transformer **❶**. In this case, a nipple screws into the bracket and runs through the center of the transformer housing. The supply wires sticking out of the box will connect to the primary leads on the transformer.

➡ **For more on mounting boxes, see p. 79.**

Feed the supply wires into the center of the transformer housing **❷**, push the top piece of the housing snug against the ceiling box, slip a washer over the end of the nipple, and then tighten the inside nut that secures the transformer housing **❸**. The circular mass inside the housing is a magnetic transformer, which has a series of copper coils.

>> >> >>

MOUNTING & WIRING THE TRANSFORMER (CONTINUED)

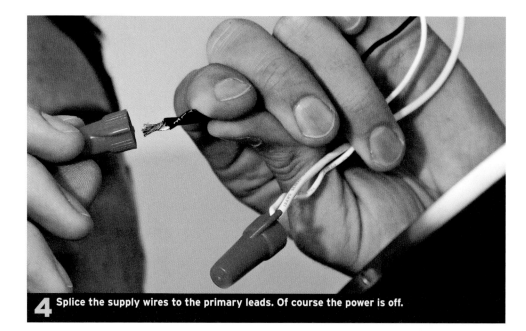

4 Splice the supply wires to the primary leads. Of course the power is off.

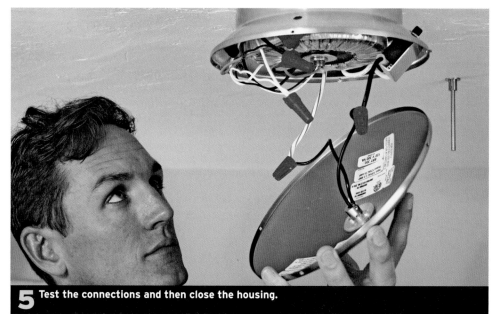

5 Test the connections and then close the housing.

Many transformers come with secondary leads preattached, so that the installer need only splice supply wires to the primary fixture leads. Using the wire connectors provided, splice the ground wires first, then the neutral leads, and finally the hot wires ❹. When all the wire connections are snug—gently tug on spliced wires to be sure—close the transformer housing by snapping the bottom to the top and installing the screws provided ❺. (By the way, the fat striped wires are secondary leads, which run from the transformer to the lo-vo power feed that energizes the track.)

HANGING THE TRACK

1 Place the track into the track housing.

2 Use conductive connectors to join the sections.

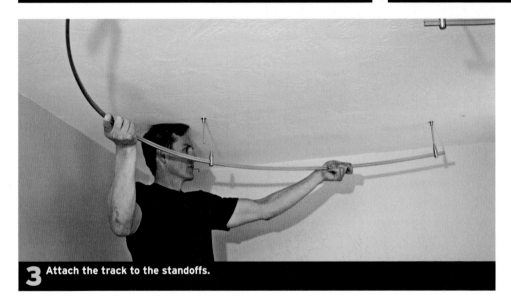

3 Attach the track to the standoffs.

PRO TIP

If you can't find anyone to help you support the track, bend short lengths of coat hanger into Z-shaped hanger brackets. Drill a 1/4-in. hole into the ceiling and insert one end of the bracket; the other end supports the track. Once the track is up, remove the hangers and patch the holes with joint compound.

With the transformer secured and the standoffs installed in the ceiling, you're ready to hang the track. Get help supporting the track until you have two or three points secured. Place the track into the track housing—the lowest piece on that assembly—then screw on the housing nipple **1**. Once that's done, tighten the setscrew that holds the nipple to the standoff post.

Where track sections meet, join them with conductive connectors and support the junction with a standoff **2**. Once the track is supported at several points, loosely attach the track housing and nipple assemblies at several points, slide them beneath the support rails, and use an Allen wrench to tighten the setscrews that join the nipples to the standoff posts **3**. Make sure the connections are tight.

Because the housing on the bottom of the transformer has setscrews on the side and the bottom, you'll need two different sizes of Allen wrenches. Loosen the small screw on the side of the housing nipple so you can

>> >> >>

HANGING THE TRACK (CONTINUED)

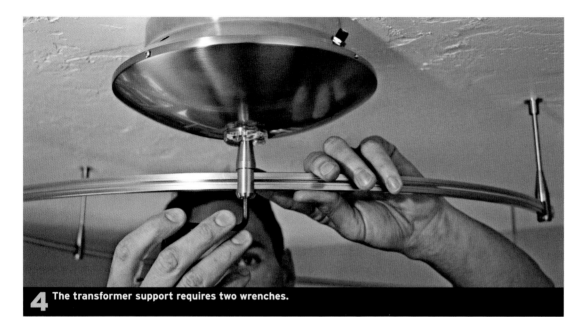

4 The transformer support requires two wrenches.

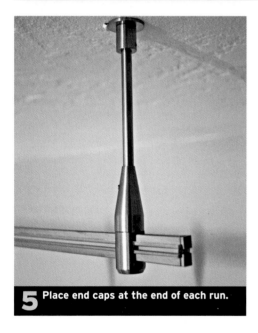

5 Place end caps at the end of each run.

turn it onto the threads of the housing. Once the nipple is tight on the housing, retighten that small screw. Then use a $3/16$-in. Allen wrench to tighten the setscrew on the bottom of the housing **4**. Finally, retighten all connections and place end caps on the ends of the track **5**.

INSTALLING THE LIGHT FIXTURES

1 To attach lights, invert the track housing and screw on the nipple.

2 Insert the shaft of the light fixture.

3 Support pendant lights with braided cable.

4 Pendant light supports screw into housing nipples.

5 Energize the system for 20 minutes, then make sure the connections aren't overheated.

Once the monorail tracks are installed, you can add the light fixtures. The fixtures require a two-part assembly that straddles the monorail track; note that in this case the housing and nipples are inverted. Insert the housing on top of the track and the nipple on the bottom **1**. Screw the pieces together, insert the shaft of the light fixture into the inverted nipple **2**, then screw the fixture nipple onto the threaded housing nipple and hand tighten it.

Attaching the pendant lights is similar, although the light pendants use braided cable rather than a solid shaft. Braided cable can be shortened if necessary, allowing you to install the pendant lights at the same or varying heights **3**. Once you've adjusted the pendant cables, tighten the fixture nipple to the housing nipple on the track **4**.

Most manufacturers recommend energizing the system and turning the lights on for 20 minutes or 30 minutes before checking the monorail connections to see if any are hot to the touch. Warm is normal, but hot connections should be retightened **5**. Do not, however, touch any halogen lights; they are certain to be hot enough to burn you (which is normal).

PRO TIP

After installing a complex assembly such as monorail track lighting, disconnect the power and retighten all connections after the first 10 to 20 hours of use.

REPAIRING LOW-VOLTAGE CONTROLS

REPAIRING LOW-VOLTAGE CONTROLS will be familiar territory if you've read the earlier chapters on switches and installing light fixtures. Basically, doorbell buttons and thermostats are switches.

To repair or replace doorbell units and thermostats, you'll need only basic tools such as those needed to install switches or lighting. And like low-voltage lighting, doorbell units and thermostats are energized by a transformer,

which reduces house voltage. You can safely test or handle existing low-voltage wires without turning off the power.

However, because transformers are energized with 120v house current, you must always turn off the power before testing or repairing a transformer or wires upstream—those that run from the transformer to a power source. Thus a noncontact tester (p. 16) and a multimeter are essential tools to keep you safe.

DOORBELLS

Troubleshooting a doorbell, p. 106

Replacing a doorbell switch, p. 109

Installing a chime unit, p. 110

THERMOSTATS

Replacing an old thermostat, p. 112

Installing a programmable thermostat, p. 113

TROUBLESHOOTING A DOORBELL

TEST THE SWITCH

1 Unscrew the doorbell switch cover to expose the wiring.

2 Use a continuity tester to test the switch.

TEST MULTIPLE COMPONENTS

3 Join the two bare ends of wire to test the system.

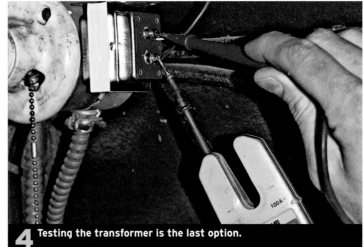

4 Testing the transformer is the last option.

Troubleshooting a doorbell system takes a little detective work. On older systems, the problem is usually the chime or bell unit—we'll use the term chimes to denote either. In many cases, the plunger springs on the chimes become compressed, resulting in chimes that no longer ring predictably—or at all. Corrosion or dust buildup can also silence chimes. Try the tests given here to determine whether the problem is the switch, the chimes, the transformer, or the wiring between the transformer and the switch.

Start by testing the doorbell switch. Unscrew it and gently pull it out from the wall to expose its connections on the back side **❶**. Disconnect one of the wires and, using a continuity tester, touch the

tester clip to one switch terminal and the tester point to the other. Press the button: If the tester lights as you depress the button, the switch works **❷**. If not, the switch is faulty and should be replaced.

A more thorough testing
Alternatively, you can detach both wires from the switch and touch their bare ends together to perform several tests. If the chimes sound when you join the wires, the switch is defective **❸**. If the switch wires spark when you touch them but the chimes don't ring, test the chimes as shown in "Testing Chimes," on p. 108.

SINGLE DOORBELL WIRING

In a single doorbell system, the circuit runs from the transformer to the doorbell switch, from the switch to the chime unit, and then back to the transformer. By pressing the doorbell, you complete the circuit, and the chime unit rings.

Outlet box

Power source (120v)

Front terminal

Transformer

Doorbell switch

Trans terminal

Rear terminal (unused)

Chime unit

FRONT TRANS REAR

The wireless alternative

Installing a wireless replacement system often makes a lot of sense. Radio-frequency (RF) wireless doorbell systems have been available since the 1990s. Most wireless systems consist of a radio doorbell/transmitter located by an exterior door and a receiver/chime set inside the house. Wireless doorbells are an easy alternative to running wire. Less expensive wireless units are typically battery-powered, which you'll have to check periodically. Whereas other wireless models plug into a nearby outlet. Most systems offer multiple chime units. *Note:* Check the unit's transmitting range to be sure it will reach your chime's proposed location(s).

If there's no spark when you touch the switch wires, the transformer may be defective. Turn off power to the circuit serving the transformer. Use a multimeter to test the transformer output ❹. Being careful not to touch transformer terminals, try to find a manufacturer and serial number, which will, in turn, enable you to look up the transformer's output specs on the internet. If the transformer is more than a decade or two old, you probably won't find specs for it.

At that point, you may want to have a licensed electrician replace the transformer, because it is attached to house current (120V) and the parts may be corroded. Alternatively, if the electrician determines that the transformer is working, you'll need to replace the wiring to the doorbell switch or install a wireless system.

Perhaps the trickiest part of low-voltage repairs is running the cable. If you're replacing broken or shorted lo-vo wires, such as those running to a doorbell, you may be able to twist and tape new low-voltage wires to the old ones and pull them through the walls. Because low-voltage wire is thin, it's flexible and much easier to pull than Romex. But, as likely, the old wires will be stapled in place.

➡ See "Pulling Cable," p. 199, and "Fishing Cable Behind Finished Walls," p. 201

>> >> >>

TROUBLESHOOTING A DOORBELL (CONTINUED)

DOUBLE DOORBELL WIRING

A double doorbell system has two circuits, each controlled by a doorbell switch, whose power comes from the transformer. Thus the chime unit for a double doorbell has three terminals. Typically, the chime unit has two different ring patterns (*ding* and *ding-dong*) so you can tell whether the visitor is at the front or rear door.

Outlet box

Power source (120v)

Transformer

Front terminal

Front doorbell switch

Back doorbell switch

Chime unit

Rear terminal

Trans terminal

Testing chimes If the chimes don't ring when you touch the doorbell switch wires together, remove the chime cover and vacuum out accumulated crud. If the chime plungers are rusty or corroded, spray them with WD-40® or a similar lubricant and move them by hand to get them sliding freely. Rubbing screw terminals with steel wool may improve electrical contacts. But chances are the old unit is worn out and needs to be replaced. To find out, dial a multimeter AC setting that's close to the low-voltage rating on the chime unit, then touch the tester probes to the trans and front terminals and to the trans and rear terminals, as shown in the photo. If you get a reading close to the unit's rating but the chimes won't ring, the transformer is delivering power, but the chime unit is defective. Replace it.

Test the chime terminals using a multimeter.

REPLACING A DOORBELL SWITCH

Replace a doorbell switch if it sticks, it is damaged, or continuity no longer exists between the contacts when the switch is depressed. You may also decide to upgrade simply because you want a newer style.

Unscrew the low-voltage wires from the doorbell. If they show corrosion, scrape or sand the wires lightly. Once the wires are clean and exposed, screw them to the terminals on the new doorbell switch. Then screw the new switch to the wall.

Screw the old wires to the terminals on the new switch.

Choosing a new doorbell When replacing a doorbell switch/button pay close attention to the existing mounting holes. Purchase a replacement button that has the same hole pattern or a larger hole pattern. Installing a replacement button that is smaller than the original will require patching and painting of the original holes, which can be difficult and, depending on the mounting surface, may add to the amount of work necessary to complete the project. Installing a button with a hole pattern that does not match the existing button, but is close, can lead to problems when trying to install new screws too close to the existing screw holes.

INSTALLING A CHIME UNIT

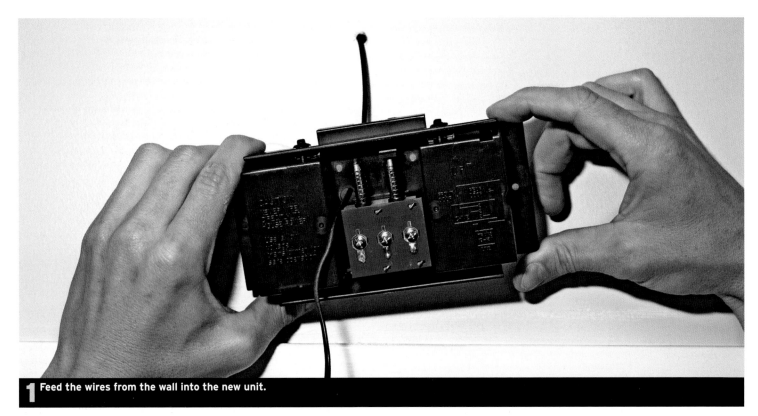

1 Feed the wires from the wall into the new unit.

Turn the power off before working on a chime unit. Once you've determined that the old chime is defective, unscrew the low-voltage wires from their terminals and unscrew the mounting screws that secure the unit to the wall. As you carefully remove the old unit, hold on to the low-voltage wires so they don't fall into the wall. If the exposed wires are especially short, it's a good idea to tape them to the wall with duct tape.

After making sure the new unit has the same voltage rating as the old unit, remove it from the packaging. Feed the low-voltage wires through the access hole in the new unit ❶. Level the unit's housing and then screw it to the wall. Because chime units are lightweight and installed in out-of-the-way places, it's seldom necessary to screw the chimes to the framing. It's usually sufficient simply to screw them to drywall or plaster ❷.

If the low-voltage wires look corroded or cracked and there's enough extra wire, snip their bare ends and restrip them. Then use needle-nose pliers to loop the ends clockwise ❸. Place the looped ends on the unit's terminals, exerting a slight pressure on the wires to keep them from slipping off as you tighten the screw terminals ❹. After you tighten the screw terminals, press the doorbell switch to test the new chimes. If they work correctly, snap on the unit's protective cover ❺.

PRO TIP
The power to the transformer should be shut off. If you're working with the power on and the leads touch and stay in contact, it could cause the transformer to overheat and burn out.

2 Level and mount the chime unit on the wall.

3 Strip and loop the low-voltage wires.

4 Attach the wires to the screw terminals.

5 Snap the cover into place and turn on the power.

REPLACING AN OLD THERMOSTAT

If your thermostat is a low-voltage unit, it gets its reduced voltage from a transformer. If the thermostat doesn't manually turn the furnace on and off, remove its cover to see if it's clogged with dust or if the wires are loose ❶. Remove dust using a small painter's brush and reattach loose wires.

If the old thermostat still doesn't work, you might test it with a multimeter set to ohms (resistance), but pros rarely bother—they just replace the unit. New thermostats can be programmed to conserve energy and, considering their multiple functions, their cost is negligible. Before disconnecting the wires, photograph or make a sketch of the wire connections. Thermostats have terminal codes (R, C, W, Y, G, etc.) that are standard, so the wires will probably attach to the same terminal-letters on the new unit.

Disconnect the remaining wire(s) ❷ and remove the unit.

1 Remove the cover of the existing thermostat.

2 Photograph the old thermostat wiring, disconnect the wires, and remove the wall plate.

SAFETY ALERT

Thermostats are specialized switches that open or close a circuit in response to temperature changes. Although most thermostats are low-voltage units that are safe to handle, your unit may be unsafe to handle if it mounts to an electrical box and is connected to house wiring (120V). Shut off the power, test to be sure it's off, disconnect the thermostat, and have a heating professional assess it.

SAFETY ALERT

Old thermostats may contain mercury—which is very toxic—so don't throw it in the trash. To find a recycler who can dispose of it safely, please go to www.thermostat-recycle.org or call 888-266-0550.

INSTALLING A PROGRAMMABLE THERMOSTAT

1 Level the new thermostat and trace mounting screw holes so you can predrill them.

2 Attach the existing wires to the designated terminals on the thermostat. They will probably be the same as the old thermostat.

3 This wireless unit's electronic components enable it to communicate with a whole-house system.

4 Remove the protective plastic from the face and pull the plastic tab at left to activate the battery.

The thermostat being installed in the photo sequence above is a Lutron Touch-Pro Wireless—wireless in the sense that it can be controlled by and report back to a whole-house system (p. 140). However, the thermostat is still hard-wired to the heating/cooling system by the tiny low-voltage wires. Chances are, those wires will attach to terminals with the same designation codes as the old thermostat, but consult installation instructions to be sure.

Thermostats must be leveled to function properly. Level the wall plate of the new unit and trace its mounting holes on to the wall **1**. Set aside the wall plate and predrill holes and insert wall anchors, as needed.

Once the wall plate is secured to the wall, attach the existing low-voltage wires to the designated terminals on the new unit **2**. Insert the stripped wire ends into push-in clamps or loop them clockwise around screw terminals.

You may also need to set a switch on the back of the thermostat plate to select the type of heat (electric, oil, or gas) **3**. Many modern units are shipped with coin-type batteries installed; pull out the plastic tab over the battery to activate it. Replace the thermostat's cover, and remove any protective coverings **4**. Consult the instructions, and program the unit.

PRO TIP
If the thermostat works but its temperature settings are too high or low, it may need to be plumbed or leveled. Remove its cover and look for a pair of plumb or leveling marks on the base.

MULTIMEDIA

MULTIMEDIA ENCOMPASSES various types of audio, video, voice, and data signals. The tools and methods used to install multimedia cables are similar to those used to install basic residential electrical circuits. Whether you're adding a phone jack to existing service or installing a media distribution panel, you'll need only a few specialized tools. Multimedia connections are extremely precise, so it's important to follow installation instructions exactly to ensure strong signals throughout your sound, video, phone, and data networks.

TOOLS & MATERIALS

Multimedia cable & connectors, p. 116

Stripping cable, p. 117

ADDING PHONE JACKS

Extending a phone line, p. 118

Mounting a new jack, p. 121

DISTRIBUTION PANELS

Mounting a media distribution panel, p. 122

Running cables to a media distribution panel, p. 125

Connecting cables at the panel, p. 126

INSTALLING A MULTIMEDIA OUTLET

Locating the multimedia outlet, p. 127

Installing cable connectors, p. 128

Connecting Panduit jacks, p. 129

Installing Leviton jacks, p. 130

Attaching jacks to an outlet plate, p. 131

SPEAKERS

Retrofitting a speaker, p. 133

USB CHARGER/ RECEPTACLE COMBOS

Retrofitting a USB charger/receptacle combo, p. 135

WALL-HUNG TELEVISIONS

Installing a wall-hung television, p. 137

WHOLE-HOUSE SYSTEMS

Whole-house control systems, p. 140

Integrating whole-house systems, p. 142

A typical installation, p. 144

Multi-room audio systems, p. 145

Setting up the whole-house system, p. 147

MULTIMEDIA CABLE & CONNECTORS

Here's an overview of the cable and connectors you'll need to wire your house for sound, video, data, and telephone service.

Coaxial cable is most often quad-shielded RG6, although double-shielded RG59 cable is still used. RG6 cable has a slightly thicker wire gauge than does RG59. Used for video distribution (cable TV), coaxial cable has been around for years. Video cable terminates in an F-connector such as the watertight RG6 connector shown in the photo at right. To simplify life and forestall callbacks, many professional electricians install watertight F-connectors inside and out.

Data cable can carry data or phone signals; it is typically 24-gauge, solid-wire unshielded twisted pair (UTP) cable. Category (Cat) 5e cable is the workhorse of data networking, but cable is constantly evolving: Cat 6 and Cat 6a are increasingly specified. In general, higher cable numbers denote faster data-transmission capabilities. Data cable contains four pairs of wires, thus RJ-45 data jacks contain eight pins.

Telephone cable is usually Cat 3 cable, which is not twisted; it is solid wire. RJ-11 phone jacks contain six pins. Although data cable can carry phone or data signals, Cat 3 phone cable is not rated for high-speed data transmission.

Audio (speaker) cable is usually 18-gauge to 12-gauge finely stranded wire. Speaker wire terminations vary from bare wires compressed between stacked washers to screw-on or crimped jacks that plug into speaker ports. Plug-in jacks are color striped to match speaker polarity: red-striped jacks for positive terminals and black-striped jacks for negative terminals.

Each multimedia connector is to the left of the cable it terminates. From left: RG6 F-connector, dual-shielded RG6 coaxial cable; RJ-45 (eight-pin) jack, Cat 6 UTP data cable; RJ-11 (six-pin) jack, Cat 3 phone cable; two RCA audio jacks (sometimes called banana jacks), 14-gauge low-loss audio cable.

Signal strength: coming in loud and clear

Although solid connections are as important to multimedia as they are to all electrical wiring, signal strength—not voltage—is the objective when connecting data, audio, video, and phone components. In fact, most multimedia input is not impelled by AC, as is house wiring. Rather, video and phone signals are generated by cable or phone companies. Computers and routers amplify data signals, and stereo amplifiers boost sound signals; but although those devices run on house current, the signals themselves are not AC. Thus the cables that carry multimedia signals are dramatically different from, say, Romex cables, and require different connecting devices and a few specialized tools.

 PRO TIP

Pros use watertight connectors on all coaxial cable connections, even those installed indoors. Watertight connectors such as the RG6 shown in the photo above don't cost much more and they always provide a solid connection.

STRIPPING CABLE

Electricians generally favor one type of stripper and use it to strip everything, thus reducing the number of tools in their belts.

Splicing scissors can trim tiny wires, but they can also score sheathing: Hold the cable in one hand, and, with the other, hold a scissors blade perpendicular to the cable and rotate it around the cable **A**. It's not necessary to cut through the sheathing. Once scored, the sheathing will strip off when you pull on the scored sections **B**. In fact, merely scoring the sheathing is less likely to damage individual wire insulation.

The cable scorer shown in photo **C** is specifically designed for stripping cables, but pros who perform a lot of terminations save time by using scissors skillfully. Wire strippers are the most reliable way to strip insulation off individual wires because you can choose a stripper setting that matches the wire gauge **D**. Finally, whether stripping wire, drilling holes, or doing any other wiring task, wear eye protection and sturdy gloves.

Multimedia installation tools. From left: low-voltage cut-in ring template, splicing scissors, wire strippers, and punch-down tool.

TWISTED WIRES

Remove the sheathing from Cat 5e or Cat 6 cable, and you'll discover twisted wires within. Twisting wires reduces the occurrence of *cross-talk*, in which electromagnetic signals jump from wire to wire. Although it is necessary to straighten some data cable wires to attach them to some jacks, the twisting must be maintained to within ¼ in. of the termination on the jack.

Cat 5e and 6 cables are examples of UTP cable, which is twisted to prevent signals from jumping between wires.

A To score sheathing, lightly rotate splicing scissors around the cable.

B Properly scored, the sheathing should slide off with a gentle tug.

C Lightly twirl a cable scoring tool around the sheathing.

D Wire strippers have settings that match wire gauges.

EXTENDING A PHONE LINE

Thanks to cell phones and remotes, we're no longer tied to the room where the phone line ends. But for clear, reliable service you can't beat a hard-wired phone plugged into a nearby jack. Happily, almost anyone can run an extension from an existing jack, thereby saving a hefty installation fee from the phone company.

The only tricky part of the job is running the cable to the new jack. You can tuck it under carpets, tack it atop baseboards, or run it around door jambs, but it won't look great. For the cleanest job, route that extension line into the attic or basement or—as shown here—drill through the wall and run it outside.

Before you start, disconnect the main incoming line at the interface. Then find the shortest route between the existing jack and the new one. Measure that route carefully and add enough extra cable for drip loops and at least 1 ft. extra on each end for the thickness of walls and for stripping and connecting to the jacks. Buy Cat 3 or 5e cable, which contains four pairs of solid-conductor, 24-gauge wire.

Never work on a phone line during a storm: lightning striking an aerial phone cable could electrocute you.

Connecting to an existing jack

Start by unscrewing the cover on the jack and the mounting screws that hold the jack to the wall. Gently pull the jack out from the wall, being carefull not to pull loose the wires attached to the jack terminals ❶.

If the jack is surface mounted, drill a hole for the extension cable that will be covered by the jack. If the jack is flush mounted, drill anywhere inside the ring, because the hole will be covered by the jack cover. Drill at a downward angle ❷ so that exterior water will tend to run out of the hole. Look into the outlet opening before drilling to avoid elec-

1 Gently pull the jack out from the wall.

2 Drill downward to prevent water from traveling to the interior.

3 Strip the cable sheathing and wire insulation.

Cat 5e and Cat 6 cables have four pairs of color-coded copper wires, which require 8-pin plugs (RJ45). RJ45 fittings, wired in T568A or T568B configurations, can be used for data or phone cable. Cat 3 cable, used only for phone lines, requires 6-pin, RJ11 fittings.

T568A RJ45

1 2 3 4 5 6 7 8

T568B RJ45

1 2 3 4 5 6 7 8

RJ11 OSOC

1 2 3 4 5 6

trical cables in the wall. Use a ¼-in. extension bit in a cordless drill for the job.

After drilling through the wall, use duct tape to attach a piece of string to the bit and pull the bit back through the wall. Then tie the new Cat 3 or 5e phone cable to the string and pull it into the hole behind the jack. Once you've pulled the new cable to the existing jack, strip about 2 in. of the cable sheathing and separate the cable wires into pairs **3**. >> >> >>

EXTENDING A PHONE LINE (CONTINUED)

Using splicing scissors or a wire stripper, strip about ½ in. of insulation from a wire pair (for example, a blue and a blue-white wire), loop the bare wire ends clockwise, and attach one wire to each of the two jack terminals that are presently wired ❹. Typically, terminals have stacked washers that hold several wires.

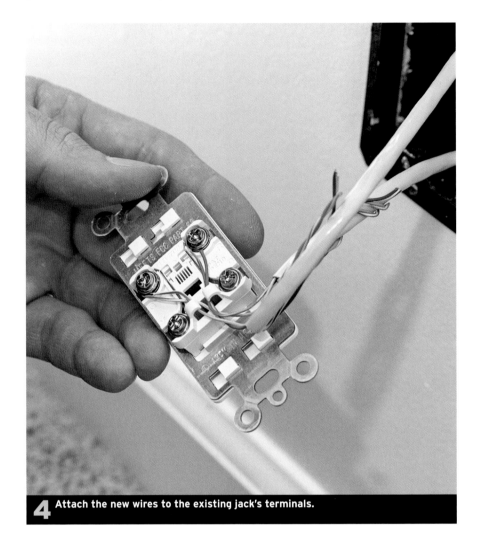

4 Attach the new wires to the existing jack's terminals.

Wiring techniques

When connecting to an existing phone line, avoid bending existing wires repeatedly because they can become weak and break off. Screw terminals come with multiple washers and are intended to have one wire under each washer. It is not recommended to twist wires together and install them under one washer. Finally, always wrap wires around screw terminals in a clockwise direction.

PRO TIP

Many electricians install Cat 5e cable for both data and phone lines to allow future expansion or modification. That is, Cat 3 is fine for phone service but inadequate for data, whereas Cat 5e can carry both signals.

Keep line and lo-vo cables apart! To avoid electromagnetic interference between lines, keep line-voltage (120v) and lo-vo cables separate. The NEC requires 2 in. of separation between line-voltage and low-voltage wiring. Do not secure them under the same staples nor run them through the same holes drilled in framing. If you must house both cable types in a two-gang box, use a snap-in plastic box divider to isolate their signals.

MOUNTING A NEW JACK

Before pushing the cables into the wall and remounting the existing jack, staple the new cable so it can't move and stress electrical connections. If the cable runs outside, loop it downward so water will drip off, and staple it with insulated cable staples ❶. Then fill the hole in the siding with siliconized latex caulk.

Locate the new jack and drill through the wall to bring cable to the location ❷. As described earlier, tape a string to the end of the drill bit before withdrawing it, then tie the new cable to the string. Once you've pulled the new cable into the room, remove its sheathing, strip insulation from a pair of wire ends, feed the cable through the new jack, and screw the jack to the wall ❸.

Loop the bare wire ends clockwise, insert them between the stacked washers on the jack, and screw them tight ❹. Finally, tug gently on the wires to be sure they're well attached, tuck the wires neatly out of the way, and snap on the jack cover ❺.

1 Form a drip loop, then staple the cable to the wall.

2 Drill a hole at the new jack location and pull in phone cable.

3 Mount the new jack in the opening.

4 Screw the stripped wire ends to the jack.

5 Snap on the jack cover and double-check to make sure it works.

PRO TIP

Low-voltage wire and multimedia cable are not stiff, so staple them at least every foot to prevent sagging, strains on connections, and an unsightly appearance.

PRO TIP

If you must drill through an exterior wall to bring lo-vo wiring or media cables into a room, drill downward to keep water from running into the walls. After inserting the wire or cable, fill the hole with siliconized latex caulk which, unlike pure silicone, is paintable.

MOUNTING A MEDIA DISTRIBUTION PANEL

A distribution panel is the heart of a home multimedia network because it receives incoming signals from phone, cable, and data companies and distributes them throughout a house. Panels can also distribute the signals from a stereo or sound system to speakers in many rooms. Many panel makers offer solutions with prewired modules, so a homeowner can configure a multimedia network today that can be easily changed tomorrow. To successfully install your system, closely follow the instructions provided, using the recommended tools.

As with other electrical installations, connect the power last, after wiring the panel and running cable to the outlets. Wear safety glasses at all times and work gloves to protect your hands. Panel edges can slice your hands in a flash; metal shards dislodged by hammers or drills are also dangerous. Finally, sturdy gloves enable you to grip and pull cables more easily.

Mounting the panel

Locate the distribution panel centrally so you'll have shorter cable runs: None should be longer than 300 ft. from the panel to an outlet. To minimize electrical interference, locate the multimedia panel away from the service entrance panel or a subpanel. Ideally, place the distribution panel on an interior wall to minimize temperature fluctuations—never locate it in an attic or unheated garage. You'll build in future flexibility if you run Cat 5e or Cat 6 cable for all data and telephone lines.

Install the rough-in box for the multimedia distribution center by screwing it to adjacent studs ❶. If you've already pulled most of the cables to feed the panel, as shown here, tack them to one side so they'll be out of the way. Slide the panel in or out so its edges will be flush with the drywall ❷.

Remove the knockout(s) for the power supply ❸. If your panel will house only telephone and cable TV, you may not need a power supply, but routers require line voltage, so installing a power-supply module will

1 Screw the panel to the studs.

2 Set the edges of the panel flush with the drywall.

> **PRO TIP**
> When mounting panels, install screws loosely at the top to hold the panel in place. Set and secure the bottom, then reset the top screws as needed.

provide future flexibility. Drop the power-supply unit into the opening, run Romex cable to it, and screw the module to the panel housing ❹.

Install the final locknut on the utility conduit ❺. The conduit may run outside to the utility pole or to an underground pull box. Depending on your utility's main point of entry (MPOE) or demarcation, you may need an exterior box to which the utility will run the service. Or the utility may install the MPOE inside, in the distribution panel.

>> >> >>

SAFETY ALERT

Plan your interior layout before removing panel knockouts. That way you know where and how you want your cables to come in and you don't have to go back to reroute cables or seal unused knockouts.

3 Remove a power-supply knockout.

4 Attach a power-supply module to the panel.

5 Tighten the locknut to secure the utility conduit to the panel.

MOUNTING A MEDIA DISTRIBUTION PANEL (CONTINUED)

A TYPICAL MULTIMEDIA PANEL

From this one multimedia panel (its outgoing low-voltage wiring has been completed), cables distribute video, sound, telephone, and data signals throughout the house. In this panel, the incoming utility and cable services are not yet installed–they will be pulled in through the conduit at the lower left.

Patch cables

Multimedia distribution block

Coaxial cable (video)

Conduit (Yellow line is a pull string.)

Router

Telephone lines

Data lines

Speaker cables

Bridging module

Passive splitter

Power-supply module

Panel basics

A router distributes digital subscriber line (DSL) or broadband signals from a modem (not shown) throughout the house so you can have several people accessing the Internet at one time. Patch cords make connections from the router to jacks on the data/phone distribution block. The multimedia distribution block is a prebuilt unit: One side has banks of jacks and punch-down blocks that distribute data signals to outlets; its other side distributes telephone lines. A passive splitter distributes video signals from a cable company throughout the house; an amplified splitter boosts the video signal before distributing it. A bridging module distributes sound signals to speakers around the house. The power-supply module is fed with 120v house current; it has receptacles that router or amplified splitter cords (not shown) can plug into.

RUNNING CABLES TO A MEDIA DISTRIBUTION PANEL

There's no one right way to run multi-media cable to a multimedia distribution panel. In new construction, electricians typically start from the distribution panel and pull cable outward. But remodel wiring is rarely predictable because you can't see obstructions hidden in walls and floors.

Before pulling cable into the panel, snap plastic bushings into the panel knockouts so sharp edges won't chafe the cable sheathing ❶. As you pull cable into the panel, loop it gently so that you don't crimp it ❷. If you have a lot of cables entering a panel, roughly divide them between two or more knockouts so the box will look neater.

Install prewired data and phone distribution boards and other modules. In photo ❸, the two columns on the left are jacks with 110-type punchdowns to which you'll attach data cables. Incoming phone lines terminate in the center of the module, which are then distributed to phone jacks throughout the house, permitting multiple lines at different locations.

As you route cable through the panel, tie-wrap cable bundles to free up workspace and enable you to see connections easily ❹. Labeling both ends of every cable is also essential, so you'll know which cable is which should you need to repair or modify the multimedia wiring ❺. Finally, create a numbered house map to show the cable locations.

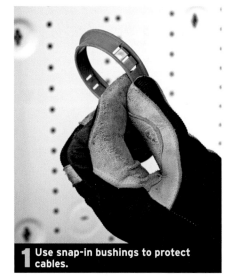

1 Use snap-in bushings to protect cables.

2 Loop the cable to avoid crimping it.

3 Install modules in the panel.

4 Bundle the cables to conserve space.

5 Label the cables at both panel and outlets.

CONNECTING CABLES AT THE PANEL

Because different types of cables converge at the distribution panel, there are, naturally, different connectors used to attach each one.

Speaker wires are typically stranded. Strip the ends as indicated by the panel maker—¼ in. is typical—insert them into the connectors' screw-down terminals, and tighten them securely ❶. Some panels will terminate speaker wires in a banana jack, as shown in the photo on p. 116; here, a plastic jack snaps to a bridging module ❷.

Using a combination stripping and crimping tool, strip the coaxial cable that carries data or phone signals and crimp an F-connector into the cable ❸. Plug coaxial cables into the passive splitter and tighten them snug ❹. (Note: The capped blue terminal is for input from the cable company.)

Strip approximately 3 in. of sheathing from the ends of Cat 5e and Cat 6 cable (data and phone); separate the stranded wire pairs; and, using a punchdown tool, press the individual wires onto the insulation displacement connector (IDC) prongs on the data and phone board ❺. The punchdown tool also removes excess wire. The blue cables in the foreground are data cables; the beige cables are phone lines ❻. Finally, plug in patch cords that connect router input to jacks on the data and phone board ❼.

1 Screw down the speaker wires in the terminal.

2 Insert the speaker jack into the bridging module.

3 Strip and crimp the coaxial cable.

4 Plug the coaxial cables onto the splitter terminals.

5 Install the data and phone wires.

6 Once connected, group and strap the cables to keep the panel neat.

7 Use patch cords to connect the router to the data.

LOCATING THE MULTIMEDIA OUTLET

1 Place the new outlet at the same height as nearby receptacles.

2 Level the cut-in ring.

3 Cut on the waste side of the line.

4 Use a flexibit to drill access holes for the cables.

5 Hook the kellum to the bit and pull the cable to the outlet.

6 Route the cables through the cut-in ring and install it on the wall.

In general, electricians run one data, one phone, and one video cable to each outlet. In the example here, however, specs dictated two data lines (green and blue cables) and a coaxial cable for video.

When locating the cut-in ring for a new outlet set alongside an existing receptacle, always measure from the center of the existing box, so the center screws on the cover plates will line up **❶**. The two types of cover plates may be different sizes, so lining up their tops or bottoms won't look good. Level the cut-in ring and trace its outline on the wall. (The template shown in the top photo

on p. 117 is another option.) Don't try to eyeball level: If you're even slightly off, the outlet will look cockeyed **❷**.

Use a jab saw (drywall saw) to cut out the opening. To start the cut accurately, strike the heel of your hand against the saw handle. To avoid cutting too large a hole, cut on the waste side of the outline **❸**.

To bring cables from the distribution panel, drill holes into the wall plate using a flexibit **❹**. Use a drilling guide to protect your hands while guiding the bit. Flexibits have a hole in the point. After the bit emerges through the wall plate, have someone tape

the cables together, slide a swivel kellum over the taped wires, and hook the kellum to the bit **❺**. The kellum swivels, so the wires won't twist up as you reverse the drill and pull them back up through the hole. Install the cut-in ring to provide a mounting surface for the outlet plate **❻**.

➜ **For more on running wires, see pp. 198-203.**

INSTALLING CABLE CONNECTORS

In the next few pages, we'll discuss the installation of several different types of cable connectors: F-connectors used on coaxial cable (video), as well as two popular systems (from Panduit® and Leviton®) that connect to Cat 3 cable (phone), Cat 5e, and Cat 6 cables (telephone or data). Each connector maker specifies tools and methods of assembly, so follow its installation instructions closely.

There are several types of F-connector styles, including twist, push-on, crimp, and (shown in the photo sequence at right) compression fittings. Each type has its merits, but in our opinion, compression fittings are the most reliable and the least likely to damage coax cable. Whatever style you choose, be sure it's compatible with the cable being installed.

Use a combination stripper-crimper to strip insulation off the end of the coaxial cable. Stick the cable in the end of the tool, spin it, and peel off both types of insulation from the outer sheathing ❶. The tool leaves about ½ in. of bare copper and ¼ in. of white insulation with the shielding on it. Slide an F-connector over the stripped end of the coaxial ❷. Place an F-connector in the crimping bay, insert the stripped cable, and squeeze the tool to crimp the connector tight to the cable ❸. (Note: The F-connector shown here is a watertight variety.)

1 Spin the stripper-crimper on the coaxial cable.

2 Use an F-connector to cap the coaxial cable.

 PRO TIP

It's not necessary to house lo-vo multimedia connections in covered junction boxes (required for high-voltage splices). Install flush-mounted cut-in rings (data rings) to provide a secure device to which you can attach outlet plates and insert jacks. A brush faceplate (p. 131) is an inexpensive way to finish the data ring. Whether you're mounting doorbell chimes or a multimedia wall outlet, take the time to level and plumb the device and, if there's another outlet nearby, to align the height of the new outlet.

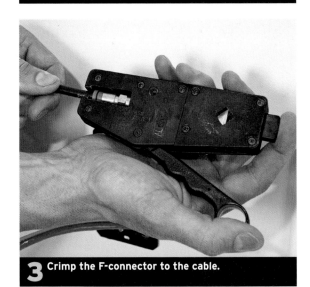

3 Crimp the F-connector to the cable.

CONNECTING PANDUIT JACKS

1 Separate and straighten the wire pairs.

2 Cut the wire ends diagonally.

3 Push the wires in all the way.

4 Trim the wire ends square.

Connecting phone or data cable jacks to a multimedia outlet requires a few steps. Start by reviewing cable stripping (see p. 117). Cat 5e and Cat 6 cable are UTP cable, so after stripping about 3 in. of sheathing, separate the wire pairs before attaching them to a jack. If you use Panduit jacks (often referred to as Pan jacks), you'll also need to unwind (untwist) the wires.

Use stripping scissors to unwind the individual cable wires before attaching them to a Pan jack ❶. Using light pressure, pull the wires across a scissor blade to straighten them. Next, slide the wires into a plastic cap, which is color coded to indicate where the wires go. Flatten the wires and cut their ends diagonally so they'll slide easily into the cap ❷. Push the wires all the way into

>> >> >>

CONNECTING PANDUIT JACKS (CONTINUED)

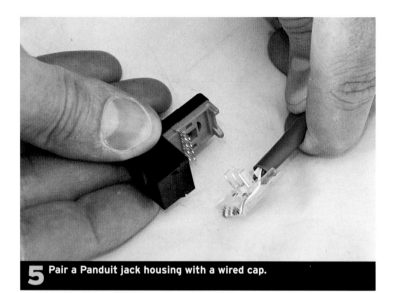

5 Pair a Panduit jack housing with a wired cap.

6 Snap the housing and cap together.

the cap **❸**, then trim the wire ends straight across **❹**.

The wired cap snaps into a jack housing, forcing the wires into V-shaped IDC prongs that slice the wire insulation to make the electrical contact **❺**. Place the wired cap onto the jack housing and use the small plastic lever provided to snap the assembly together **❻**. Panduit jacks are reliable because they make secure connections.

INSTALLING LEVITON JACKS

The Leviton jack system uses the 110 punchdown tool required to punch down wires in the distribution panel (see photo 5 on p. 126). But the system takes practice to avoid loose wires, so amateur electricians might get more predictable results using Panduit jacks.

In the Leviton system, there's no need to untwist wires. Separate the wire pairs and punch them directly into the IDC prongs built into the jack. Use the plastic disc provided to back the jack as you punch down **❶**. The punchdown tool comes with 110 and 66 blade sizes; each blade has a side that punches the wire down and a side that cuts off excess wire. For best results, work from back to front to avoid disturbing wires that are already down. Once you've connected the wires, snap on the jack's trim cap, which keeps wires in place and relieves strain on the connection **❷**.

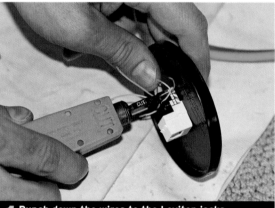

1 Punch down the wires to the Leviton jacks.

2 Snap the trim cap into place.

ATTACHING JACKS TO AN OUTLET PLATE

In the project shown here, we're installing both Leviton and the Panduit jacks to show that despite variations in jack wiring, both snap into the most common type of face-plate, the keystone style.

To install coaxial terminals, snap the threaded coupling into the faceplate ❶. The coaxial cable's F-connector screws to the coupling, creating a clean termination instead of having cable hanging out of the wall ❷. Snap a RJ-45 (eight-pin) Leviton jack into the faceplate ❸. Note the color coding on the side of the jack to indicate the order of wires you

punched down earlier. Finally, snap a RJ-45 Panduit jack into the remaining port in the keystone plate ❹.

Carefully feed the cable into the wall, hold the faceplate flush to the wall, and screw it to the cut-in ring ❺. The outlet shown uses phone and data jacks that are different colors so that users can quickly differentiate which jack is which. This differentiation is not an issue in residences, but it's imperative in business installations.

>> >> >>

FACEPLATE OPTIONS

There are many types of faceplates on the market for mounting telephone, data, coaxial, and specialty jacks. They come designed to match the adjacent electrical outlet (for example, duplex or Decora® style) and in various colors.

There are also faceplates and adapters for specific applications such as video (HDMI, S-video, component video, VGA), sound, and fiber optics. One favorite is infinitely flexible: A brush faceplate accepts up to four cables—just feed them through and its brushes fill the space between cables to give a finished look.

1 Snap on the screw-in coupling for coaxial cable.

2 Screw an F-connector to the snap-in terminal.

ATTACHING JACKS TO AN OUTLET PLATE (CONTINUED)

3 Snap in the Leviton data jack.

4 Snap in the Panduit jack.

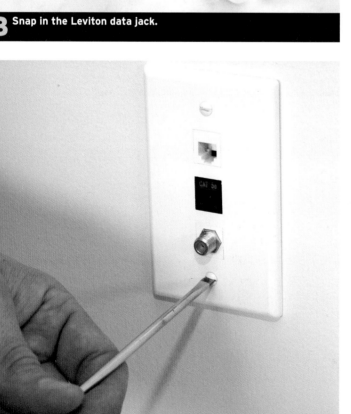

5 Screw the faceplate into place.

RETROFITTING A SPEAKER

Adding a speaker is largely a matter of running wire between two points and making solid electrical connections at both ends. You may also need to drill holes in framing to run wire and cut a hole in a wall or ceiling to inset the speaker.

To size speaker wire correctly, read the manufacturer's specs to find the *maximum output ratings* for the audio equipment you are connecting. Then determine the distance from the amplifier or sound-system control-ler to the speaker. For runs up to 80 ft., use 16-ga. wire; for runs 80 ft. to 200 ft., 14-ga. wire; longer than 200 ft., 12-ga. wire.

To minimize repairs, try to run speaker wire through unfinished attic or basement spaces. If you must fish wire (p. 201), use a long flexible drill bit and a swivel kellum grip to simplify the task. To locate speakers in finish surfaces, drill a small exploratory hole and insert a piece of coat hanger bent at a right angle to help locate studs or ceiling joists: That is, move speakers (as needed) to avoid cutting into framing. Most in-wall speakers are held in place by spring clips or swivel ears.

Typically, left and right speaker wires are identical and are not color-coded. But seri-ous audiophiles with complex sound separa-tion or surround-sound systems should iden-tify L and R speaker wires with colored tape before fishing them through walls and con-nect them to appropriate terminals on both ends. Follow your system's set-up diagrams.

These in-wall speakers have spring clips or *spring-loaded binding posts* that receive bare wire ends ❶. Use wire strippers to remove $3/8$ in. to $1/2$ in. of insulation from the end of the stranded wires. Place the speaker into the wall or ceiling hole ❷, being careful not to pinch the speaker wires. Next tighten

>> >> >>

1 Close-up of speaker wire connectors, with spring clips to hold wire temporarily in place, secured by swivel ears not unlike those on cut-in boxes.

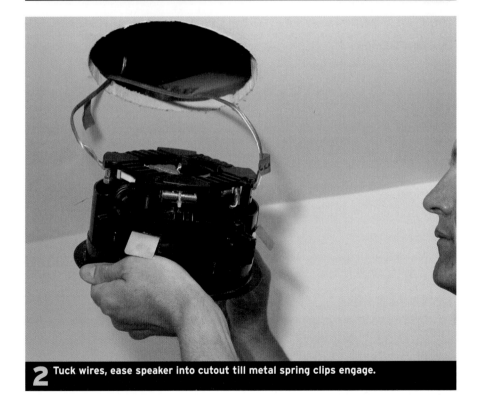

2 Tuck wires, ease speaker into cutout till metal spring clips engage.

RETROFITTING A SPEAKER (CONTINUED)

the mounting screws, which will extend swivel ears out from the speaker body and pull the unit's lip tight to the finish surface ❸. Attach the speaker face ❹, which is usually held on with magnets.

If your speakers are free-standing (not inset), choose fittings that will look good. The RCA audio jacks shown in the photo on p. 116 are popular and easy to install. The jacks fit into an audio wall plate and receive a gold-plated banana plug. (Fittings are gold-plated, by the way, to improve conductivity.)

3 Tighten swivel ears.

4 The acoustic cover is held in place by magnets.

RETROFITTING A USB CHARGER/RECEPTACLE COMBO

1 Cut power to the outlet and use a noncontact tester to be sure the power is off. Test all three slots in the receptacle.

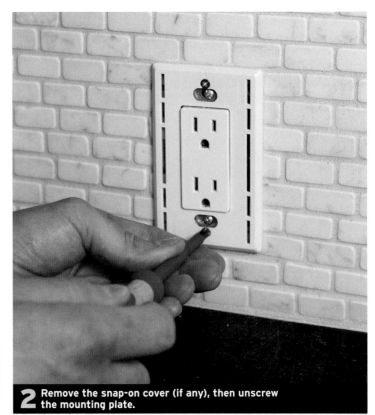

2 Remove the snap-on cover (if any), then unscrew the mounting plate.

Mobile electronic devices go everywhere, yet, being battery-powered, they must stop from time to time to get recharged. In this section we will show how to replace a standard duplex receptacle with an ingenious Leviton USB charger/receptacle combo that speeds recharging and gets more use out of a one-gang outlet. As a bonus, the receptacle portion of the combo is tamper-resistant (TR). For more about TR receptacles, see p. 38.

What it's not

Though the upper portion of this combo device has two USB ports, these ports do *not* enable you to transfer data. The USB ports exist solely to recharge mobile devices. Because the combo has a built-in transformer, you no longer need the cube-like adaptor into which an iPad®, iPhone®, Kindle®, etc., USB cord inserts.

What it is

The combo shown in the photo sequence above has a TR outlet rated 15A, 125v; its USB ports are rated 2.1A (DC), 5v (DC). Quoting Leviton specs, "The right USB port is specifically designed for use with larger battery devices . . . The left USB port is ideal for changing smaller battery devices."

Installation

Turn off the power to an existing outlet and use a noncontact voltage tester ❶ to be sure the outlet is de-energized. Lock the breaker panel or remove the fuse controlling the outlet to be sure that no one inadvertently re-energizes the circuit while you are working on it.

Remove the cover plate ❷, unscrew the mounting screws holding the existing receptacle to the outlet box, and gently pull

>> >> >>

RETROFITTING A USB CHARGER/RECEPTACLE COMBO (CONTINUED)

3 Without touching the sides of the receptacle, unscrew the mounting screws.

4 Remove wires from the old receptacle; attach them to the new device.

5 Clamps next to screw terminals receive the stripped wire ends.

the device out from the wall. Disconnect its wires in this order: hot (black), neutral (white), ground (green or bare copper) **3**.

Reconnect wires to the new USB combo in the reverse order: First connect the ground wire to the green grounding screw **4**, then connect the neutral wire, then the hot wire. As shown here, the installer reused the existing loop to attach the ground wire, but he elected to back-wire the neutral and hot wires. He used needle-nose pliers to straighten their loops, then snipped them so the stripped portion of each wire was 1/2 in. long. He then inserted each straightened wire end into a clamp next to a terminal screw. The neutral (white) wire attached to the clamp next to the silver screw; the hot (black) wire attached to the clamp next to the brass screw **5**. Tighten terminal screws to grip wires firmly in the clamps.

Carefully fold the combo receptacle into the box, tighten mounting screws, and install the cover plate. Re-energize the circuit and you are ready to charge your mobile devices.

This USB charger/TR receptacle combo **charges more quickly than a standard USB adaptor; you can also charge two mobile devices on the top of the combo.**

INSTALLING A WALL-HUNG TELEVISION

Securing the wall-hung TV bracket is the key to all that follows: locating the outlet box, running cables to the box and, of course, mounting the TV. Get help; wall-hung TVs are heavy.

The principal challenge to installing a wall-hung TV is structural, not electrical, because flat-panel displays are heavy. Only once you have secured the TV's mounting bracket to the framing can you decide exactly where to place the outlet box that will supply power (120v) and low-voltage A/V cables. Correctly located, those cables won't be seen, even though the TV will be the most visible object in the room.

Note: All electrical work in this section must be done with the power off. Before you begin, test to be sure cables are de-energized (p. 42).

Install the bracket

Read bracket-mounting instructions carefully and make small exploratory holes to determine exactly where the stud centers are located. Lag screws used to mount brackets are hefty ($5/16$ in. to $3/16$ in. by 3 in.), and you want to be sure that they sink into the middle of studs; otherwise, you risk splitting them. Drill pilot holes. In most cases, you can install flat-panel TV brackets without having to open the wall and add blocking.

Locate the outlet box

The outlet box should be located so that cables won't interfere with the bracket's movement. As a

---

CHOOSING A WALL-HUNG TV BRACKET

TV brackets usually come with the television, rated for the weight of the unit. This bracket will likely be a standard, nontilting type that allows no adjustments once the screen is mounted. Consequently, many people buy a separate bracket that tilts, or tilts and pivots on an articulating arm.

If the screen is more or less at eye level, you can get by with a fixed bracket. But if the TV is mounted up high on the wall, at least get a tilting bracket so that you can tilt the screen to achieve an optimal viewing angle—roughly 10 to 20 degrees from your line of sight (when seated) to the top of the screen. If you like having friends over for movie night or

sports events, consider an articulating bracket that enables you to pull the screen out from the wall, and tilt and pivot it till there's not a bad seat in the house.

Not surprisingly, durable, multidirectional brackets are pricey—$500 is not unheard of. If you watch a lot of TV, spend the money: Replacing a bracket later on may be a major pain, because it could require moving the outlet box, too. *Important:* When shopping for brackets, take the TV's technical literature to ensure that the new bracket can support the weight and that bracket holes will align with mounting hardware on the back of the set.

An articulating bracket allows you to pivot and tilt the TV screen for optimal viewing.

---

rule of thumb, putting the box over the bracket will keep cables from getting pinched when the top of the screen tilts forward. Expensive brackets often have cut-outs in the frame to accommodate a one-gang or two-gang box, and places in the articulating arm through which to run cable. So when the arm is pulled out, the cable(s) are hardly visible. These cut-outs typically line up with input jacks in the back of the TV.   >> >> >>

INSTALLING A WALL-HUNG TELEVISION (CONTINUED)

Run power to the outlet box

After locating the new outlet but before cutting into finish surfaces, find the nearest existing outlet to tap into. (It must be on a circuit with unused capacity.) Think 3D: A power source might be on the other side of a wall, in a built-in cabinet, or on the floor above or below. If possible, run power down from an attic or up from a basement because drilling through wall plates to reach a stud bay will minimize patching finish surfaces later. (Drilling and fishing cable are discussed on pp. 198–203.)

The new box will contain both a line voltage cable (120v) and low-voltage cable(s)—most commonly, *high-definition multimedia interface* (HDMI) cable. (Keep line and lo-vo cables isolated from each other, as explained on the facing page. To house both types of cables you will need either a two-gang box with a snap-in divider, or a one-gang box paired with a data ring. We like the second option because the side of the one-gang box isolates the Romex cable from the lo-vo, and the data ring has 1-in. knockouts that receive 1-in. ENT conduit, which we'll explain next.

Wire for the future

High-tech equipment changes so often that it's impossible to know what data lines or A/V cable you will need five or ten years from now. However, if you run electrical nonmetallic tubing (ENT) to the outlet box and feed A/V cables through the ENT, future upgrades will be easy. ENT is a corrugated plastic conduit that offers little friction so it's easy to snake new wires through it. It has the secondary benefit of isolating lo-vo lines, too. ENT connects to outlet boxes and data rings via a screw-on connector that fits into a 1-in. knockout. Use PVC straps to secure ENT to the sides of studs, but remember to locate the ENT at least 1¼ in. back from stud edges so the ENT can't get perforated by drywall screws or nails.

Making connections

Trace the outlet box onto the wall. Use a jab saw to cut an opening into drywall (p. 127) or an oscillating multi-tool if the wall is plaster. Pull the cables (and the ENT) through the opening and feed them through knockouts in the cut-in box (p. 26), tighten

Locate the outlet box only after the bracket is secured to the wall. This installer is tracing the outline of a two-gang box; you can also use a data ring clipped onto a one-gang box.

Running low-voltage cables through flexible ENT conduit will make replacing cables someday much easier.

PRO TIP

A pro notes: "Until the TV bracket is mounted, don't install the outlet box: It will *always* be in the wrong place. If we're roughing out a room that will have a wall-hung, we run cable into the stud bay and tape it off, so that after the homeowner chooses the bracket, an electrician can cut a hole into the wall in the correct place, reach in and retrieve the cable, and mount the box where he *knows* it won't interfere with the bracket."

1-in. diameter ENT connectors will fit into most box or data ring knockouts. In retrofits, attach the connector to the box (or data ring) before securing the box to the wall.

Don't Mix Signals Keep

line-voltage (120v) and low-voltage cables isolated from each other to avoid electromagnetic interference between lines. To achieve isolation:

1. Keep cables at least 2 in. to 6 in. apart when they run parallel.
2. Don't run cables through the same holes or under the same staples.
3. Where cables must cross, do it at a right angle to minimize contact.
4. If cables share a two-gang box, isolate them by inserting a plastic divider in the middle of the box. Alternately, you can feed the line voltage into a one-gang box and run A/V cables into a data ring next to it.

cable connectors (if any), and then secure the box to the wall. Remove Romex cable sheathing, strip insulation from individual wires, and attach them to the screw-terminals of a duplex receptacle, as described on p. 43.

Because the receptacle will be hidden by the TV screen, spend a bit extra to get a *transient-voltage surge-suppressor* (TVSS) receptacle with an audible alarm. Should outlet protection or function fail, the receptacle will sound a warning. TVSS receptacles are about the size of a GFCI receptacle, so you may need to remove the receptacle's mounting ears to allow the cover plate to sit flush. To finish off the data ring, we suggest using the brush faceplate shown on p. 131. It cleanly finishes the opening and accommodates a number of lo-vo cables.

Before energizing the new outlet, use a multimeter to test the new circuit for dead shorts.

Showtime

Once the electrical connections are complete, get several helpers to mount the wall-hung television onto its bracket and plug cables into the receptacle and inputs on the back of the set. This takes at least three people.

This TVSS receptacle will sound an audible alarm should the outlet protection fail. Audible alarms are especially appropriate if the receptacle is hidden by the TV screen.

WHOLE-HOUSE CONTROL SYSTEMS

Whole-house systems have been around for a while, mostly to control lighting and distribute music in high-end homes where entertaining was common, there were multiple lighting types in each room, and there were more rooms than one person could reasonably monitor. The solution to this privileged problem was automation, but it was complicated, typically installed during new construction and major remodels, and best left to professionals. And it cost the moon: $30K or $40K installations were nothing unusual.

Technology has changed all that. Solid-state devices now pack processing power in switches and other devices that were previously very basic. As important, wireless communication—specifically low-frequency radio waves that can penetrate walls and other solid barriers—has spawned a host of options for controlling lighting, shades, HVAC systems, and appliances such as televisions, computers, satellite dishes, and sound systems. New control systems are increasingly affordable, scalable, suitable for existing homes or retrofits, and (except for a few tasks) something do-it-yourselfers can take on.

Today, whole-house systems are installed mostly for convenience and comfort, though energy conservation is an increasingly important reason to do so, as federal and state agencies mandate conservation measures such as replacing incandescent bulbs with CFLs and LEDs, and utilities incorporate smart-grid technologies.

Security will be another big growth area. To cite one example, some control systems offer one-button "Away" settings that simulate the cycles of a busy household even when no one is at home. Lights come on at dusk and wink on and off in different rooms till bedtime when they all go out; shades go up and down; music plays in different rooms. A business person suddenly called out of town will have one less thing to worry about. And if you're away from home when a bad storm is approaching, you can change thermostat settings from your iPad.

Understanding whole-house systems

"Whole-house system" is a bit of a misnomer, because different home functions require separate systems, each with its own controller. Thus a house may contain a lighting control system, a distributive audio system, an A/V system with a surround-sound processor that converts data from a DVD, an HVAC system, and so on.

Systems can communicate with each other to a limited degree, but true interconnectivity and seamless user interfaces are still works in progress—and a great engine of growth. To better understand whole-house control, we'll look at multi-room music systems, which are among the most developed and come in a variety of configurations and options (see pp. 145-146).

Smart grids In many areas, electrical grids operate at close to maximum output and adding capacity isn't economically feasible. One way to optimize existing capacity is to reduce electrical demand during peak hours—by charging more for peak-hour electricity and charging less for off-peak usage. The key to monitoring this usage is a *smart grid*, in which there is an ongoing, two-way conversation between each energy user and energy suppliers (utility companies). In such a grid, each household has a *smart meter* that notes both use and time of use and bills customers accordingly.

Whole-house control systems would, in turn, interface with smart meters, inform homeowners about usage patterns, and suggest ways to save money by automatically cutting back on energy use during peak hours. But while smart-grid goals are generally lauded, smart meters are often lambasted as an invasion of privacy, an injury to health, and worse. Will the smarties prevail? Stay tuned.

INSTALLING REPEATERS

Repeaters are the brains of a whole-house control system. Lutron recommends installing repeaters in out-of-sight locations that will not be disturbed, such as closets and cabinets. All wireless devices must be located within 30 ft. (9 m.) of a repeater, so large homes may require auxiliary repeaters.

INSTALLING DEVICES

Repeaters communicate with multiple wireless devices such as dimmer/switches, shade/drapery controls, zone controls, occupancy/vacancy sensors, auto transmitters, and so on.

Drawings adapted from Lutron RadioRA 2 "Manual Setup Guide," with permission of Lutron Electronics Co., Inc. Lutron, RadioRA, Sivoia, GRAFIK Eye, and Pico are registered trademarks and RadioRA 2, and Radio Powr Savr are trademarks of Lutron Electronics Co., Inc.

INTEGRATING WHOLE-HOUSE SYSTEMS

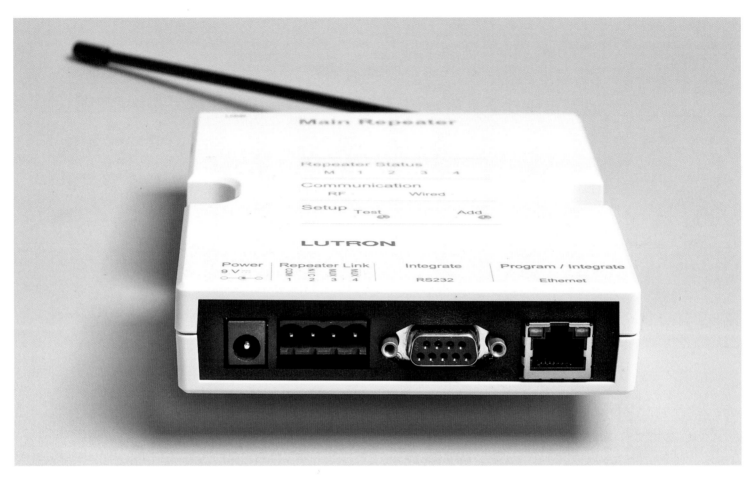

Multiple cables feed into the bottom of a main repeater. From left: power input; links to auxiliary repeaters (to extend signal); RS232 port (integrates different systems); Ethernet RJ45 port to connect to LAN, program and integrate devices into the system, etc.

Integrating whole-house control systems is complex. One logical set of systems to integrate are those impacting energy consumption—namely, lighting controls, raising and lowering shades (for solar gain and heat retention), and HVAC.

Lutron's RadioRA® 2 product (along with their shade line) is an interesting solution because it's relatively affordable, integrates several functions, can be retrofit using existing wiring, and, with a little help setting it up, can be largely installed by a homeowner. (Ballpark estimate for a DIY installation: $2,000 to $2,500 for equipment, plus electrician fees to set up and activate the system.) The bulk of the installation is replacing existing devices with smart devices that communicate wirelessly, or adding in devices that do not require wiring at all. Reduced to bullets, it looks like this:

- Replace existing switches with smart switches or hybrid keypads (keypads that don't just act as control points but also switch and dim light sources).

- Install stand-alone keypads or controls.
- Install dimming modules and switching modules at lamps and media-type appliances. (It's worth noting that when you switch off TV or computer screens, those appliances are on stand-by mode, drawing "phantom power." A keypad that controls the whole room turns appliances completely off, saving a considerable amount of energy.)
- Install motorized wireless shades.
- Replace conventional HVAC controls with smart thermostats and sensors.

All of these devices communicate with a central (programmable) *repeater* that creates a wireless network of communication and control that, once programmed, can perform multiple functions with a single button, monitor and conserve energy, and communicate two-way with utility company smart grids.

This motorized shade requires 24v, which the cable at top supplies. The clip in hand connects to the shade motor; the clip attached to the pigtail connects to a wireless dongle.

This Lutron wireless dongle communicates to a wireless controller via the RadioRA 2 system. The capped wire hanging down is the antenna lead.

Living-area shades are typically filtered; blackout shades are often spec'd for bedrooms. Tucked behind the shade, power and wireless dongle cables are invisible.

Basic wireless controls *Basic wireless controls* communicate with other devices on a limited basis— as distinguished from wireless controls that oversee whole-house functions. The Maestro wireless switch and Pico controller shown on p. 58 are examples of basic wireless controls. Typically, such controls are programmed directly by pressing switch and/or program buttons.

Other types of basic wireless controls include the following:

- Wireless motion sensors that talk to a local wireless switch used in a storage room, porch, or other space where occupancy sensing would be useful.

- Keypads that control a lamp, installed next to an existing light switch in a living room, dining room, or bedroom.

- Wireless switches retrofitted to replace inconveniently located manual ones.

A TYPICAL INSTALLATION

This wireless keypad communicates with the main repeater and so—via the repeater—this keypad can be programmed to control wireless switches and shades anywhere in the house. Though communicating wirelessly, the keypad is powered by line voltage (120v).

Turn power off before changing faceplates. (To illustrate this keypad's lo-vo LED lights, we turned the power back on briefly.) After a system has been activated and homeowners have tried it for a month, the manufacturer will engrave custom keypad buttons.

Just as there is no average family, there are no typical installations, but yours might include these tasks: (1) swap out switches in major rooms and bedrooms with hybrid keypads; (2) where there are groups of switches in a room, replace one switch with a hybrid keypad and change out the others to wireless switches; (3) plug in dimming modules between wall outlets and the floor and table lamps; (4) for appliances with phantom loads, plug in switching units between the equipment and the receptacle serving them; (5) install wireless shades (light-filtering shades in family rooms, living rooms, and kitchens; perhaps blackout shades in bedrooms); (6) upgrade HVAC controls (such as thermostats) and add stand-alone controls by bedside tables.

With this system, entire rooms (lights, lamps, shades, or any other appliance that has a cord connection) can be controlled from a single location or via remote control; lights, shades, and HVAC can be programmed to operate automatically; a single button can gently turn up all of the lights in your home, drop the shades for privacy, and turn the heater on; if you like, monitor and control the system via your smartphone or tablet.

MULTI-ROOM AUDIO SYSTEMS

Distributed audio allows homeowners to (a) play music (or any sound signals) from multiple sources simultaneously, (b) balance the level of sound throughout a home, and (c) control what's playing in individual rooms or zones.

Generally speaking, there are two types of multi-room audio systems: wired and wireless. A wired system has wires to power speakers and low-voltage cables (Cat5e) to controls such as keypads. A wireless system sends radio-frequency signals to components that are not physically connected. (Most audio systems have wired and wireless elements, but let's keep things simple for now.) Each type has benefits and challenges.

Wired systems

Wired systems have (1) a central unit that powers the speakers and controls multiple speaker pairs, (2) keypad controllers that control each room or any room on the system, (3) speakers, and (4) auxiliary source equipment such as iPods, digital media streamers, Internet radio, CD players, turntables, etc. (Some systems can be controlled by mobile devices.)

Benefits:
- Speakers physically connect to the system so you can install them in walls and ceilings.
- Often have more input options, e.g., you can play music simultaneously from many different sources (MP3, CD, Internet radio, etc.).
- Have individual keypad controls in each room.
- Have applications that enable control from (wireless) smartphones and devices.
- Generally cost less on a per-zone basis.

Challenges:
- More labor-intensive to install.
- Walls and ceilings must be opened to run speaker cables, or you must fish cables behind finish surfaces.

Wireless systems

Wireless systems typically include (1) a transmitter/repeater, (2) stand-alone internally amplified speakers, and/or (3) individual amplifiers that connect to conventional speakers. With wireless systems, the transmitter sends wireless signals (or music) to the internally amplified speakers or stand-alone amplifiers. The speakers and amplifiers require AC power. The transmitter can be

Control keypad for a multi-room audio system. The keypad controls the zone to which it is programmed, displays and allows selection of music from multiple sources, controls volume, and has global control of every zone.

connected to various sources and in general can be controlled via a PC, tablet, or smartphone, but often cannot be connected to multiple sources simultaneously.

Benefits:
- Can be installed in existing construction without the need to run speaker cables.
- Less labor-intensive to install.

Challenges:
- Speakers on wireless systems aren't powered by a central source, so they must plug into a nearby outlet (120v) or get power (and signals) from an auxiliary transceiver.
- Because they need to plug into a nearby power source, speakers are not typically installed in walls or ceilings.
- Can play multiple songs in multiple rooms, but typically from fewer sources.
- Typically more costly on a per-zone basis.

MULTI-ROOM AUDIO SYSTEMS (CONTINUED)

Sound choices

When planning a multi-room system consider the following: Where is the best place to locate the music source, how many zones will you need, how much control do you want, and how easy will it be to run wiring and install speakers? For example, can you run speaker cables through an attic or fish lo-vo cable down into the walls for control keypads? Or is an unfinished basement a better route? How much cutting, patching, and painting will be required?

Speakers vary in output (loudness) and are rated in watts (or energy used). High-wattage speakers can provide bigger sound. Wired systems deliver specific watts per channel (a channel is one speaker). Speakers driven at levels beyond system capability will require secondary amplification. If all of this is new to you, a reputable audio store can help you choose components and configure the system. These sites are also great resources:

www.nuvotechnologies.com

www.russound.com

www.sonos.com/system

www.aperionaudio.com

Multi-room audio components **are wired with low-voltage Cat5e UTP cable.**

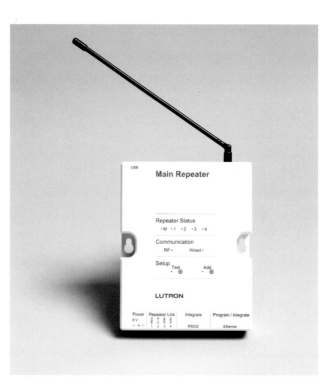

This main repeater **is the brain of a whole-house control system; it holds the program and tells other devices what to do.**

SETTING UP THE WHOLE-HOUSE SYSTEM

Setting up whole-house control systems such as RadioRA 2 is largely menu-driven and fairly intuitive once you get the hang of it. But the menu is complex and thus daunting to many people. More to the point, most homeowners won't know what the system can do or what their options are. So hire a pro to help set up the system–typically, a licensed electrician company-trained in the system he or she is installing.

An installer will start by sitting down with the homeowners to get a sense of their needs and to tell them what the system can do. From that input, the installer pieces together a system room by room. A basic floor plan emerges locating the repeater (main controller), keypad controllers, and all the devices you'll need to swap out. From a floor plan you can ballpark the costs of different options and estimate how complex programming will be.

If the homeowner wants to save money by installing most of the components (based upon the floor plan), the electrician will work up a list of equipment to buy. In general, installing devices is no more difficult than, say, replacing a switch. Once the new devices are in, the electrician will upload the software program and commission (activate) the system.

There are typically many steps to activate and fine-tune the system–it's not hard but you must go through the software and respond to many prompts that enable the controller to recognize installed components. After homeowners use the system for a month, they often have the installer return to tweak the system–make this button do this, turn on the furnace a little earlier, make the shades lower more slowly. The electrician makes and uploads those changes. Finally, when functions are all settled and everything works well, the manufacturer will engrave the names of functions onto keypad keys for free. Turn off the power, snap the engraved keys onto proper locations, turn power on, and you're done.

Menu-driven design/programming by manufacturer-trained professionals expands the options available and reduces the time required to set up and commission the system; solves compatibility issues as you go; develops complete parts lists; facilitates changes; allows for back-up; and, if properly networked, allows changes to be made remotely.

Getting it together

Since PCs became widespread in the 1980s, computer users have been part of one ongoing, occasionally buggy beta test. Interconnectivity–getting software and hardware to work together–has always been a challenge, and whole-house control systems are no exception. In our opinion, several companies are ahead of the pack on interconnectivity:

www.crestron.com

www.lutron.com

www.elanhomesystems.com

www.savantsystems.com

Clockwise, from upper right: HVAC controller mounts on and is wired to HVAC unit; duct sensor reads temperature of return air; wireless temperature sensor can be placed throughout the house; temperature control can be manually set, talks to HVAC controller.

FANS

RESIDENTIAL FANS CAN BE DIVIDED into two groups. The first group might be better called exhaust or vent fans, because their primary function is to remove moist or odor-laden air from living spaces, route it through ducts, and expel it outside. Commonly installed bath fans and range hoods both fall into this category. By removing excessive interior moisture, these fans help forestall mold and other unhealthy conditions.

The second group, primarily ceiling fans, circulate still, summer air and thus increase comfort by evaporating moisture on your skin. In cold climates, these fans push warm air down from the ceiling where it collects, so it can once again warm the bodies below. Whole-house fans, installed in attics in warm regions, also circulate hot air, but because they typically push it out roof or gable-end vents, whole-house fans are more like exhaust fans without ducts.

WIRING TIPS

Before you begin, p. 150

BATHROOM VENT FANS

Choosing a bathroom fan, p. 151

Locating a bathroom fan, p. 152

Installing the roof vent, p. 153

Mounting the fan box, p. 155

Retrofitting a bathroom fan, p. 156

Wiring a bathroom fan, p. 157

RANGE HOODS

Mounting & ducting a range hood, p. 159

Wiring the range hood, p. 160

CEILING FANS

Installing the ceiling fan box, p. 162

Mounting the ceiling fan, p. 164

BEFORE YOU BEGIN

There are two important tips to note before wiring any type of fan. First, check out the wiring schematic that comes with the unit **A**. In most cases, the schematic is affixed either to the fan housing or to the backside of a cover. Or it may be included in the installation instructions. You'll also find essential information such as the fan's rating, expressed in amperes.

SAFETY ALERT

When installing or replacing a fan of any type, always turn off the electrical power to that location. Then test with a voltage tester to be sure the power is off.

Second, most units have an integral junction box, like the one seen in photo **B**. The junction box contains wire leads that you'll splice to the incoming house wiring. All metal boxes—including fan housings—must be grounded.

PRO TIP

Never assume that all the parts you need for assembly and installation are in the box. Check the contents before you start by comparing the parts in the box to the inventory list included in the owner's manual. Smaller parts, such as screws, are typically packaged in clear plastic so you can count them without having to open the packet—a good idea because they're easy to lose.

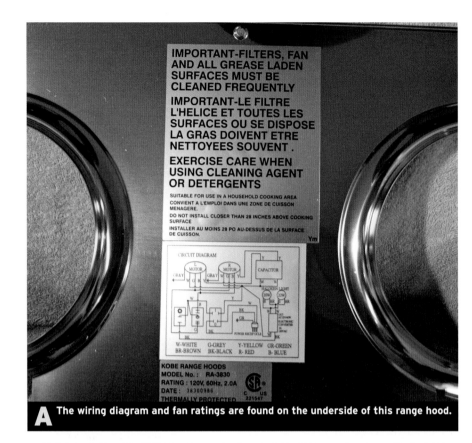

A The wiring diagram and fan ratings are found on the underside of this range hood.

B An integral junction box is in the housing of this bathroom vent fan. The second green wire grounds the metal housing.

CHOOSING A BATHROOM FAN

Bathroom fans are increasingly power-ful, quiet, and available with numerous bells and whistles. When considering all the extra features, however, remember that the primary function of a bathroom fan is to remove moisture. Energy-efficiency is a close second, thus Panasonic®, Delta®, Broan®, Nutone®, and other major fan makers offer a wide range of energy-conserving models.

There are complex formulas for sizing bath fans, but a good rule of thumb is 1 cfm (cubic foot per minute) per square foot for bathrooms 100 sq. ft. or smaller. For bath-rooms larger than 100 sq. ft., allot 50 cfm for each fixture (toilet, lavatory, shower) and 100 cfm for hot tubs.

Also, get a quiet fan. Whereas cheaper bath fans are rated at 3 sones to 4 sones, some energy-efficient models run at less than 0.3 sone. Two sones is tolerable, and 1 sone is very quiet. (By comparison, refrig-erators average about 1 sone.) And remote inline fans, typically installed in attics some distance above bathrooms, are quieter still. Consequently, you can install a larger fan inline and still have a quiet bathroom.

Next, consider switches. Fans usually need to continue venting after you leave the shower or use the toilet, so get an electronic switch with an integral timer so that the fan continues running after the light is turned off. You can also connect the fan to a *humid-istat*, which is a moisture sensor that turns the fan off once a preset moisture level is attained.

SAFETY ALERT

Never install a rheostat—commonly called a dimmer switch—to control an exhaust fan. Fan motors are designed to run on a fixed voltage, and if you reduce the voltage by using a rheostat, you may burn out the fan motor.

FAN COVERS

Most exhaust fans come with plastic covers, but they can be replaced with metal plates. Here, an antique wall register was plated to match the other fixtures in the room.

REMOTE INLINE FANS

Even a well-made bathroom fan will be relatively noisy if the motor is 2 ft. from your head in the bathroom ceiling. But if you install the fan some distance from the bathroom, you'll reduce the noise considerably. That remote location may mean that you have longer duct and wiring runs, but routing them is rarely a problem. In fact, with a large-enough fan motor and a duct Y-connector, you can vent two bathrooms with one fan. Because longer duct runs can mean greater air resistance, consider installing rigid-metal or polyvinyl chloride (PVC) ducts, whose smooth surfaces offer less resistance, rather than flexible metal ducts. Alternatively, you could oversize the fan slightly. Better fan makers, such as Fantech and American Aldes®, offer acoustically insulated cases to deaden sound further.

Remote inline fans **require longer ducting, but they're quieter because they're located farther away from the bathroom.**

LOCATING A BATHROOM FAN

There are three primary considerations when locating a bath fan. First, place the fan where it can expel moisture effectively—ideally, near the shower, where most of the moisture is generated.

Second, locate the fan so that its duct run is as short as possible and minimizes cut-outs in the blocking or framing members—especially rafters. Vent the ductwork from the fan out the roof or through a gable-end wall. Avoid sidewall vents because moist air expelled by them could be drawn up into the attic by soffit vents in roof overhangs.

Third, locate roof vents away from problem areas such as skylight and valley flashing. Water usually dams up on the uphill side of a skylight, creating a leak-prone area that must be carefully flashed. Typically, skylight flashing consists of two pieces: a base flashing and a counterflashing that goes over it. Locate a roof vent near skylight flashing and you're inviting trouble. Valley flashing, on the other hand, may consist of a single broad piece of metal or elastomeric material folded up the middle. But because this flashing is located where roof planes converge, it channels an enormous amount of water during rainy seasons. So keep things simple: Locate roof vents away from obstructions in the roof or concentrations of water. Don't put a roof vent near an operable window, either.

A BATHROOM FAN

To keep moisture from leaking into the attic, apply silicone caulk between the fan box flanges and the ceiling drywall. Use metal foil tape to ensure airtight joints where ducting attaches to fan and vent takeoffs.

Roof vent

Flexible metal duct

Metal foil tape

Fan box (housing)

Silicone caulk between flange and drywall

Ceiling drywall

PRO TIP
Before you cut a hole in the ceiling, be sure there are no obstructions along the way. Tentatively locate the fan and use a $1/4$-in. extension bit to drill along the proposed duct path. You'll also want to drill an exploratory hole up through the roofing.

INSTALLING THE ROOF VENT

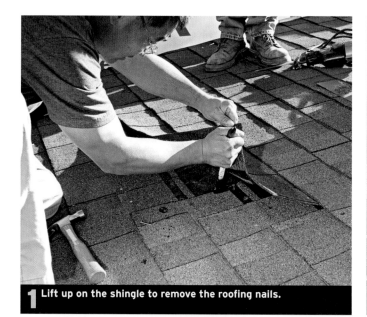

1 Lift up on the shingle to remove the roofing nails.

2 Remove the shingles over the entire section.

3 With the vent in place, trim the shingles to fit the upper arc of the vent.

4 Use a utility knife to cut the shape of the vent hole through the roofing paper.

In the installation shown here, there was enough clearance around the exploratory hole and there happened to be a roofer on site, so the crew decided to install the roof vent first. (Roof vents vary; the model shown has a round stack and a weatherproof cap.)

Go onto the roof and find the ¼-in. exploratory hole drilled while locating the fan. The hole represents the center of the vent hole you'll need to cut.

Most ducting and roof-vent takeoffs are 4 in. diameter, so sketch that circle onto the roof. If the circle would cut into

the tabs of any shingle—roughly the bottom half of a shingle strip—use a shingle ripper or a cat's paw to remove the nails holding those shingles in place before cutting the vent hole ❶. Be gentle when removing shingles so you can reuse them ❷.

Slide the upper flange of the roof vent under the shingle courses above and use a utility knife to trim its arc onto the shingles above ❸, then cut out the vent's circle into any remaining shingles and the roofing paper ❹. Next, use a reciprocating saw to cut through the sheathing ❺ (on the following page).

>> >> >>

INSTALLING THE ROOF VENT (CONTINUED)

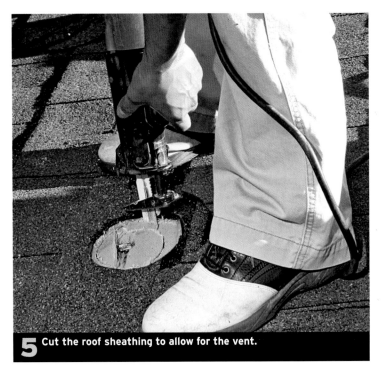

5 Cut the roof sheathing to allow for the vent.

6 On low-pitch roofs, caulk the vents to help prevent leaks.

If the roof pitch is 4:12 or greater, it usually isn't necessary to caulk the vent edges. Here, a 2:12 pitch required caulking to forestall leaks **6**. Carefully lift the shingle course above the vent and nail the two corners of the vent's upper flange into place **7**. Do not nail the lower corners of the vent: those nails would be exposed to weather and could leak. Cut and replace removed shingles and renail them.

PRO TIP
Keeping fan-expelled moisture out of attics and wall cavities is crucial, and the only way to do so is to create airtight connections: Caulk the fan housing to the ceiling and seal each duct joint with aluminum foil tape, not fabric duct tape.

7 Nail only the top corners of the vent—shingles cover these nails.

MOUNTING THE FAN BOX

1 If needed, add blocking between the framing members.

2 When positioning the fan, a scrap of drywall acts as a stand-in for the finished ceiling.

3 Slide on the flex duct and tape it in place.

If bathroom framing is exposed, mounting the fan is pretty straight-forward. If you remove the fan assembly from the fan box, the box will be lighter and easier to hold in place one-handed while you use your other hand to screw the unit to the ceiling joists. Most fans have expandable brackets which extend between joists spaced 16 in. on-center (o.c.). But you should always screw at least one side of the fan box to a joist, to ensure that it's anchored securely. For ceiling joist (or rafter) spacing greater than 16 in. o.c., it's a good idea to add blocking **1**.

If the fan-box flange mounts flush to the underside of the ceiling, use a piece of drywall scrap to gauge the depth of the unit relative to the finished ceiling **2**. Regardless of whether the box flange sits above or below the ceiling drywall, caulk the flange with polyurethane sealant to create an airtight seal between the two materials. If you removed the fan assembly earlier, reinstall it now.

Keep duct runs as short as possible to reduce air resistance. Slide the lower end of the flexible duct to the fan's exhaust port **3** and seal the joint with metal duct tape, then attach the other end to the roof vent takeoff. Or, if you haven't yet cut the hole in the roof, hold the free end of the duct to the underside of the roof sheathing and trace its outline onto the surface.

RETROFITTING A BATHROOM FAN

If you are remodeling or installing a bath fan and the finished ceiling is already in place, begin by creating a cardboard template of the fan housing. Mark the approximate position of the fan by driving a screw or nail through the ceiling and then go up into the space above the bathroom and find the marker. If there is an insulated attic above, take along a dustpan to shovel loose insulation out of the way and be sure to wear a dust mask and gloves. After you've located the marker, place the fan template next to the nearest joist and trace around it. Most fan boxes mount to ceiling joists. If the fan box has an adjustable mounting bar, you have more latitude in placing the fan. Use a jab saw or reciprocating saw to cut out the opening. To keep the drywall cutout from falling to the floor below, take a piece of scrap wood slightly longer than the cutout and screw it to the drywall.

Before placing the fan box on top of the ceiling drywall, caulk around the perimeter of the opening to create an airtight bond to the box flange ❶. Once the box is wired and the ceiling has been painted, install the trim piece to cover any gaps around the fan opening ❷.

1 Apply a bead of caulk under the flanges before you set the fan box in place.

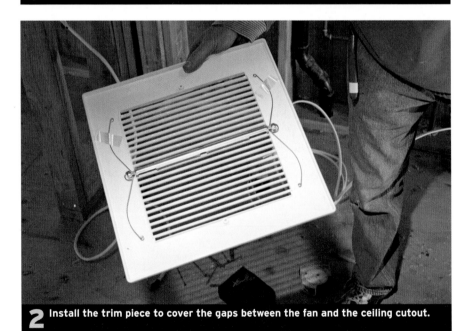
2 Install the trim piece to cover the gaps between the fan and the ceiling cutout.

PRO TIP

If there's an existing ceiling light in the bathroom, a fan-and-light combination unit may simplify your remodel. If you want the fan and light to operate at the same time, you can reuse the 2-wire cable that's presently controlling the light switch. Another option is to install a fan/light with a built-in occupancy sensor (p. 64). The light is controlled by the switch on the existing 2-wire cable and the fan turns on or off automatically when someone comes into the room.

WIRING A BATHROOM FAN

1 Staple cable no more than 1 ft. from the fan box.

2 Strip the sheathing off the wires.

3 Splice like-wire groups, starting with the ground wires, then neutrals, then hot wires. (At this stage the wires are not energized.)

4 Fold the spliced wires into the junction box and install the cover.

Before making any connections in the fan's junction box, make sure the power is off. Follow the wiring diagrams provided by the fan manufacturer. In general, it's easier if the incoming power runs through a switch box first; then you don't have to try to splice the switch legs in the fan junction box—junction boxes inside fan housings tend to be cramped and may not be rated for the additional wires. Bathroom fans should also have GFCI protection if installed in a shower whose ceilings are 8 ft. or less above the finish floor.

If the duct space is tight, it's usually best to wire the fan box before installing the duct. When running cable to the fan box, allow a generous loop of cable, just in case. As with light fixtures and receptacles, staple the cable within 1 ft. of the fan box **❶**. Insert a cable connector into a junction box knockout, feed the cable through it, and strip the cable sheathing **❷**.

Using wire connectors, first splice the incoming ground wire to the fixture ground **❸**. (If the fixture lead wires are stranded, extend them slightly beyond the solid wire so that the wire connector will engage them first.) Splice the neutral wires and then the hot wires. If the light and fan are wired separately, there will be two sets of hot wires.

Tug each wire group gently to be sure the splices are secure. When all groups are spliced, carefully fold the wires into the fan junction box and cover the box **❹**.

PRO TIP

In tight spaces like a junction box, almost all the pros use a utility knife to remove sheathing from the wires.

RANGE HOODS

Choosing a Range Hood

All cooktops and stoves should be vented by a range hood. In addition to sucking up the smoke of a charred steak, range hoods exhaust airborne grease that might otherwise migrate to a cool corner and feed mold or adhere to woodwork and discolor its finish. Range hoods come in many configurations but basically there's a *hood* to collect smells and smoke, a *fan* to expel them, *ducts* to carry exhaust out, and *shrouds* and other trim pieces. Range hoods vary from low-powered and inexpensive (less than $50) to custom-designed units (which cost thousands).

Range hoods are most often *wall-mounted* directly over a range. Alternatively, there are *downdraft* and *side-draft* vents that pop up from a counter area to suck away fumes. Over island and peninsula ranges, you can install *chimney-type* vents. In general, install the type of vent that will carry exhaust gases outdoors with the shortest and straightest duct run possible. Because heated air rises, wall-mounted and chimney types are inherently efficient, whereas downdraft and side-draft vents pull heated gases in directions they wouldn't go naturally and can even pull burner flames sideways.

Ideally, a range hood should be slightly wider than the range, say, 3 in. wider on each end, and mounted 30 in. above the range, but follow the hood maker's suggested mounting height. More powerful hoods can be installed higher. Finally, buy a unit with a good-quality filter that can withstand regular washing with soap and water. Most filters are aluminum mesh, better ones are stainless steel; many can be popped into the dishwasher. In general, be skeptical of range hoods that recirculate air through a series of filters rather than venting it outside.

Range hoods can be handsome additions to kitchen decor. This one is a European-style wall-mounted hood from Kobe®.

The height of the fan and the fact that it is not against a wall mean that the hood needs to draw more air to be effective. This stylish design is set higher than a typical range hood to provide sight lines across the room.

SIZING THE HOOD

A 100-cfm wall-mounted hood should be adequate to vent the average four-burner, 30-in.-wide range. But if that same range is located on a kitchen island, its range vent should draw 125 cfm to 150 cfm. More is not better when sizing range hoods. For one thing, larger hoods are noisier. Midsize range hoods average 3 sones to 3.5 sones, which is too noisy to have a conversation nearby; monster hoods can reach 8 sones. (In comparison, refrigerators register 1 sone.) Oversize hoods can also expel so much air that they create *back-drafting,* in which negative in-house air pressure draws furnace or fireplace exhaust gases back down the chimney.

MOUNTING & DUCTING A RANGE HOOD

1 Slide the duct into the thimble.

2 Level, center, and mount the hood.

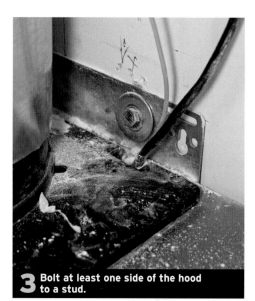

3 Bolt at least one side of the hood to a stud.

4 Lower the duct over the hood takeoff and seal the joint with metal tape.

> **PRO TIP**
> A well-sized hood should extend about 3 in. beyond the range on both ends.

Range hoods are typically screwed to the underside of a cabinet or mounted directly to a wall. A hood should be mounted about 30 in. above the range, and the ducting that vents it should exit the house as directly as possible. As you plan your duct route, use a stud finder to locate studs in the wall behind the stove or through ceiling joists above. The duct run should exit through the siding or the roofing. To locate the hole for the duct work, level the hood and center it over the range.

Cut a hole in the wall or ceiling and insert a thimble—a specialized fitting that creates an opening through a wall or ceiling into which the duct fits. If there already is a thimble in place, insert the duct from the range hood up into the thimble 3 in. to 4 in. above its final position **1**. Friction should hold the duct in place.

Level the hood, center it over the range, and bolt it to the wall **2**. Mount the hood in at least two points: If the studs behind the hood are 16 in. o.c., you may have to bolt one side of the hood to a stud **3** and secure the other side of the hood with a toggle bolt. After the hood is mounted, slide the duct down over the takeoff atop the hood **4**. Tape all of the joints with self-adhering metal tape.

WIRING THE RANGE HOOD

Many range hoods have discrete electrical junction boxes with knockouts, into which you insert cable clamps and cables. In the example shown here, the shroud that encloses the duct doubles as a junction box. The lead wires from the fan and light emerge through a bushing on the top of the hood and attach to wires in a Romex supply cable, which emerges from the wall cavity.

Strip and splice like wire pairs using wire connectors. Splice the ground wires first–be sure there's a grounding pigtail to the hood itself–then neutral wires, and then hot wires ❶.

To minimize weight and avoid marring shiny trim pieces, many pros install the fan filters, trim, and other trappings after the hood shell is mounted. Most of the parts simply snap into place–just follow the instructions provided ❷. Then, if your hood has a bottom casing, screw it into place ❸. Finally, fit the shroud over the ducting and the wire connection–they're usually held in place with one pair of screws at the top and another pair at the bottom ❹.

SAFETY ALERT

Most hoods aren't heavy but they're unwieldy, so get help installing one.

1 Splice the grounds, then neutrals, and then hot wires.

2 Snap on the fans, filters, and trim pieces.

3 Attach the bottom casing onto the hood.

4 Use screws to secure the shroud in place.

CEILING FANS

Choosing a Ceiling Fan

These days, you can find fan styles that match almost any architectural style; the Internet is a good place to start looking. As you might expect, quality correlates closely to cost. Good-quality fans will be balanced, so they don't wobble, and will run quieter, thanks to features like sealed steel bearings.

Most fan companies offer three mounting profiles: *standard* (which employs extension downrods to situate fan blades at an optimal height), *flush* (for low ceilings), and *angled* (for sloping ceilings). To operate safely, fan blades must be located at least 7 ft. above the floor; optimally, fan blades should be 8 ft. to 10 ft. above the floor. To attain that height from ceilings higher than 9 ft., fan makers offer extension downrods of varying length. Most downrods are 1/2 in. in diameter; better-quality units use rods that are 3/4 in. in diameter. For safety reasons, fan blades must be at least 18 in. away from the nearest wall or sloping ceiling.

Ceiling fan blade spans range from 32 in. to 60 in. There are, of course, complicated formulas for determining fan size, and ideally you should center any fan over the area in which people are most likely to congregate in a room. The chart on p. 165 will help you determine the right size.

In general, more fan blades won't move more air. More important is the blade angle. The steeper the pitch of the blade, the more air it will move. Less-expensive fan blades will have a 10-degree pitch and spin faster; better-quality fans will have a 12-degree to 14-degree pitch.

Another important consideration is the switch that controls the fan. Most fans have a multiple-speed pull-chain switch built into the bottom of the housing. If the fan is too high for you to reach the chain comfortably or you just don't like the look of a pull chain, install a wall switch or remote control. Among the more popular fan controls are fan-speed wall switches and remote wireless controls. Do not use standard dimmer switches (rheostats) to control a fan, however, as rheostats frequently cause fan motors to hum or, in some cases, burn out. Follow manufacturer's recommendations for appropriate switches.

This low-profile Nouvelle® fan comes with a bronze patina and walnut blades.

Remote controls, like this Adapt-Touch®, allow you to forgo long pull chains.

CEILING FAN LIGHTS

Many homes are designed with a single light outlet in the center of each room. If homeowners want both a fan and a ceiling light in a given room, installing a ceiling fan light is a straightforward and cost-effective solution. Thus many fan makers offer light kits, or fans with integral lights. Until recently, this all-in-one solution resembled a man wearing two hats because the light looked glued onto the fan. Fortunately, some fan makers are now designing combo units that look more integrated—search for them, they're out there. If you still don't find a combo fan and light that fits your taste, add a separate lighting outlet.

The integrated LED light fixture of this Scandia® fan can be modulated by a dimmer switch.

INSTALLING THE CEILING FAN BOX

CEILING FAN ELEMENTS

Mounting details and fan assemblies vary: Follow the installation instructions that come with your unit. Add down-rod extensions as needed to locate the fan blades 8 ft. to 10 ft. above the floor.

Fan-rated box

Supply wires

Wire leads from fan

Mounting bracket

Ball hanger

Down rod

Canopy

Fan motor

Blade holder

Blade

SAFETY ALERT

Although there are plastic ceiling boxes rated for fans, many installers won't touch them. Spooked by the possibility of stripped screw holes and crashing fans, they insist on using a metal fan box.

All fans must be securely mounted to framing, but this is especially true of ceiling fans, which are weighty and subject to vibration and wobbling. All fans must be installed in a ceiling box rated for fan use—that is, capable of supporting 50 lb. or more. Check your fan's installation specs. If your fan is particularly heavy or complex, it may require a box with a higher weight rating or additional bracing.

If ceiling joists are exposed, you have several options. You can install a piece of 2×4 or 2×6 blocking to the ceiling joists (or rafters), then mount a fan-rated 2-in.-deep octagonal metal box to the blocking. Mark the location of the blocking so the box will be flush to the finished ceiling surface. Then drive three 3-in. toenailed wood screws through each end of the blocking and into the joists, keeping the blocking on your marks.

If you must hang a fan from a ceiling joist's edge, screw a fan-rated 1/2-in.-deep metal pancake box directly to the joist. Before doing so, however, be sure there is enough room inside the fan's canopy to hide electrical connections—because there's no room for them in the pancake box! If not, move the fan or modify your plans.

An alternative is to mount an adjustable hanger to the framing. Bar hangers are strong, easier than nailing up blocking, and easily positioned by sliding the box along its support bar. Remodel bar hangers are also available.

➔ **For more on bar hangers, see p. 27.**

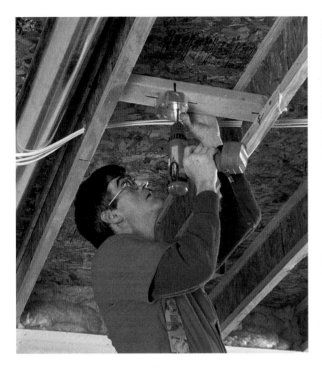

If joists are exposed, **install the blocking and mount a fan box.**

SAFETY ALERT

If there's an existing fan box, turn off the power to it and test before proceeding. If the box is plastic, check the screw holes that the fan mounting bracket attaches to. If the screw holes are at all stripped, if the box is cracked or deformed, or if you have any doubts that it can support the new fan, replace the box.

If joists are not exposed, install a remodel bar (aka a *braced box*) if there's a finish ceiling. Locate the fan, cut a 4-in.-diameter hole in the ceiling, insert the bar into the hole ❶, and maneuver it until its feet stand on top of the drywall. Then hand-turn the bar to expand it. When the bar touches a joist on both ends, turn the bar with a wrench to drive the bar points into the joists ❷. Finally, bolt the ceiling box to the remodel bar using the hardware provided ❸.

1 Insert a remodel bar through the ceiling cutout.

2 Expand the remodel bar by hand. Then force the pointed ends into the joists by turning the bar with a wrench.

3 Attach the fan box to the remodel bar.

MOUNTING THE CEILING FAN

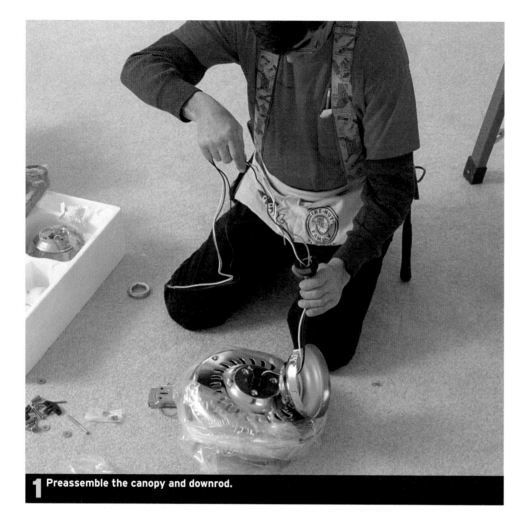

1 Preassemble the canopy and downrod.

2 Insert the downrod into the bracket.

3 Bolt the blade holders to the fan motor.

Fan assemblies differ greatly, so be sure to follow the installation instructions that come with your fan. After testing to be sure the power is off, feed the ceiling wires through the opening in the mounting bracket and screw the bracket to the fan box. *Note:* For some assemblies, the mounting bracket is simply a flat crossbar that spans the fan box; for other types, the fan's weight is supported by a bracket that is somewhat like a slotted dome, into which a ball hanger fits.

Preassemble the parts necessary for hanging the fan motor and housing. Typically, you feed the fan's wire leads up through a canopy and a hollow downrod. The downrod has a ball head that slips into, and is supported by, a slotted mounting bracket screwed to a ceiling outlet box ❶.

Carefully lift the fan motor toward the mounting bracket in the ceiling. Being careful not to pinch the wires from the ceiling or those from the fan motor, insert the ball head of the downrod into the opening of the mounting bracket ❷. On some models, you may need to rotate the fan body until a slot in the ball head aligns with a pin in the bracket. If there is a locking bolt or hanging pin that secures the assembly, be sure to attach it or the unit may fall.

Now wire the unit. Because all metal boxes must be grounded, attach a grounding pigtail to the bracket. Use wire connectors to join like wire pairs, starting with the grounding wires, then the neutral wires, and then the hot wires. If there's a fan light, there will be two hot wire leads: The black lead typically connects to the fan and the blue or red lead controls the light. Tuck the spliced wires behind the canopy, slide the canopy up the downrod until the canopy is flush to the ceiling, and then tighten the setscrew that holds it in place.

Attach the fan blades last. Typically, four machine screws attach a blade to each blade holder; each screw hole is lined with a rubber grommet that cushions the screw-and-nut assembly and forestalls vibration. Each blade holder then bolts to the underside of the fan motor ❸. Because fan blades are prebalanced at the factory, never use blades from other fans. Once you've tightened and checked all bolts and screws, turn the fan on its slowest speed to check for wobbling.

PRO TIP

The most common cause of wobbling is a blade holder that's become misaligned. To check for that, turn off the fan and use a yardstick to see if all blade holders are the same height from the ceiling. If any part of a ceiling fan doesn't fit due to misalignment, take the whole fixture back to the store for an exchange. Fan makers also have websites that describe how to balance and troubleshoot their fans.

WIRING A FAN-LIGHT COMBINATION

The fan types discussed in this section are frequently configured with both fans and lights. Running a 3-wire cable (12/3 with ground or 14/3 with ground) enables you to operate the fan and light separately. When a ceiling fan's junction box is closer to the power source than to the switch box, as shown in the drawing below right, the switch is called a "back-fed switch." *Note:* Because of code changes, back-fed switches are not suitable for *new* construction.

INCOMING POWER THROUGH SWITCH BOX

Switch leg to fan · Switch leg to light · 12/3 or 14/3 cable · Ground · Fan switch · Light switch · Hot · Incoming power · Neutral

BACK-FED SWITCH

Ground · Hot to switches · Incoming power · Switch leg to fan · Neutral · Switch leg to light · 12/3 or 14/3 cable · Fan switch · Light switch · Hot white wire taped black

FAN SIZES	
Blade span (in.)	Room size (sq. ft.), max*
32 or 36	100
42 or 44	144
48	225
50 or 52	400
54 to 60	> 400

* Output may also be expressed in cfm (cubic feet per minute). For example, a good-quality fan with a 36-in. span will move 2,500 cfm to 4,000 cfm.

PLANNING

BEING DETAIL ORIENTED IS AS important to planning as it is to installation. When you plan a wiring project, be methodical: Assess the existing system, calculate electrical loads, check local codes, and draw a wiring floor plan.

If you are only replacing existing devices—changing a light fixture, replacing a faulty switch, or upgrading a receptacle, for example—you seldom need a permit from the local building department. However, if you extend or add any circuit, you must pull (or file) a permit.

Most local electrical codes are based on the NEC. When it's necessary to pull a permit, local code authorities will want to approve your plans and later inspect the wiring to be sure it's correct. Don't shortcut this process: Codes and inspections protect you and your home.

Whatever the scope of your project, if you work on existing circuits, first turn off the power and test to be sure it's off, and tag or lock the panel.

BEFORE YOU BEGIN

Inspecting the fuse box or breaker panel, p. 168

Assessing the condition of wiring, p. 170

Is the system adequately sized? p. 171

ACCORDING TO CODE

General wiring guidelines, p. 173

General-use circuit requirements, p. 174

Requirements room by room, p. 175

WORKING DRAWINGS

Developing a floor plan, p. 176

Electrical notation, p. 178

Wiring schematics, p. 180

INSPECTING THE FUSE BOX OR BREAKER PANEL

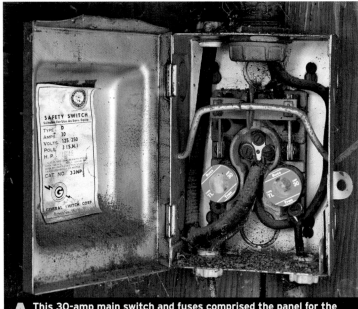

A This 30-amp main switch and fuses comprised the panel for the whole house. Even if it were safe, it would be dramatically undersize.

B Replace older panel brands that have had widespread failures. This panel cover is missing knockouts—very dangerous.

By looking at the outside of the service panel and wiring that's exposed in the basement and attic, you can get a basic overview of the system's condition. If the panel has unused breaker spaces and the wiring insulation is in decent shape, you can probably continue using it and safely add an outlet or two if there is sufficient capacity. However, if the system seems unsafe or inadequate, hire a licensed electrician to open the panel and do a more thorough examination.

Here's what to look for.

Start your investigation at the fuse box or breaker panel. You can learn a lot about the condition of the system by examining the outside of the service box. Examining the inside of a panel or fuse box is best left to a licensed electrician, however.

Rust and corrosion on the outside of a service box or on the armored cable or conduit feeding it can indicate corroded connections inside **A**. Such connections can lead to arcing and house fires, so have a licensed electrician replace the fuse box or panel. Likewise, if you see scorch marks on breakers or a panel—or near a receptacle cover—have a pro examine it.

Melted wire insulation is a sign either of an overheated circuit—usually caused by too many appliances in use at the same time—or of a poor wire connection in which arcing has occurred. In the first case, a homeowner typically installs an oversize fuse or breaker to keep an overloaded circuit from blowing so often; but this "remedy" exceeds the current-carrying capacity of the wire. The wire overheats and melts its insulation, which can lead to arcing, house fires, or—if someone touches that bare copper wire—electrocution.

An oversize fuse may not melt wires where you can see them, but it may have damaged wire insulation in a place where you can't. Have an electrician inspect the electrical system. Installing type-S fuse socket inserts can prevent overfusing.

"Pennying" a fuse is another unsafe way to deal with an overloaded circuit that keeps blowing fuses. In this case, someone unscrews a fuse, inserts a penny or a blank metal slug into the bottom of the socket—a dangerous act in itself—and then reinstalls the fuse. The penny allows current to bypass the fuse and the protection it offers. Here,

again, have an electrician examine the circuits for damage to the wire insulation.

Panel covers that don't fit, have gaps, or are missing are unsafe. So if you see covers that have been cut to fit a breaker, housing knockouts that are missing, bus bars that are visible when the panel cover is on, or mismatched components, hire a licensed electrician to assess and correct those problems. Some older brands of panels and breakers, such as Federal Pacific® and Zinsco®, have a host of well-documented failures and so should be carefully checked and, where necessary, replaced **B**.

Missing cable connectors or unfilled knockouts enable mice and vermin to enter the panel and nest in it, which can be a fire hazard. Missing connectors also allow cables to be yanked, stressing electrical connections inside the panel **C**. A missing cable clamp may also allow the sharp edge of the panel to slice through thermoplastic cable sheathing, which could energize the panel (if the grounding of the system is not correct) and electrocute anyone who touches it **D**.

A properly grounded panel will have a large grounding wire running from the panel

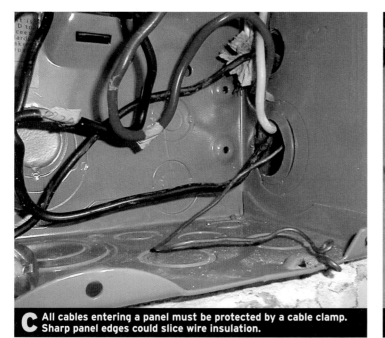

C All cables entering a panel must be protected by a cable clamp. Sharp panel edges could slice wire insulation.

D Service entrance cable enters a panel through a defective bushing. The sharp edge has nearly cut through the cable sheathing.

UNSAFE!

These fuses are too large (30 amps) for the load rating of the circuit wires, which could melt and start a fire.

The scorch marks on this receptacle indicate arcing inside the outlet—electrical leaps between connections that have worked loose.

Stay out of panels!

Only a licensed electrician should work in a service panel or sub-panel—or even remove the cover. Even with the main fuse or breaker turned off, some parts inside a panel are always *hot* (p. 10) and could electrocute you. The panel may not be correctly grounded. Or the inside of a panel may be so crowded (see "Play it safe," on p. 11) that it will be difficult to get a cover back on without pinching (and possibly damaging) wires.

to a grounding electrode (which could be a metal underground water pipe, a ground rod driven into the earth, or a Ufer electrode). For the entire electrical system to be grounded, there must be a continuous ground wire or other effective grounding path running from each device or fixture to the service panel and, by extension, to the grounding electrode. Cold water and gas pipes must also be connected (bonded) to the grounding bus in the panel.

➜ **For more on grounding, see p. 12.**

ASSESSING THE CONDITION OF WIRING

Cables may be visible as they near the service panel and as they run through attics and basements. If there are covered junction boxes, carefully remove the covers and examine the wire splices inside—without touching them. You can also turn off power and pull a few receptacles out to better examine the wires.

Deteriorated sheathing is a potential shock hazard, so note brittle fiber insulation and bare wire, but avoid touching it. If cable sheathing has been chewed on by mice, rats, or squirrels, it should be replaced.

NM cable (cable protected by nonmetallic sheathing) must be stapled within 8 in. of single-gang boxes that don't have cable clamps, and within 12 in. of other boxes, and supported by stapling or another method at least every 4½ ft. (54 in.). A cable running through a drilled hole is considered supported. Sagging wire is hazardous because it can get inadvertently strained, jeopardizing electrical connections. Likewise, all boxes must be securely mounted. All NM cable entering metal boxes must be gripped by cable clamps. Single-gang plastic boxes do not require the strain relief of cable clamps, but double-gang (and larger) plastic boxes have integral plastic tension clamps that afford some strain relief on cable.

Small-gauge aluminum wiring (10 or 12 gauge) is a fire hazard unless it is correctly spliced to a copper wire with a COPALUM® connector, or terminated to CO/ALR-rated outlets and switches. If it is incorrectly terminated in a copper-rated-only device, the two metals will expand and contract at different rates each time the circuit is under load. This can lead to loose connections, arcing, overheating, and house fires. Aluminum-to-aluminum splices require special splicing techniques, either COPALUM connectors or another listed and approved method.

Wire splices (whether copper to copper, copper to aluminum, or aluminum to aluminum) must be housed within a covered junction box or outlet box. Wires that are spliced outside a box or inside an uncovered box can be a fire hazard because of the dangers of arcing. Loose connections not contained in a cover box can easily ignite combustibles nearby because arcs approach 2,000°F.

Knob-and-tube (K & T) wiring, although outdated, is usually safe unless individual wire insulation is deteriorated, splices are incorrectly made, the wiring is overloaded, or the wiring is buried in thermal insulation. Typically, splices that were part of the original installation will not be in a junction box but must be wrapped with electrical (friction) tape and supported by porcelain knobs on both sides of each splice. Nonoriginal splices must be housed in covered boxes. Have knob-and-tube wiring assessed or modified by an electrician familiar with it; it's quirky stuff. The NEC does not allow knob-and-tube wiring to be buried in insulation.

Knob-and-tube wiring lacks an equipment ground (a separate grounding wire), so it offers no protection should a faulty appliance get plugged into a receptacle. On the other hand, a knob-and-tube system is run completely on insulators, a plus. The conductors of K&T wiring were copper, coated with a thin layer of tin (to protect the copper from sulfur in the rubber wire insulation). Uninformed inspectors often mistake the tinned copper wire for aluminum wire.

Unstapled cable and unsecured boxes can be inadvertently yanked and stress electrical connections. Work this sloppy suggests substandard wiring throughout the house.

A 30-YEAR PRO'S TAKE ON REWIRING

If the wiring in an older home appears to be sound and in good repair (see the warning signs below), it's probably OK to continue using it, even though it may not meet code requirements for a new installation. If you are planning to gut the house completely, it makes sense to rip out all the old wiring and completely rewire the house. If you're remodeling only part of the house, leave most of the old wiring in place if it is sound and spend your money rewiring the kitchen, baths, and laundry circuits. That will give you more bang for your buck.

However, you should replace old wiring that's unsafe. If you observe any of these conditions, the wiring should be replaced:

- Circuits that have been extended improperly, as evidenced by loose connections, unprotected splices, or insufficient support.

- Circuits that contain mismatched wire types or sizes, such as NM cable spliced to knob-and-tube wiring outside of a junction box.

- Knob-and-tube wiring whose insulation has deteriorated or that has been damaged. Also, if knob-and-tube wiring in the attic has been covered with loose-fill insulation or insulation batts, that is a serious code violation that could lead to overheating and fire danger.

- Circuits wired with unsheathed wires (other than properly done knob-and-tube) rather than with sheathed cable or conduit.

IS THE SYSTEM ADEQUATELY SIZED?

If receptacles in your house teem with multiplugs and extension cords, you probably need to add outlets. But there are more subtle clues: If you blow fuses or trip breakers regularly, or if the lights brown out when you plug in a toaster or an electric hair dryer, you may need to add new circuits to relieve the overload on existing circuits. This section will help you figure out whether your system has the capacity to do so.

> **For more on how electrical service works, see p. 8.**

These days, 3-wire service feeding a 100-amp service panel is the minimum required by the NEC, and many electricians install 150-amp or 200-amp panels if the homeowners plan to enlarge the house at some point or acquire a lot of heavy-energy–using appliances, such as electric ranges and hot tubs. If there are only two large wires running from the utility pole to the house, they deliver only 120v service.

A house with 2-wire service probably has a 30-amp or 60-amp main fuse or breaker, which is inadequate for modern usage.

Rules of thumb

The only sure way to know if you've got enough capacity to add an outlet or a circuit is to calculate electrical loads (p. 172). But for the benefit of those who wish that an electrician would just offer an offhand opinion of what works most of the time, here are a few rules of thumb.

Fuse-box service. If you've got a fuse box with a 30-amp or 60-amp main fuse, the best advice we can give is to upgrade your service. Don't add outlets or circuits until you replace the fuse box with a breaker panel. Fused mains are often abused by people trying to bypass its protection, so insurance companies often charge higher premiums on houses with fuse boxes.

Adding outlets. If you have a breaker panel with space to add an additional breaker, you can most likely add a circuit to feed a new outlet or two or more lights. If, for example, you have 3-wire service and a

>> >> >>

(calculate electrical loads (p. 172))

ASSESSING A CIRCUIT'S CAPACITY

To recap briefly, electricity, impelled by *voltage*, flows from the power source. (*Amperes* are the rate of electron flow.) Along the way (at outlets), it encounters resistance and does work. (*Watts* are a measure of power consumed.) It then returns to the power source, its voltage reduced or spent.

Or, expressed as mathematical formulas:

watts = voltage × amperes

amperes = watts ÷ voltage

To determine the capacity of a circuit you want to extend, identify the circuit breaker controlling the circuit and note the rating of the breaker. If it's a general-purpose circuit, the breaker will probably be 15 amp or 20 amp. A circuit controlled by a 15-amp breaker has a capacity of 1,800w (15 amp × 120v); one controlled by a 20-amp breaker has 2,400w.

The total wattage of all loads on the circuit (including the extension) must not exceed these capacities; otherwise, you risk overheating wires. To avoid overloading, it's a good idea to reduce the capacity by 20 percent. For example, 80% of 1,800w is 1,440w for a 15-amp circuit; 80% of 2,400w equals 1,920w for a 20-amp circuit.

CIRCUIT CAPACITIES

Amperes × Volts*	Total capacity	Safe capacity**
	(watts)	(watts)
15 × 120	1,800	1,440
20 × 120	2,400	1,920
30 × 120	3,600	2,990

*Amperes multiplied by volts equals watts. **Safe capacity = 80 percent of total capacity

3-wire service, made up of two large, insulated hot conductors wrapped around a stranded bare wire messenger cable (neutral), supplies enough power for modern needs.

IS THE SYSTEM ADEQUATELY SIZED? (CONTINUED)

100-amp main, you may have excess capacity.

Adding a circuit for general use. If there is an unused space in the panel, have an electrician determine whether the panel can handle another circuit.

Adding a kitchen or bath circuit. If you want to add a bath fan or some new light fixtures, and there's space in the panel, have an electrician see if you can add a circuit. Adding a 20-amp, small-appliance circuit to reduce the load on an existing circuit is smart.

Remodeling a kitchen. Kitchens are complicated and often full of big energy users. Use the chart at right to help you add up the loads. If there aren't many open spaces for breakers, you may need to upgrade to a larger panel.

Adding dedicated circuits. If you need to add dedicated circuits for heavy-use items such as an electric range (50 amps) or a hot tub (60 amps), get out the calculator and do the math.

EXAMPLE OF LOAD CALCULATION FOR SINGLE-FAMILY DWELLING

CALCULATING GENERAL LIGHTING LOAD

Type of Load	NEC Reference	Calculation	Total VA
Lighting Load	Table 220.12	2,000 sq. ft. X 3 VA	6,000 VA
Small Appliance Load	Section 220.52	2 circuits X 1,500 VA	3,000 VA
Laundry Load	Section 220.52	1 circuit X 1,500 VA	1,500 VA
Total General Lighting			**10,500 VA***

Ⓐ CALCULATING DEMAND FOR GENERAL LIGHTING LOAD

Type of Load	Calculation	Demand Factor (DF)	Total VA
General Lighting	First 3,000 VA X DF	100%	3,000 VA
General Lighting	7,500‡ X DF	35%	2,625 VA
Total Lighting, Small Appliances & Laundry		**Ⓐ**	**5,625 VA**

Ⓑ CALCULATING DEMAND FOR LARGE-LOAD APPLIANCES

Type of Load	Nameplate Rating	Demand Factor (DF)	Total VA
Electric Range	Not Over 12KVA	Use 8KVA	8,000 VA
Clothes Dryer	6,600 VA X DF	100%	6,600 VA
Water Heater	6,600 VA X DF	100%	6,600 VA
Other Fixed Appliances	0 VA X DF	100%	0 VA
Total Load for Large Appliances		**Ⓑ**	**21,200 VA**

	Total VA (Ⓐ+Ⓑ)	**26,825 VA**
Minimum Service Size	Total VA /240V	**111.77 VA**

The minimum service size is the next standard size above the total VA calculated. Based upon these calculations, the minimum service size is 125 amps.

*Use this to calculate Ⓐ
‡Total General Lighting Load 10,500 VA – First 3,000 VA = 7,500 VA

USING THIS TABLE
1. Square ft. for general lighting load is for the entire dwelling including habitable basements or attics.
2. NEC requires a minimum of two small appliance loads, but it is important to add small fixed kitchen appliances such as microwaves, disposals, dishwashers, large range hood, computers, etc.
3. Minimum of one laundry load is required for a single-family dwelling.
4. The demand factor calculation is designed to take actual use into account (e.g. it is unlikely all lights and small appliances will be running at one time).
5. All large load appliances (high wattage) are added at 100%.
6. The final load calculation is the minimum. Often increasing capacity has little cost impact and is a good practice.

GENERAL WIRING GUIDELINES

GROUNDING REQUIREMENTS!

In a service panel, connect ground and neutral wires to a neutral/ground bus.

Large copper ground wire is clamped to a grounding electrode (rod).

All metal boxes and metal appliance housings require grounding.

The main water pipe must be properly bonded.

Attach ground pigtails to green ground screws on devices.

Electricians follow the NEC, as adopted (or amended) by local jurisdictions, which was compiled to promote safe practices and prevent house fires. Consider these requirements before you start drawing plans, but be sure to consult local electrical code—it is the final authority in your area.

The guidelines given here apply to all circuits in the house, whether general lighting or heavy-use appliance circuits. Local codes rarely require you to change existing circuits—as long as they are safe—but new electrical work should reflect current electrical code.

Circuit wiring

Wire gauge must be large enough to carry the circuit load and be protected by a comparably sized breaker or fuse at the panel. General-use and lighting circuits are typically 14AWG wire, protected by 15-amp breakers; kitchen, bath, and workshop circuits usu-

ally have 12AWG wire, protected by 20-amp breakers.

See the facing page for more on calculating circuit loads.

Acceptable cable

Most circuits are wired with NM cable because the cable is protected behind a finish surface such as drywall or plaster. When circuit wiring is to be left unprotected and exposed, it must be armored cable or in conduit.

➤ For more on cable and conduit, see p. 28.

Grounding

All receptacles, appliances, and electrical equipment must be connected (bonded) to the service panel via an equipment grounding conductor (ground wire). NM cable contains a separate ground wire, whereas armored cable sheathing and metal con-

duit provide the path to ground if properly installed.

Boxes

All electrical connections must take place in covered boxes. Boxes where connections are made must be accessible, that is, not buried in a wall or ceiling. Based on local code requirements, boxes may be plastic or metal. If metal, the box must also be connected to the equipment grounding conductor (bonded). If NM cable is used, the ground wire must be connected to a metal box with either a ground screw or a ground clip. If AC cable or metal conduit is used, it must be properly attached to the box to ensure effective bonding. If the box is plastic, it does not need to be (and cannot be) grounded; run a ground wire to the device or fixture only.

GENERAL-USE CIRCUIT REQUIREMENTS

General-use circuits are intended primarily for lighting, but small loads that are connected via a cord and plug, such as televisions, fans, and vacuums, are allowed—as long as the power they draw doesn't exceed the capacity of the circuit.

Lighting and small loads

Though 14AWG wire is sufficient for lighting, electricians often run 12AWG wire on general-use circuits to accommodate future uses. Calculate lighting loads at 3w per square foot, or roughly one 15-amp circuit for every 500 sq. ft. of floor space. When laying out the lighting circuits, do not put all the lights on a floor on one circuit. Otherwise, should a breaker trip, the entire floor would be without lights.

Receptacles

There must be a receptacle within 6 ft. of each doorway, and spaced at least every 12 ft. along a wall. (This is also stated as, "No space on a wall should be more than 6 ft. from a receptacle.") Any wall at least 2 ft. wide must have a receptacle; and a receptacle is required in hallway walls 10 ft. or longer. Finally, any foyer of more than 60 sq. ft. must have a receptacle on any wall 3 ft. or longer.

Outlets

The NEC does not specify a maximum number of lighting or receptacle outlets on a residential lighting or appliance circuit, though local jurisdictions may.

Figure roughly 9 outlets per 15-amp circuit and 10 outlets per 20-amp circuit.

Light switches

There must be at least one wall switch that controls lighting in each habitable room, in the garage (if wired for electricity), and in storage areas (including attics and basements). There must be a switch controlling an outside light near each outdoor entrance. Three-way switches are required at each end of corridors and at the top and bottom of stairs with six steps or more. When possible, put switches near the lights they control. It should be noted that the light switch may control a receptacle (considered "lighting") in habitable rooms except in kitchens and bathrooms.

GFCI protection

The NEC requires GFCI protection for all bathroom receptacles; all receptacles serving kitchens; all outdoor receptacles; accessible basement or garage receptacles; and receptacles near pools and hot tubs. (Check the current NEC for a complete listing.)

AFCI protection

Since the 2008 NEC, AFCI protection is required for branch circuits in all areas inside the house except bathrooms, kitchen, garage, and unfinished basements and attics.

KITCHEN LIGHTING BASICS

Kitchen lighting should be designed to utilize natural light during the day and achieve a balance of general lighting and task lighting at night. Do not be afraid of energy-efficient lighting such as fluorescent. Today's energy-efficient lighting is instant, dimmable, and available in colors that match incandescent light. Kitchen lighting is often highly regulated for energy efficiency. Check with local building officials before you begin your design.

GENERAL LIGHTING
General lighting is meant to illuminate the space generally and can come from recessed cans, surface-mounted fixtures, track lighting, or cove uplighting. Consider cabinetry and appliances when laying out new light fixtures. A general rule is 2w incandescent or 1w fluorescent per square foot of kitchen area, but even illumination is the goal.

TASK LIGHTING
Task lighting is meant to provide a higher level of illumination at work areas (sinks, countertops, and islands) and can be achieved with recessed cans, pendants, or undercabinet fixtures. If cabinets are over countertops, undercabinet fixtures (T5 fluorescent or LED strips) are by far the best choice and should be spaced for even illumination of the counter surface. For islands and sinks choose a recessed can with a slightly higher wattage and narrower lamp beam spread, or install pendants with similar attributes.

Arc-fault breakers are designed to detect arcing patterns of current for very short time intervals.

REQUIREMENTS ROOM BY ROOM

Kitchen and bath appliances are heavy power users, so their circuits must be sized accordingly.

Bathroom circuits

Bathroom receptacles must be supplied by a 20-amp circuit. The NEC allows the 20-amp circuit to supply the receptacles of more than one bathroom or to supply the receptacles, lights, and fans (excluding heating fans) in one bathroom. Receptacles in bathrooms must be GFCI-protected, either by a GFCI receptacle or a GFCI breaker. Bathroom ventilation fans are required in new and remodeled bathrooms in many jurisdictions regardless of whether there are operable windows. So always check local codes.

Small-appliance circuits

There must be at least two 20-amp small-appliance circuits in the kitchen serving the kitchen countertops. No point along a kitchen countertop should be more than 2 ft. from an outlet—in other words, space countertop receptacles at least every 4 ft. Every counter at least 12 in. wide must have a receptacle.

Kitchen lighting

Adequate lighting is particularly important in kitchens so people can work safely and efficiently. Lay out a good balance of general and task lighting. Be aware that many jurisdictions have energy-efficiency requirements for lighting in kitchens, so check with your local building authority first.

Bathroom lighting

It is important to illuminate the face evenly in mirrors. Common practice is to place good-quality light sources either above the vanity mirror or on either side of it. Be careful when using recessed cans over the vanity because they can leave shadows across the face. Many jurisdictions also have energy-efficiency requirements for lighting in bathrooms, including the use of high-efficacy lighting and vacancy sensors.

Dedicated circuits

All critical-use and fixed appliances should and in some cases (depending on the demand of the appliances and size of the circuit) must have their own dedicated (separate) circuits. These fixed appliances may include the water pump, freezer, refrigerator, oven, cooktop, microwave, furnace and/or whole-house air-conditioning unit, window air conditioners, and electric water heater. A bathroom heater requires a dedicated circuit, whether it is a separate unit or part of a light/fan. Laundry room receptacles must be on a dedicated circuit; so must an electric clothes dryer.

PRO TIP

Map your electrical system and place a copy near the panel so that you can quickly identify an outlet later if a circuit breaker trips or a fuse blows. Be specific when labeling each breaker.

DEVELOPING A FLOOR PLAN

Drawing a set of project plans can help you anticipate problems, find optimal routes for running cable, minimize mess and disruption, and make the most of your time and money. A carefully drawn set of plans is also an important part of the code compliance and inspection process.

If you're replacing only a receptacle, switch, or light fixture, you usually don't need to involve the local building department. But if you run cable to extend a circuit, add a new circuit, or plan extensive upgrades, visit the building department to learn local code requirements and take out a permit. Your wiring plans should be approved by a local building inspector before you start the project.

Phone first

Call the building department and ask if local codes allow homeowners to do electrical work or if it must be done by a licensed electrician. You may be required to take a test to prove basic competency. This is also a good time to ask if the municipality has pamphlets that give an overview of local electrical code requirements.

Read up

Make a rough sketch of the work you propose, develop a rudimentary materials list, and then apply for a permit. At the time you apply, the building department clerk may be able to answer questions generated by the legwork you've done thus far. This feedback often proves invaluable.

MATERIALS LIST: LIGHTING AND SWITCHES	
This materials list was derived from "Electrical Plan: Lighting and Switches Layer," on p. 179.	

ROUGH	
Fixture housings	Type 4, 5, and 6
4 ea.	3/0 or 4/0 metal boxes with bar hangers (verify fixture requirements)
3 ea.	4/0 NM boxes with bar hangers (wall fixtures only)
4 ea.	One-gang NM adjustable boxes
2 ea.	Two-gang NM adjustable boxes
4 ea.	Three-gang NM boxes
17 ea.	Romex connectors
500 ft.	14/2 NM Romex: 24 fixtures × 15 ft. ave. = 360 ft. (use excess for home runs, 3 × 50 = 150 ft.)
105 ft.	12/3 NM Romex (use remaining from power rough)

NOTE:
Staples, screws, and nail plates from power rough materials list.

Recommendations:
Verify all surface-mounted fixtures before rough. Some have very small canopies and must have a 3/0 or even a one-gang box.

For undercabinet lights, do not install a box. Stub cable out of wall approximately 6 in. higher than the bottom of the upper cabinet. This way the drywall can be notched and the cable brought down to the perfect height by the cabinet installer. If undercabinet fixtures are to be installed at the front of the cabinet, some trim piece or metal sheath must be put over the NM cable to protect it from the wall to the fixture.

For recessed and other ceiling lighting, layout fixtures on the floor and use a plumb bob or laser to set fixtures on the ceiling.

To align straight rows of ceiling fixtures, use a taut line.

TRIM	
Trims and lamps	Type 4, 6, 5
Fixtures and lamps	Type 1, 2, 3, 5, 8, 9,10
6 ea.	Single-pole Decora switches
5 ea.	Three-way Decora switches
2 ea.	Single-pole Decora dimmers
1 ea.	Four-way Decora dimmer
1 ea.	Decora timer
3 ea.	Three-gang plastic Decora plates
1 ea.	Two-gang Decora plate
4 ea.	One-gang plastic plates
4 ea.	Romex connectors

Inspectors inspect

Inspectors are not on staff to tell you how to plan or execute a job, so make your questions as specific as possible. Present your rough sketch, discuss the materials you intend to use, and ask if there are specific requirements for the room(s) you'll be rewiring. For example, must bedroom receptacles have AFCI protection? Must kitchen wall receptacles be GFCIs if they are not over a counter? Be specific.

Draw up plans

Based on the feedback you've gotten, draw detailed plans. They should include each switch, receptacle, and fixture as well as the paths between switches and the device(s) they control. From this drawing, you can develop your materials list. Number each circuit or, better yet, assign a different color to each circuit. When you feel the plans are complete, schedule an appointment with an inspector to review them.

Listen well and take notes

Be low-key and respectful when you meet with the inspector to review your plans. First, you're more likely to get your questions answered. Second, you'll begin to develop a personal rapport. Because one inspector will often track a project from start to finish, this is a person who can ease your way or make it much more difficult. So play it straight, ask questions, listen well, take notes, and—above all—don't argue or come in with an attitude.

On-site inspections

Once the building department approves your plans, you can start working. In most cases, the inspector will visit your site when the wiring is roughed in and again when the wiring is finished. Don't call for an inspection until each stage is complete.

MATERIALS LIST: POWER	
This materials list was determined from "Electrical Plan: The Power Layer," on p. 179.	
ROUGH	
18 ea.	One-gang NM adjustable boxes
1 ea.	One-gang metal cut-in box
1 ea.	Two-gang NM adjustable box (oven)
3 ea	Boxes NM (Romex) connectors
1 ea.	Box (500) $3/4$-in. staples (to be used in rough lighting also)
1 ea.	Box (100) nail plates (to be used in rough lighting also)
500 ft.	12/2 NM Romex (2 × 250 ft. rolls): 20 units @ 15 ft. ave. = 300 ft. (4 home runs @ 50 ft. ave. = 200 ft.)
250 ft.	12/3 NM Romex (1 × 250 ft. roll): 2 home runs @ 50 ft. ave. = 100 ft. (use remainder in rough lighting)
50 ft.	10/3 NM (purchase cut to length): 1 home run @ 50 ft.
1	Bag (250) red wire connectors (to be used in rough lighting also)
1	Container (500) wafer-head #10 × $3/4$-in. screws
TRIM	
16 ea.	Duplex receptacles 15-amp or 20-amp rated
3 ea.	GFCI receptacles (15 amp with 20-amp feed through)
1 ea.	30-amp/220v receptacle (verify with range manufacturer)
16 ea.	One-gang plastic duplex plates
1 ea.	30-amp/220v plate

NOTE:
GFCIs are packaged with their plates.

PRO TIP

If you're remodeling, keep in mind that every finish surface you drill or cut into is a surface that you'll have to patch later. So minimize cutting and drilling.

ELECTRICAL NOTATION

Start by making an accurate floor plan of the room or rooms to be rewired on graph paper using a scale of ¼ in. = 1 ft. Indicate walls and permanent fixtures such as countertops, kitchen islands, cabinets, and any large appliances. By photocopying this floor plan, you can quickly generate to-scale sketches of various wiring schemes.

Use the appropriate electrical symbols to indicate the locations of receptacles, switches, light fixtures, and appliances.

➡ **For a key of electrical symbols, see "Common Electrical Symbols," at right.**

Especially when drawing kitchens, which can be incredibly complex, use colored pencils to indicate different circuits. You can also number circuits, but colored circuits are distinguishable at a glance. Use solid lines to indicate cable runs between receptacles and switches and dotted lines to indicate the cables that run between switches and the light fixtures or receptacles they control.

The beauty of photocopies is that you can experiment with different options quickly. As you refine the drawings, refer back to the list of requirements given earlier to be sure that you have an adequate number of receptacles, that you have GFCI receptacles over kitchen counters, that there are switches near doorways, and so on. Ultimately, you'll need a final master drawing with everything on it. But you may also find it helpful to make individual drawings—say, one for lighting and one for receptacles—if the master drawing gets too busy to read.

If you have questions or want to highlight a fixture type, use callouts on the floor plan. As you decide which fixtures and devices you want to install, develop a separate materials list and use numbered keys to indicate where each piece goes on the master drawing. Finally, develop a list of all materials, so you'll also have enough boxes, cable connectors, wire connectors, staples, and so on. In short, list all you need to do the job.

COMMON ELECTRICAL SYMBOLS

Symbol	Name
Duplex receptacle	
GFCI duplex receptacle	GFCI
Fourplex receptacle	
240v receptacle	
Weatherproof duplex receptacle	WP
Duplex receptacle, split-wired	
Single-pole switch	S
Three-way switch	S_3
Switch leg	
Home run (to service panel)	
Recessed light fixture	Ⓡ
Wall-mounted fixture	
Ceiling outlet	
Ceiling pull switch	Ⓢ
Junction box	Ⓙ
Vent fan	VF
Ceiling fan	CF
Telephone outlet	▶
2-wire cable	
3-wire cable	

LIGHTING AND SWITCHES LAYER

Ⓐ Running 12/2 cable will accommodate the disposal circuit.

Ⓑ Use 14/2 cable for all general lighting home runs (cable runs back to the service panel).

Ⓒ Verify the dimmer load; dimmers must be de-rated when ganged together.

POWER LAYER

Ⓐ Wire the GFCI receptacle at the beginning of the run so it affords protection to receptacles downstream.

Ⓑ Dishwasher circuit. Install under the sink in the cabinet.

Ⓒ Single-location GFCI protection.

Ⓓ Stove is gas, so the receptacle is only for the igniter and clock and is OK to run with the hood. Leave NM cable stubbed at the ceiling, and leave 3 ft. to 4 ft. of slack for termination in the hood/trim. (Note: Never run a stove igniter off a GFCI-protected circuit because it will trip the GFCI every time the stove is turned on.)

Ⓔ Use 12/3 cable for the home run, so a single cable takes care of the dedicated refrigerator circuit and the countertop receptacle (small-appliance) circuit.

Ⓕ Home run for counter (small-appliance) circuit 2.

Ⓖ Oven outlet. Refer to unit specifications to verify receptacle or hard-wired connection.

ELECTRICAL PLAN: LIGHTING AND SWITCHES LAYER

A professional's electrical floor plan may be daunting at first, but it will start to make sense as you become familiar with the symbols used. To make the plans easier to read, they have been divided into two layers: (1) lighting and switches and (2) power, which consists of receptacles and dedicated circuits. (There's some overlap.) The circled letters are callouts that indicate areas warranting special attention. The circled numbers correspond to a master list of lighting fixtures that the electrician developed with the architect. Drawing switch legs and circuits in different colors makes a plan much easier to read.

Pendant lights in the dining area are noted by a dotted green switch leg running from the two ceiling boxes to the single-pole switch on the wall.

All circuits for recessed, drop, and undercabinet lighting are noted in different colors. Be certain to track each circuit back to the appropriate wall switch.

ELECTRICAL PLAN: THE POWER LAYER

This kitchen remodel is typical in that it has many dedicated circuits (also called designated circuits) and, per code, at least two 20-amp small-appliance circuits wired with #12 cable. Circled letters are callouts that correspond to the lettered notes.

Whether for 120v wall outlets or 240v appliance outlets, each circuit should end with a home run back to the service panel.

Any receptacle that serves the countertop must be GFCI-protected. Refrigerators, however, should be run on a non-GFCI receptacle.

WIRING SCHEMATICS

RECEPTACLE IN MIDCIRCUIT

By splicing like wire groups and running *pigtails* (short wires) to the receptacle in this conventional method, you ensure continuous current downstream.

Incoming power

Outgoing power (downstream)

Twist-on wire connectors

Neutral pigtail

Hot pigtail

Ground

RECEPTACLE AT END OF CIRCUIT

Incoming power

Because there are no receptacles downstream, attach all wires directly to the device.

The diagrams in this section show most of the circuit wiring variations that you're likely to need when wiring receptacles, fixtures, and switches. Unless otherwise noted, assume that incoming cable (from the power source) and all others are 2-wire cable with ground, such as 14/2 w/grd or 12/2 w/grd (#14 wire should be protected by 15-amp breakers; #12 wire should be protected by 20-amp breakers).

➡ See "Appliances," on p. 220, for more wiring schematics.

All metal boxes must be grounded. Assume that nongrounded boxes in the wiring diagrams are nonmetallic (plastic) unless otherwise specified. In sheathed cables, ground wires are bare copper. Black and red wires indicate hot conductors. White wires indicate neutral conductors, unless taped black to indicate that the wire is being used as a hot conductor in a switch loop (p. 52).

GANGED RECEPTACLES IN METAL BOX

A two-gang metal box with fourplex *(double duplex)* receptacles uses a ground screw or ground clip to connect a ground pigtail to the box.

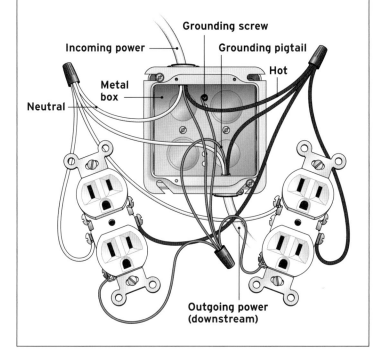

Grounding screw

Incoming power

Grounding pigtail

Hot

Metal box

Neutral

Outgoing power (downstream)

GFCI RECEPTACLE, MULTIPLE-LOCATION PROTECTION

A GFCI receptacle can protect devices* downstream if wired as shown. Attach wires from the power source to terminals marked "line." Attach wires continuing downstream to terminals marked "load." As with any receptacle, attach hot wires to brass screws, white wires to silver screws, and a grounding pigtail to the ground screw. *Note:* Here, only ground wires are spliced; hot and neutral wires attach directly to screw terminals.

From power source

Spliced ground wires

To devices downstream

Neutral

Hot

* Devices include receptacles, switches, and light fixtures.

GFCI RECEPTACLE, SINGLE-LOCATION PROTECTION

This configuration provides GFCI protection only at the GFCI receptacle. All devices downstream remain unprotected. Here, splice hot and neutral wires so the power downstream is continuous and attach pigtails to the GFCI's "line" screw terminals. With this setup, receptacle use downstream won't cause nuisance tripping of the GFCI receptacle.

Incoming power

To devices downstream

Neutral wires spliced

Hot wires spliced

Line brass

Ground wires spliced

Line silver

Ground screw

WIRING SCHEMATICS (CONTINUED)

LIGHT FIXTURE AT END OF CABLE RUN

Switch wiring at its simplest: Incoming and outgoing hot wires attach to the terminals of a single-pole switch. Neutrals and grounds are spliced through.

Grounding screw

Metal box

Ground

Nonmetallic box

Neutral

Incoming power

Hot

A SIMPLE SWITCH WITH A "SWITCH LOOP": THE MODERN METHOD

The 2011 NEC requires that there be a neutral in every switch box because some electronic timer switches and other energy-saving controls need a neutral. Thus, if you want to use a switch-loop approach, you must use 3-wire cable, connect the neutral at the power source, and then cap off the neutral in the switch box.

Ground

Incoming power

Metal box

Grounding screw

Neutral

Hot

3-wire cable

Hot wire

Ground

Unused neutral capped in box

Nonmetallic box

Switch leg

GANGED SWITCHES, TWO FIXTURES

This is a typical setup for switches by exterior doors. For example, one single-pole switch controls an exterior light fixture, while the second switch controls and interior fixture.

Neutral

To fixtures

Two-gang nonmetallic box

Hot

Ground

Incoming power

Switch legs

CLOSEUP: THREE-WAY SWITCH

Three-way switches control a fixture from two locations. Each switch has two brass screws and a black screw (common terminal). The hot wire from the source attaches to the common terminal of the first switch. Traveler wires between the switches attach to the brass screws. Finally, a wire runs from the common terminal of the second switch to the hot lead of the fixture.

Traveler wires attach to brass screws.

Common (COM) terminal

THREE-WAY SWITCHES, LIGHT FIXTURE BETWEEN

Travelers

3-wire cable

3-wire cable

Incoming power (2-wire cable)

Switch leg

Neutral

White wire taped black (switch leg)

Ground

Common (COM) terminal

Neutral

Common (COM) terminal

Ground screw

Travelers

Ground screw

Travelers

In this existing setup, two three-way switches control a light fixture placed between them. Run 3-wire cables between each switch and the fixture. Whenever you use a white wire as a switch leg, *tape it black* to indicate that it's hot. Although this wiring configuration does not meet NEC 2011 requirements for new work, it is very common in older homes and is acceptable as part of existing wiring.

THREE-WAY SWITCHES, LIGHT FIXTURE AT START OF CABLE RUN

Here, incoming power enters through the fixture box. Acceptable in existing wiring, but does not meet NEC 2011 requirements for new work.

Incoming power (2-wire cable)

Grounding screw in metal box

Hot white wire taped black

Neutral

Hot

2-wire cable

3-wire cable

Hot white wire taped black

Switch leg

Common (COM) terminal

Hot white wire taped black

Common (COM) terminal

Travelers

Travelers

WIRING SCHEMATICS (CONTINUED)

THREE-WAY SWITCHES, LIGHT FIXTURE AT END OF CABLE RUN

Two three-way switches precede the fixture on the circuit. Meets NEC 2011 requirements for new work.

Incoming power (2-wire cable)

3-wire cable

2-wire cable

Grounding screw in metal box

Ground wires

Hot

Neutral

Common (COM) terminal

Common (COM) terminal

Travelers

Travelers

SPLIT-TAB RECEPTACLE CONTROLLED BY SWITCH, SWITCH UPSTREAM, REGULAR RECEPTACLE DOWNSTREAM

This setup is commonly used to meet NEC requirements if there is no switch-controlled ceiling fixture. As shown, the switch controls only the bottom half of the split-tab receptacle. The top half of the split-tab receptacle and all receptacles downstream are always hot. Removing the tab is shown in photo 1 on p. 47.

3-wire cable

Incoming power (2-wire cable)

Top half always hot

2-wire cable

Ground

Always hot

Neutral

Switch leg

Hot

Controlled by switch

Tab removed

SPLIT-TAB RECEPTACLE CONTROLLED BY SWITCH, SWITCH AT END OF CABLE RUN

Incoming power

3-wire cable

Neutral

Tab removed

Hot

Top half always hot

Switch leg

Ground

Controlled by switch

Unused neutral capped in box

The switch controls the bottom half of the split-tab receptacle. The white wire feeding the switch is taped black to indicate that it is being used as a hot wire.

120/240V DRYER RECEPTACLE

This dedicated circuit requires a 10/3 cable with ground and a two-pole 30-amp breaker. Two 120v hot wires terminate to "hot" setscrews on the receptacle and the breaker poles; the neutral wire terminater to the "neut" setscrew on the receptacle and the neutral/ground bus bar in the service panel.

Ground

10/3 cable

Ground

Hot

Neutral/ground bus bar in service panel

30-amp two-pole breaker

Neutral

ROUGH-IN WIRING

ROUGH-IN WIRING REFERS TO THE first phase of a wiring installation. It is the stage at which you set outlet boxes and run electrical cable to them—as opposed to finish wiring, or connecting wires to devices and fixtures.

Rough-in wiring is pretty straightforward when studs and joists are exposed. Whether a house is new or old, running wires through exposed framing is called *new work,* or new construction. If the framing is covered with finish surfaces such as plaster and drywall, however, the job is referred to as *remodel wiring* or *old work.* Remodel wiring is almost always more complicated and costly because first you must drill through or cut into finish surfaces to install boxes and run cable, and later you need to patch the holes you made.

GETTING STARTED

Rough-in basics, p. 188

Tools for rough-in, p. 190

Materials for rough-in, p. 192

Laying out the job, p. 194

OUTLET BOXES

Installing new work boxes, p. 196

Installing ceiling boxes, p. 197

RUNNING CABLE

Drilling for cable, p. 198

Pulling cable, p. 199

Feeding cable through corners, p. 200

Fishing cable behind finish walls, p. 201

Fishing cable to a ceiling fixture, p. 202

RETROFIT WORK

Cutting a wall box into plaster, p. 204

Cutting a wall box into drywall, p. 204

Retrofitting a ceiling box, p. 205

Creating a wiring trench, p. 206

Pulling cable to retrofit boxes, p. 207

MAKING UP BOXES

Making up an outlet box, p. 208

Making up a can light, p. 209

Making up a single-gang switch box, p. 210

Making up a multigang switch box, p. 211

METAL CABLE & CONDUIT

Flexible metal cable, p. 212

Installing AC cable, p. 213

Installing MC cable, p. 214

Working with EMT steel conduit (interior), p. 215

Making bends with metal conduit (interior), p. 216

Fishing wire through conduit, p. 217

Prepping receptacles for surface metal boxes, p. 218

Wiring outlets, p. 219

ROUGH-IN BASICS

Wait until rough carpentry is complete before you begin rough-in wiring. Part of an electrician's job is setting boxes so they'll be flush to finished surfaces. Before an electrician starts working, modifications to the framing—such as furring out or planing down irregular studs and ceiling joists—must be complete.

Where to start

Wait until the plumbers are gone. Waste pipes are large and often difficult to locate, which usually means a lot of drilling and cutting into studs and joists. Once the plumbing pipes are in place, you'll clearly see what obstacles you face and will have more room to move around.

Check your plans often. If there's not a table on-site where you can roll out your electrical plans, staple them to a stud—preferably at eye level so you can read them easily. Checking and rechecking the plans is particularly important if you're not a professional electrician.

Be flexible. As you lay out devices, you'll realize that not everything specified on the plans is possible; most plans are developed without knowing exactly what the framing looks like or where obstructions are. Do all the rough-in wiring with the power off.

Organize your work

Perform one task at a time. Each task—such as setting boxes or drilling—requires a different set of tools. So once you have the tools out to do a given task, go around the room and complete all similar tasks. You'll become more proficient as you go: You waste less time changing tools, and the job goes much faster. In general, the sequence of rough-in tasks looks like this:

1. Walk the room with plans, marking outlet locations on walls and floor.
2. Snap chalklines or shoot laser lines to pinpoint box elevations.
3. Attach boxes to studs and ceiling joists.
4. Drill holes for cable runs.
5. Pull cable through holes and into boxes.
6. Make up boxes—strip wire ends, splice grounds, splice current-carrying conductors, attach mud rings, and push wires into boxes.
7. Rough-in inspection.

After the inspection, finish surfaces are installed. Then, at the trim-out or finish stage, wires are attached to the devices and fixtures.

The rough-in inspection

At the rough-in stage, inspectors look for a few key signs of a job well done: cables properly sized for the loads they'll carry; the requisite number and type of outlets specified by code; cables protected by nail plates as needed; neat, consistent work throughout the system; and, above all, ground wires spliced and, in metal boxes, secured to a ground screw. If grounds aren't complete, you won't pass the rough-in inspection.

When running cable around doors and windows, find the easiest path. Consider drilling through top or bottom plates and running cable in the space above or below.

During the rough-in inspection, inspectors demand solid ground-wire splices and, in metal boxes, a ground screw or clip that secures the ground wire.

At this inspection, only grounds need to be spliced. But since you've got the tools out, it makes sense to splice neutrals and continuous hot wires (those not attached to switches).

➔ For more on grounding, see p. 12.

When all splices are complete, carefully fold the wire groups into the box. When you come back to do the trim-out stage, simply pull the wires out of the box, connect wires to devices, and install devices and cover plates.

Connecting circuit wires to a main panel or subpanel is the very last step of an installation. As noted throughout this book, you should **avoid handling energized cables or devices**.

REMODEL WIRING SAFETY ESSENTIALS

Before removing box covers or handling wires, turn off the power to the area and use a voltage tester to be sure it's off.

First remove the fuse or flip off the circuit breaker controlling the circuit and post a sign on the main panel warning people of work in progress. Better yet, if you've got circuit breakers, do as the pros do and install a breaker lockout so it will be impossible for anyone to turn it on. Breaker lockouts are available at electrical supply houses and most home centers.

➔ For more on lockouts, see p. 248.

Testing for power is particularly important in remodel wiring, because walls and ceilings often contain old cables that are energized. Always test the tester first–on an outlet you know is energized–to be sure the tester is working correctly. A noncontact tester is especially useful in remodel situations. Simply touch the tester tip to cable sheathing or wire insulation. That is, you don't have to touch the tester tip to bare wires to get a reading: If a cable, wire, or electrical device is energized, the tip will glow. A noncontact tester can detect voltage through cable sheathing.

Whatever tester you use, test it first on an outlet that you know is live to make sure the tester is working properly.

Always use a voltage tester to test for power before touching cables, devices, or fixtures. Here, a noncontact tester detects voltage through cable insulation.

⚠ SAFETY ALERT

Make an emergency plan. It may be as simple as carrying a cell phone or having a friend close by—never do electrical work alone. Calling 911 is an obvious first step if an emergency occurs. On the job site, you should also post directions to the nearest hospital and a list of phone numbers of people to contact.

TOOLS FOR ROUGH-IN

Most of the tools you'll need for rough-in wiring are discussed in "Tools and Materials," so here we'll focus on tools that make rough-in easier and more productive. All hand tools should have cushioned handles and fit your hand.

Safety tools include voltage testers (especially a noncontact tester), eye protection, work gloves, hard-soled shoes, knee-pads, a dust mask, and a hard hat. Hard hats are clunky but essential when you're working in attics, basements, or any other location with limited headroom. Every job site should also have a fire extinguisher and a first aid kit visibly stored in a central location.

Adequate lighting, whether drop lights or light stands, is essential to both job safety and accuracy. If a site is too dark to see what color wires you're working with, your chances of wrong connections increase.

Sturdy stepladders are a must. In the electrical industry, only fiberglass stepladders are Occupational Safety and Health Administration (OSHA) compliant because they're nonconductive. Wood ladders are usually nonconductive when dry, but if they get rained on or absorb ambient moisture, wood ladders can conduct electricity.

Shop vacuums, push brooms, dust pans, and garbage cans help keep the workplace clean. And a clean site is a safe site. Clean up whenever debris makes footing unsafe, especially if you're cutting into walls or ceilings. Plaster lath is especially dangerous because it's loaded with sharp little nails that can pierce the soles of your shoes.

Layout tools include tape measures, spirit levels, chalklines, and lasers. *Rough-in* is a misleading term because there's nothing rough or crude about locating fixtures or receptacles—layout is very exacting. For that reason, levels and plumb lasers are indispensable when laying out outlets **A**.

The most used hand tools are the same pliers, cutters, strippers, levels, and screwdrivers mentioned throughout this book. It's also handy to have a wire-nut driver **B** if you've got dozens of splices to make up.

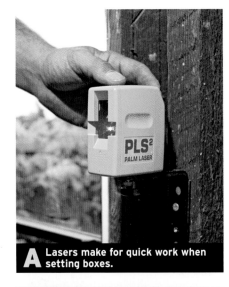

A Lasers make for quick work when setting boxes.

B A wire-connector driver speeds up wire splices.

D An 18-in. auger bit bores easily through several studs.

E A wire reel prevents kinking cable as you pull it.

There's also a nut-driver bit that fits into a screw gun **C**, but it tends to overtighten wire connectors if you're not experienced in using it. If you'll be cutting into and patching plaster or drywall, get a jab saw (drywall saw), a utility knife, and a taping knife. A flat bar (for prying) and an old, beat-up wood chisel are always busy in remodels, too.

Power tools help speed many tasks. Always wear eye protection when using them. A screw gun is preferable to nailing most of the time because you can easily remove a screw if you want to reposition, say, an outlet box.

A right-angle drill with a $1/2$-in. chuck is the workhorse of rough-in wiring because it has the muscle to drill through hard old lumber. If you will be drilling through nail-infested wood, get a "nail-eater bit"; a number of companies make them. If you use a standard 6-in.-long auger bit, the drill head and bit will fit between studs and joists spaced 16-in. on-center. It enables you to drill perpendicular to the framing to make wire pulling easier. Longer bits also have their merits: An 18-in. self-feeding auger bit **D** bores easily through several studs or doubled wall plates; it is also long enough that you probably

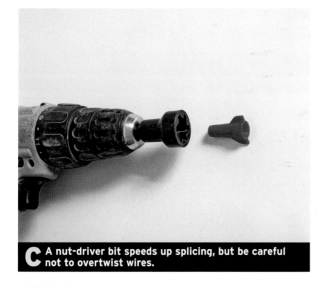

C A nut-driver bit speeds up splicing, but be careful not to overtwist wires.

F Remodel wiring tools. From right: drywall saw, flex bit, extension, flex bit steering guide, reel of fishing tape.

A well-organized tool belt prevents you from looking for tools all day long.

won't need a ladder to drill through top plates.

To cut larger holes in plaster or drywall—say, to retrofit pancake boxes or recessed light cans—use a fine-toothed hole saw.

Use a jab saw or an oscillating multi-tool to cut individual box openings into finish surfaces. Use a Universal E-cut multi-tool blade to cut through finish surfaces. When cutting through plaster lath, alternate cuts on each side of the opening rather than cutting one side completely. This will keep the lath from fluttering and cracking the plaster. Use a reciprocating saw to cut through

framing or through plaster lath to create a cable trench.

➔ **For more on creating a cable trench, see p. 206.**

Use a demolition sawblade to cut through wood that contains nails or screws. It'll hold up to such heavy work.

There are a number of specialty tools designed to ease rough-in. A wire reel, a rotating dispenser that enables you to pull cable easily to distant points, is worth having. Reels hold 250 ft. of cable **E**. A 25-ft.

fishing tape—a flexible steel, fiberglass, or nylon tape—enables you to pull cable behind finish surfaces **F**. In most cases, however, it's simpler to use a flex bit to drill through framing in one direction.

➔ **For more on pulling cable, see p. 207.**

A 48-in. drill extension will increase the effective drilling length of a flex bit. Use a flex bit steering guide to keep the flex bit from bowing excessively.

MATERIALS FOR ROUGH-IN

Single-gang cut-in box with Grip-Lok tabs (also known as "battleships")

Single-gang box with swivel ears

Goof ring (used when a box is set too deep)

Double-gang cut-in box with swivel ears

Single-gang box with screw-adjustable ears

Round fixture box with metal spring ears

Heavyweight bar

Heavyweight, fan-rated remodel bar

Lightweight bar

A Cut-in (remodel) boxes and accessories.

B Adjustable bar hangers.

C A recessed light fixture with adjustable bar hangers.

D Romex cable connectors.

As with tools, most of the materials installed during the rough-in phase are discussed in Chapter 2 and can be installed either in new construction or remodel wiring. All materials must be UL- or NRTL-listed, which indicates that they meet the safety standards of the electrical industry. There are, however, a number of specialized boxes, hanger bars, and other elements intended for remodel wiring that can be installed with minimal disruptions to existing finish surfaces.

Remodel (cut-in) boxes mount to existing finish surfaces—unlike new-work boxes, which attach to framing. Most cut-in boxes have lips (flanges) that rest on the plaster or drywall surface to keep boxes from falling into the wall or ceiling cavity. Spring clamps, folding tabs, or screw-adjustable wings on the box are then expanded to hold the box snug to the backside of the wall or ceiling. The devices that anchor boxes vary greatly **A**.

Code requires that ceiling boxes be mounted to framing. Expandable remodel bar hangers accommodate this requirement **B**. Adjustable hangers also allow you to locate recessed light fixtures exactly **C**.

Cable connectors (also called clamps) solidly connect cable to the box to prevent strain on electrical connections inside the box **D**. Cable clamps also prevent sheathing from being scraped or punctured by sharp box edges. Plastic boxes come with integral plastic spring clamps inside. If you use metal boxes, insert plastic push-in connectors into the box knockouts; no other cable connector is as quick or easy to install in tight spaces.

PRO TIP

Don't forget to leave 8 in. to 10 in. of cable sticking out of each box for connecting devices later.

Ordering materials

In general, order 10 percent extra of all boxes and cover plates (they crack easily) and the exact number of switches, receptacles, light fixtures, and other devices specified on the plans. It's okay to order one or two extra switches and receptacles, but because they're costly, pros try not to order too many extras.

Cable is another matter altogether. Calculating the amount of cable can be tricky because there are infinite ways to route cable between two points. Electricians typically measure the running distances between several pairs of boxes to come up with an average length. They then use that average to calculate a total for each room. In new work, for example, boxes spaced 12 ft. apart (per code) take 15 ft. to 20 ft. of cable to run about 2 ft. above the boxes and drop it down to each box. After you've calculated cable for the whole job, add 10 percent.

Cable for remodel jobs is tougher to calculate because it's impossible to know what obstructions hide behind finish surfaces. You may have to fish cable up to the top of wall plates, across an attic, and then down to each box. Do some exploring, measure that imaginary route, and again create an average cable length to multiply. If it takes, say, 25 ft. for each pair of wall boxes and you have eight outlets to wire, then 8 outlets × 25 ft. = 200 ft. Add 10 percent, and your total is 220 ft. Because the average roll of wire sold at home centers contains 250 ft., one roll should do it.

Have materials on hand when it's time to start installing boxes. Electricians often walk from room to room, dropping a box wherever floor plans indicate. Double-check to be sure placement meets code requirements.

Rough-in recap: Electrical code

- Circuit breakers, wiring, and devices must be correctly sized for the loads they carry. For example, 20-amp circuits require 12AWG wire and receptacles rated for no greater than 20 amps. Mismatching circuit elements can lead to house fires.

- All wire connections must be good mechanical connections. There must be good pressure between the connectors you are joining, whether wires are spliced together or connected to a device. For that reason, buy devices with screw terminals rather than back-wired (stab-in) devices whose internal clamps can deform. Deformed clamps can lead to loose wires, arcing, and house fires.

- All wire connections must be housed in a covered box.

- Boxes must be securely attached to framing so that normal use will not loosen them.

- Box edges must be flush to finish surfaces. In noncombustible surfaces (drywall, plaster) there may be a 1/4-in. gap between the box edge and the surface. But in combustible surfaces, such as wood paneling, there must be no gap.

- All newly installed devices must be grounded. Code allows you to replace an existing two-prong receptacle or to replace a nongrounded box that has become damaged. However, if you install a new three-prong receptacle, it must be grounded. The only exception: You can install a three-prong receptacle into an ungrounded box if that new device is a GFCI receptacle. If you extend a circuit, the entire circuit must be upgraded to current code.

- In new rough-in work, cable must be supported within 12 in. of any box and every 4 1/2 ft. thereafter.

LAYING OUT THE JOB

With electrical plans in hand, walk each room and mark box locations for receptacles, switches, and light fixtures. Each device must be mounted to a box that houses its wiring connections. The only exceptions are devices that come with an integral box, such as bath fans, recessed light cans, and undercabinet light fixtures ❶.

Mark receptacles and switches on the walls first. Then mark ceiling fixtures. If studs and joists are exposed, use a vividly colored crayon that will show up on the wood. If there are finish surfaces, use a pencil to mark walls at a height where you can see the notations easily—these marks will be painted over later. Near each switch box, draw a letter or number to indicate which fixture the switch controls.

Once you've roughly located boxes on the walls, use a laser level ❷ to set exact box heights for each type of box.

➡ **For more on box heights, see "Rough-in Recap: Box Locations," on the facing page.**

Use the laser to indicate the top or bottom lines of the boxes ❸. Many electricians prefer to determine level with the laser, then snap a permanent chalkline at that height so they can move the laser to other rooms ❹.

To locate ceiling fixtures, mark them on the floor ❺ and use a plumb laser ❻ to transfer that mark up to the ceiling ❼. This may seem counterintuitive, but it will save you a lot of time. Floors are flat, almost always the same size and shape as the ceilings above, and—perhaps most important—accessible and easy to mark. In complex rooms, such as kitchens, draw cabinet and island outlines onto the floor as well. Those outlines will help you fine-tune ceiling light positions to optimally illuminate work areas.

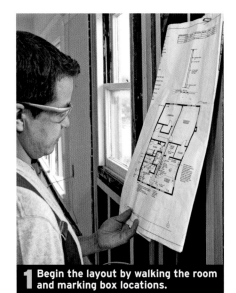

1 Begin the layout by walking the room and marking box locations.

2 Use a laser level to set box heights.

3 A hammer handle quickly establishes box heights at roughly 12 in.

4 Or, you can snap a level chalkline to indicate box tops or bottoms.

Avoiding hot wires In remodels, there may be live wires behind finish surfaces. Use a noncontact tester to test receptacles, switches, fixtures, and any visible wires. The cables feeding those devices will be nearby. Wall receptacles are usually fed by cables running 1 ft. to 3 ft. above. Switches often have cable runs up to a top plate; each ceiling fixture has cable running to the switch(es) controlling it. Avoid drilling or cutting into those areas, and minimize the risk of shock.

5 Many electricians prefer to mark ceiling fixture centers on the floor.

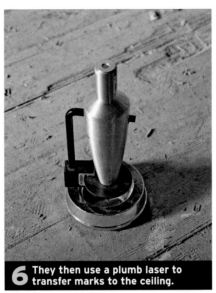

6 They then use a plumb laser to transfer marks to the ceiling.

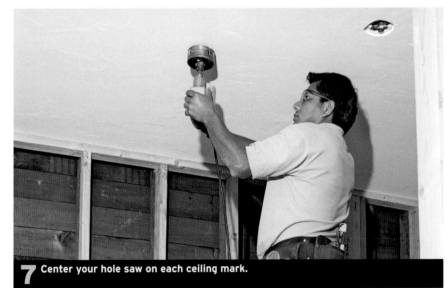

7 Center your hole saw on each ceiling mark.

PRO TIP

When marking box locations on finish surfaces, use a pencil—never a crayon, grease pencil, or a felt-tipped marker. Pencil marks won't show through new paint. Also, grease pencils and crayons can prevent paint from sticking.

Rough-in recap: Box locations

- Whatever heights you choose to set outlets and switches, be consistent.
- Code requires that no point along a wall may be more than 6 ft. from an outlet. Set the bottom of wall outlets 12 in. to 15 in. above the finished floor surface, or 18 in. above the finished floor surface to satisfy Americans with Disabilities Act (ADA) requirements.
- Place the top of switch boxes at 48 in. and they will line up with drywall seams (if sheets run horizontally), thus reducing the drywall cuts you must make.
- In kitchens and bathrooms, place the bottom of countertop receptacles 42 in. above the finished floor surface. This height ensures that each receptacle will clear the combined height of a standard countertop (36 in.) and the height of a backsplash (4 in.), with 2 in. extra to accommodate cover plates.

INSTALLING NEW WORK BOXES

1 To install an adjustable box, press its bracket flush against the stud edge and screw the bracket to the edge or side of the stud.

2 Nail-on boxes cannot be adjusted, so use the depth gauge on the side to ensure that box edges will be flush to finish surfaces.

3 Boxes with integral brackets have small points at top and bottom that sink into the stud. A mud ring brings the box flush to the wall.

4 To provide solid support for multigang boxes, first install an adjustable box bracket that spans the studs.

In this section we'll assume that framing members are exposed and that boxes will be attached directly to them. Once you've used your plans to locate receptacle, switch, and light-fixture boxes on walls and ceilings, installing them is pretty straightforward. Electrical codes dictate box capacity and composition.

→ **For more on box capacity and composition requirements, see p. 23.**

In residences, 18-cu.-in. single-gang PVC plastic boxes are by far the most commonly used. This size is large enough for a single outlet or a single switch and two cables. Otherwise, use a 22.5-cu.-in. single-gang box or a four-square box with a plaster ring.

Set each box to the correct height, then set its depth so that the box edge will be flush to the finish surface. If you use adjustable boxes, simply screw them to a stud **1**. To raise or lower the box depth, turn the adjusting screw. Side-nailing boxes typically have scales (gradated depth gauges) on the side **2**. If not, use a scrap of finish material (such as 1/2-in. drywall) as a depth gauge. Metal boxes frequently have brackets that mount the box flush to a stud edge **3**; after the box is wired, add a mud ring (plaster ring) to bring the box flush to the finish surface.

Multiple-gang boxes mount to studs in the same way. But if plans locate the box away from studs or a multigang box is particularly wide, nail blocking between the studs or install an adjustable box bracket and screw the box to it **4**. (The bracket is also called a *screw gun bracket*, because a screw gun is typically used to mount it and to attach boxes to it.)

About knockouts Once you've mounted boxes, remove the appropriate number of box knockouts and install cable clamps. Single-gang, new-construction plastic boxes don't need clamps: Simply strike a screwdriver handle with the heel of your hand to drive out the knockout. To remove a metal-box knockout, jab it with the nose of needle-nose pliers to loosen it, then use the pliers' jaws to twist it free. Page 26 shows how.

INSTALLING CEILING BOXES

INSTALLING A RECESSED CAN

1 When the can height is where you want it, fasten its hanger bars to the joists.

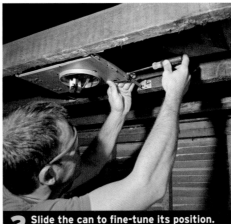

2 Slide the can to fine-tune its position. Tighten the screws to lock it in place.

INSTALLING A BOX TO THE JOIST

3 If a box position needs to be offset slightly from a joist, nail it to blocking.

INSTALLING A BOX BETWEEN JOISTS

4 For boxes that occur midway between joists, use an adjustable bar hanger.

5 Screw a metal box to the hanger. Make sure the box edge is flush to the surface.

or

6 Alternately, you can nail 2×4 blocking between the joists.

Boxes for ceiling lights are most often 4-in. octagonal or round boxes or recessed light fixtures with integrated junction boxes. Setting ceiling boxes in new work is similar to setting wall boxes, with the added concern that the ceiling box be strong enough to support the fixture. Many electricians prefer to use metal boxes for ceiling fixtures. Ceiling fans require fan-rated boxes.

➡ **For more on laying out the job, see p. 194.**

In many cases, you'll need to reposition the box to avoid obstacles or line it up to other fixtures, but it's quick work if the box has an adjustable bar hanger. To install a recessed can, for example, extend its two bar hangers to adjacent ceiling joists. Then screw or nail the hangers to the joists **1**. Slide the can along the hangers until its opening (the light well) is where you want it and then tighten the setscrews on the side **2**.

To install a 4-in. box, simply nail or screw it to the side of a joist. If you need to install it slightly away from a joist, first nail 2× blocking to the joist, then attach the box to the blocking **3**. The box edge must be flush to finish surfaces.

To install a 4-in. box between joists, first screw an adjustable hanger bar to the joists **4**, then attach the box to it **5**. Alternately, you can insert 2× blocking between the joists and screw the box to it **6**.

➡ **For a detailed look at installing hanger bars, see photo 2 on p. 79.**

DRILLING FOR CABLE

Once boxes are in place, you're ready to run cable to each of them. It's rather like connecting dots with a pencil line. To prevent screws or nails from puncturing cables, drill in the middle of studs or joists whenever possible. If the edges of any holes you drill are less than 1¼ in. from the edge of a framing member, you must install steel nail-protection plates. Always wear eye protection when drilling.

Drill for cables running horizontally (through studs) first. It doesn't matter whether you start drilling at the outlet box closest to the panel or at the last outlet on the circuit. Just be methodical: Drill holes in one direction as you go from box to box. However, if you're drilling for an appliance that has a dedicated circuit—and thus only one outlet—it's usually less work to drill a hole through a top or bottom plate and then run cable through the attic or basement instead of drilling through numerous studs to reach the outlet.

If possible, drill holes thigh high ❶. Partially rest the drill on your thigh so your arms won't get as tired. This method also helps you drill holes that are roughly the same height—making cable-pulling much easier. Moreover, when you drill about 1 ft. above a box, you have enough room to bend the cable and staple it near the box without crimping the cable and damaging its insulation.

For most drilling, use a 6-in., ³/₄-in.-diameter bit. Use an 18-in. bit to drill lumber nailed together around windows, and doorways ❷. Using an 18-in. bit is also safer because it enables you to drill through top plates without standing on a ladder. Standing on the floor is a big advantage, as the reaction torque from a heavy-duty drill can throw you off a ladder if a bit binds up ❸.

PRO TIP

Drilled holes don't need to be perfectly aligned, but the closer they line up, the easier it is to pull cable through them.

1 When drilling for cable runs, rest the drill on your thigh. This method eases drilling and places holes at a convenient height.

2 Use an 18-in. ship bit to drill through multiple studs.

3 The 18-in. ship bit also allows you to drill through top wall plates while standing on the floor.

PULLING CABLE

For greatest efficiency, install cable in two steps: (1) Pull cable between outlets, leaving roughly 1 ft. extra beyond each box for future splices and (2) then retrace your steps, stapling cable to framing and installing nail-protection plates. As with drilling, it doesn't matter whether you start pulling cable from the first box of a circuit or from the last box. If there are several circuits in a room, start at one end and proceed along each circuit, pulling cable until all the boxes are wired. Don't jump around: You may become confused and miss a box.

In new construction, electricians usually place several wire reels by the panel and pull cables from there toward the first box of each circuit **❶**. These circuit segments are called "home runs." Once electricians have run cable to all the home-run boxes, they move a reel next to each box and continue to pull cable outward until they reach the last box **❷**. When doing remodel wiring in a house with a crawlspace, however, electricians often start at the last box and pull cables toward the panel. When they reach the first boxes of several circuits, they will move the wire reels to those locations. From there, they feed, say, three cables down to a helper in the crawlspace. The helper can pull all the cables toward the panel at the same time. This method is much faster than pulling single cables three different times.

Staple cable along stud centers to prevent nail or screw punctures. It's acceptable to stack two cables under one staple **❸**, but use standoffs **❹** to fasten three or more cables traveling along the same path. (Multigang boxes are fed by multiple cables, for example.) Standoffs and ties bundle cables loosely to prevent heat buildup. As you secure cable, install nail plates where needed **❺**.

1 Place a wire reel near the beginning or end of each circuit.

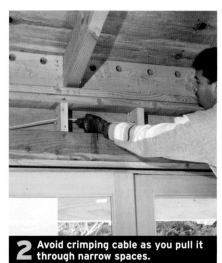

2 Avoid crimping cable as you pull it through narrow spaces.

3 Drive staples just snug to the cable.

4 When bundling two or more cables, use standoffs.

5 For cable within 1¼ in. of a stud edge, install a steel plate.

> ### PRO TIP
> Put a piece of red tape on the first box in each circuit to ensure that you run cable from it to the panel. On a complex job with many circuits, you might run cable *between* all the outlets in a circuit but forget to install the home-run cable that will energize the circuit. Not something you want to discover after the drywall is up.

FEEDING CABLE THROUGH CORNERS

1 To feed cable through a corner, drill a level hole on one side of the built-up studs.

2 Drill a second hole, at the same height, so the holes intersect.

3 Use diagonal cutters to cut through the sheathing and two of the three wires in the cable, then loop the end of the remaining wire.

4 Wrap the end of the cable so it slides through the hole easier, then work the looped wire through the holes.

Corners are usually built by nailing three or four studs together, so feeding cable through them can be tricky. Drill intersecting holes at the same height, as shown in photos **1** and **2**. Use diagonal cutters to cut through the sheathing and two of the wires, thus leaving a single wire protruding from the cable **3**.

Use pliers to loop the end of the wire. Then wrap tape around the end of the cable and onto the wire to create a tapering point that will slide easier through the hole. Push the wire through the corner holes until it emerges from the other side **4**. If the wire gets hung up midway through, insert a finger from the other side to fish for its end.

FISHING CABLE BEHIND FINISH WALLS

Most electricians hate fishing wire behind existing walls. It can be tricky to find the cable and time-consuming to patch the holes in plaster or drywall. If you're adding a box or two, try fishing cable behind the wall. But if you're rewiring an entire room, it's probably faster to cut a "wiring trench" in the wall. Before cutting into or drilling through a wall, however, turn off power to the area. If you'd like to avoid fishing altogether, see "Installing a Wireless Switch," on p. 58.

➤ **For more on cutting a wiring trench, see p. 206.**

If you're adding an outlet over an unfinished basement, fishing cable can be straightforward. Outline and cut out an opening for the new box, insert a flex bit into the opening, and then drill down through the wall's bottom plate ❶ (wear gloves to protect hands). When the bit emerges into the basement, a helper can insert one wire of the new cable into the small "fish hole" near the bit's point. As you slowly back the bit out of the box opening, you pull new cable into it ❷. No fish tape required! The only downside is that the reversing drill can twist the cable. This problem is easily avoided by sliding a swivel kellum over the cable end instead of inserting a cable wire into the flex bit hole ❸ (see p. 202). Because the kellum turns, the cable doesn't.

Alternatively, you can start by removing a wall box. The closest power source is often an existing outlet. Cut power to that outlet and test to make sure it's off. The easiest way to access the cable is to disconnect the wires to the receptacle ❹ (see p. 202) and remove it. Then remove the box ❺ (see p. 202), which may require using a metal-cutting reciprocating-saw blade to cut through the nails holding the box to the stud. Fish a new cable leg to the location and insert the new and old cables into a new cut-in box. Secure the cut-in box to the finish surface, splice the cables inside the box, and connect pigtails from the splices to the new receptacle. >> >> >>

RUNNING CABLE TO A NEW OUTLET

Top plate

New cable

Ceiling joist

New ceiling box

Existing receptacle

Cut back drywall to middle of studs

New switch box

Fishing cable to a new outlet can be time-consuming and tedious. Often, it's quicker and easier to cut back sections of drywall to the nearest studs or ceiling joists. With a stud bay exposed, you can pull wire in a hurry and staple cable to studs.

1 Use a flex bit to drill through wall plates.

2 Pull back after a helper below the floor attaches the cable.

FISHING CABLE BEHIND FINISH WALLS (CONTINUED)

3 A swivel kellum grip slides over the end of the cable being fished so the cable doesn't twist.

or

4 After testing for voltage, remove the cover plate, unscrew the receptacle from the box, and pull it out.

5 Remove the old outlet box, drill, fish new cable, and splice the old cable to the new.

FISHING CABLE TO A CEILING FIXTURE

1 To run cable to a ceiling fixture, start by drilling an exploratory hole with a small-diameter bit.

Fishing cable to ceiling fixtures or wall switches is usually a bit complicated. If there is an unfinished attic above or a basement below, run the cable across it, then route the cable through a stud bay to the new box in the ceiling. To run cable to a ceiling light, for example, drill up through the fixture location using a $3/16$-in. by 12-in. bit to minimize patching later **1**. Use a bit at least 6 in. long so a helper in the attic can see it—use a longer one if the floor of the attic is covered with insulation. Measure the distance from the bit to the wall; a helper in the attic can use that measurement to locate the nearest stud bay to drill an access hole into. If you're working alone, loop the end of a stiff piece of wire

about 1 ft. long **2** and insert it in the drilled hole; friction will keep the wire upright in the hole until you can locate it in the attic.

If there's no access above the ceiling and/or cable must cross several ceiling joists to get from a switch to a light fixture, you'll have to cut into finish surfaces at several points **3**. To access cable in a stud bay, you'll need a cutout to expose the top plate. Using a flex bit may minimize the number of holes you must cut to drill across ceiling joists. But as noted earlier, it may ultimately take less time to cut and repair a single slot running across several joists than to patch a number of isolated holes. Whatever method you choose, make cuts cleanly to facilitate repairs. First outline all cuts using a utility knife.

2 If you're working alone, jam a long, looped wire into the exploratory hole, then go aloft into the attic to look for it.

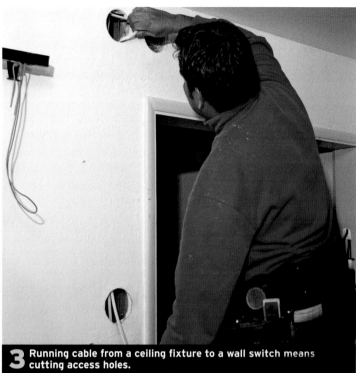

3 Running cable from a ceiling fixture to a wall switch means cutting access holes.

FISHING CABLE ACROSS CEILING JOISTS

New opening for ceiling box

Drill across ceiling joists.

Drywall cutout at top plate

New cable

Flex bit

Cutout for switch box

Cable from existing outlet supplies power.

Sometimes there is no open bay to a ceiling-fixture location. In that case, you'll have to drill across ceiling joists to run cable to the top plate of the wall. Use a 6-ft.-long flex bit (and a 48-in. extension, if needed) to drill across joists. Flex bits can wander and go off target, so be patient. When the drill bit emerges above the top plate, attach a swivel kellum taped securely to the new cable. Then slowly back the drill bit out, pulling the cable to the opening you cut in the ceiling. It's preferable to wear a heavy leather glove to protect the hand guiding the flex bit.

CUTTING A WALL BOX INTO PLASTER

If existing house wiring is in good condition and an existing circuit has the capacity for an additional outlet, turn off the power, cut a hole in the wall, fish cable to the location, and secure a remodel box (cut-in box) to the finish surface. This process is called cutting-in or retrofitting a box, and, of course, it requires boxes with special mounting mechanisms.

Hold the new box at the same height as other outlet or switch boxes and trace its outline onto the wall. Use a stud finder or drill a small exploratory hole to locate studs or wood lath behind. Look for water pipes or other wires. If you hit a stud, move the box. If you hit lath, keep drilling small holes within the opening to find the edges of the lath. If you position the box correctly, you'll need to remove only one or two lath sections **1**.

Use a utility knife to score along the outline to minimize plaster fractures. Remove the plaster within the outline using a chisel. Then cut out the lath, using a cordless jigsaw, sabersaw, or, even better, an oscillating multi-tool (p. 21) with a Universal E-cut blade **2**. As you cut through the lath strip, alternate partial cuts from one side to the other to avoid cracking the plaster. Then carefully remove the plaster beneath the box ears, so they can rest on lath. Before inserting cut-in boxes, remove box knockouts, insert cable clamps, strip sheathing off the ends of incoming cable, and feed cable into the cable clamps. If more than one cable enters the box, write the destination of each on the sheathing. Secure the box by screwing its ears to the lath **3**.

1 Position the box and then trace the box outline onto the wall.

2 After you chisel out the plaster within the outline, use a sabersaw to cut lath.

3 After fishing and pulling cable, secure the box to the wall.

CUTTING A WALL BOX INTO DRYWALL

Adding a cut-in box to drywall is essentially the same as adding one to plaster. Start by drilling a small exploratory hole near the proposed box location to make sure there's no stud in the way.

There are a number of cut-in boxes to choose from. The most common have side-mounted ears that swing out or expand as you turn their screws. Hold the box against the drywall, plumb it **1**, then trace the outline of the box onto the wall **2**. Align the blade of a jab saw (drywall saw) to the line you want to cut and hit the handle of the saw with the heel of your hand **3**.

There is no one right way to cut out a box opening; just take it slow. If the box outline is intricate or the jab saw produces a ragged line, switch to a utility knife. If you secure the cutout with a piece of painter's tape **4** as you finish the cut, the drywall's paper face will be less likely to tear and the cutout won't fall into the wall cavity–useful, should you need to patch the hole.

1 Locate the new outlet between studs, then plumb it.

2 Carefully trace the box outline onto the drywall.

3 Use a jab saw to cut the opening in drywall.

4 Attach a piece of painter's tape to the cutout.

Run cable(s) to the new outlet, remove knockout(s) in the box, and slide the box onto the cable and into the opening ❺. Code does not require that you add cable clamps for a single-gang plastic box—integral plastic clamps in the box will secure the cable.

Tighten the box mounting screws ❻, which will expand side-mounted ears to extend and draw the box tight to the drywall ❼.

5 Feed cable into the box, insert box into hole.

6 Tighten the mounting screws, which will . . .

PRO TIP

If you need to splice two or more cables, use a 4-in. octagonal or round box instead of a pancake box.

7 . . . extend side-mounted ears on the cut-in box.

RETROFITTING A CEILING BOX

As with all retrofits, turn off power to the area and explore first. Follow the mounting recommendations for your fixture. Attach the fixture box to framing.

If there's insulation in an attic above, remove it from the affected area. Be sure to wear eye protection and a dust mask when drilling through any ceiling—it's a dusty job.

Mark the box location and use a fine-tooth hole saw to cut through plaster or drywall ❶. Place the centering bit of the hole saw on the exact center of the box opening. Drill slowly so you don't damage adjoining surfaces—or fall off the ladder.

If the ceiling is drywall, you're ready to run cable through the hole in the ceiling. If the ceiling is plaster, cut through the lath or leave the lath intact and screw a pancake box through the lath and into the framing. Before attaching a pancake box, remove a knockout, test-fit the box in the hole, and trace the knockout hole onto the lath. Set the box aside and drill through the lath, creating a hole through which you can run cable ❷.

Feed cable to the location and fit a cable connector into the box. Insert the cable into the connector, slide the box up to the ceiling ❸, and secure it ❹. Strip the cable sheathing and attach the ground wire to a ground screw in the box. Strip insulation from the wire ends and you're ready to connect the light fixture.

1 Use a fine-tooth hole saw to cut the box hole.

2 Drill through the lath.

3 Fish cable through the lath and feed it through the box.

4 Screw the pancake box to framing or blocking.

CREATING A WIRING TRENCH

1 Use a chalkline to mark the top and bottom lines of the wiring trench.

2 To ensure a clean cut line and make patching easier, use a utility knife to first score along the chalklines.

3 Cut along the chalklines, holding the reciprocating saw at a low angle. Do not cut the lath.

4 If walls are drywall, simply pull out the isolated strips. If plaster, use a hammer to remove the plaster and expose the lath.

5 Use a hammer and a flat bar to pry the lath free from the studs. Work slowly to minimize damage.

6 Pull out any nails still stuck in the studs; this will make later repairs easier.

When adding multiple outlets or rewiring an entire room, cutting a wiring trench in finish surfaces instead of fishing cable behind them is much faster. Before cutting or drilling, however, turn off the power to the areas affected. Be sure to wear eye protection and a dust mask.

If there are no windows in the walls to be rewired, cut the trench about 3 ft. above the floor so you won't have to kneel while working. If there are windows, cut the trench under the windows, leaving at least 1 in. of wall material under the windowsill to facilitate repairs. If there's plaster, make the trench as wide as two strips of lath. Snap parallel chalklines to indicate the width of the trench **1**. Then use a utility knife to score along each line **2**. Scoring lines first produces a cleaner cut and easier repairs.

Next use a reciprocating saw with a demolition blade to cut through the plaster or drywall. Hold the saw at a low angle: You'll be less likely to break blades or cut into studs **3**. Using a hammer, gently crush the plaster between the lines **4**. Use a utility bar (flat bar) to pry out the lath strips or drywall section. If you expose any cables in the walls, use a noncontact tester to make sure they're not hot **5**. Next, drill through the studs so you can run cable in the trench. Wherever there's an outlet indicated, expand the trench width to accommodate the boxes.

Finally, pull any lath or drywall nails from stud edges **6**. They're easy to overlook because they're small; if you pull them now, patching the trench will go smoothly.

PULLING CABLE TO RETROFIT BOXES

Once you've cut a wiring trench and drilled the holes, installing the boxes and pulling cable are straightforward and much like the basic sequences shown in Chapter 2.

➤ **For more on installing boxes, see p. 25.**

➤ **For more on pulling cables, see p. 199.**

If you're installing metal boxes, remove knockouts and insert cable connectors into their openings **❶**. Then screw boxes to studs; screwing is less likely to damage nearby finish surfaces **❷**. Be sure that the box will be flush to finish surfaces or, if you'll install plaster rings later, flush to the stud edge. Whenever you install boxes side by side—as with the outlet and low-voltage boxes shown here—install them plumb and at the same height **❸**.

Installing cable in remodels can be tricky because space is tight and you must avoid bending cable sharply, which can damage wire insulation **❹**. Install nail plates wherever the edge of the hole is less than 1¼ in. from the stud edges. Feed cable through the cable connectors into the boxes **❺**. Finally, staple the cable to the framing within 8 in. of a single-gang box without clamps, or within 12 in. of other boxes. If there's not room to loop the cable and staple it to a stud, it's acceptable to staple it to other solid framing, such as the underside of a sill **❻**.

⚠ **SAFETY ALERT**
Before you cut into any finish surface, ascertain that it's not covered with lead paint.

1 For metal boxes, start by removing knockouts and then insert a connector.

2 Screw the box to the side of a stud.

3 For the best appearance, install outlets that are side by side at the same height.

4 Run cable to each box.

5 Feed the cable through cable connectors.

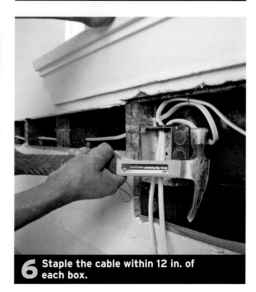

6 Staple the cable within 12 in. of each box.

MAKING UP AN OUTLET BOX

1 Use a cable ripper to slit sheathing and diagonal cutters to cut it.

2 A crimp tool may be used instead of a wire nut for the ground.

3 The long leg of the ground is looped beneath the grounding screw.

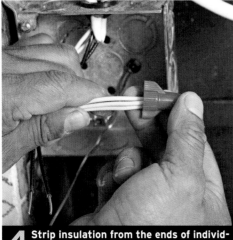

4 Strip insulation from the ends of individual wires and splice like wires together.

5 If there will be two receptacles in a box, make up two sets of pigtails.

6 Fold the wires into the box and install a plaster ring.

Electricians call the last stage of rough wiring *making up a box*. After removing sheathing from cables, rough-cut individual wires about 8 in. long, group like wires, and, to save time later, splice all wire groups.

Use a cable ripper ❶ to remove the plastic cable sheathing. (Most professional electricians favor utility knives for removing sheathing, but DIYers should use a cable ripper to avoid nicking wire insulation.) Once you've slit the sheathing with the cable ripper, pull back the sheathing and the kraft paper inside and snip off both, using diagonal cutters. Because cable clamps grip sheathing—not individual wires—there must be at least 1/4 in. of sheathing still peeking under cable clamps when you're done.

Typically, electricians start by splicing the ground wires, which are usually bare copper. (If they're green insulated wires, first strip approximately 3/4 in. of insulation off their ends.) If you use standard wire connectors (Wire-Nut is one brand), trim the ground wires and

butt their ends together, along with a 6-in. pigtail, which you'll connect later to the green ground screw of a receptacle. However, many pros prefer to twist the ground wires together, leave one ground long, and thread it through the hole in a special wire connector—or crimp the wires ❷. If the box is metal, first bond the ground wire to the box, using a grounding clip (p. 219) or a grounding screw ❸.

Splicing hot and neutral wire groups is essentially the same ❹. Trim hot wires to the same length. Strip 3/4 in. of insulation off the cable wires and the pigtail, and use lineman's pliers to twist the wires. Then screw on a wire connector. If the box will contain two receptacles, create two groups of pigtails ❺.

Once wire groups are spliced, gently accordion-fold the wires back into the box until you're ready to wire switches and receptacles ❻.

➤ **Attaching wires to receptacles and switches is covered at length in Chapter 3.**

MAKING UP A CAN LIGHT

Wiring a recessed can light or a ceiling box is essentially the same as making up an outlet box, although can lights frequently have stranded wire leads. Always follow the installation instructions supplied with your lighting unit.

Run cable to the can light, stapling it at least every 4½ ft. to the side of the ceiling joist and within 12 in. of the box. Also, make sure that the cable is at least 1¼ in. from the joist edge, so drywall screws or nails can't puncture it. Because you'll be working over your head and junction boxes are cramped, you may want to remove the sheathing before feeding cable into the box ❶. Here again, cable clamps grip sheathing—not individual wires—so there must be at least ¼ in. of sheathing still peeking under cable clamps when you're done. Then strip insulation from individual wires ❷.

Group ground wires, neutral wires, and hot wires. Then splice each group using wire connectors. Electricians typically start by splicing ground wires. Typically, a ground screw and a grounding pigtail are factory-installed in the can ❸. They then splice the neutral wires and, finally, the hot wires. When all wire groups are spliced, fold them carefully into the junction box and attach the cover.

1 Run enough cable to the light fixture so that there's about 10 in. sticking out of its junction box.

2 Feed the cable into the junction box, remove the sheathing, and strip the insulation from the ends of individual wires.

3 Use wire connectors to splice paired wire groups, starting with the ground wire group. Fold the spliced wires into the box.

PRO TIP

The ground screw must compress the ground wire evenly. Never cross the ground wire (or any other wire) over itself, because the screw would touch only that high spot.

MAKING UP A SINGLE-GANG SWITCH BOX

1 Use a cable ripper or score the sheathing lightly on both sides and give it a quick tug to slide it off the wires.

2 Use lineman's pliers to twist the grounds together. Leave one ground longer to be attached to the device.

3 Use a twist-on wire connector to splice the neutrals. Do not splice the hot wires; they are attached to the switch later.

4 Fold the wires in an accordion pattern and tuck them into the box.

Single-gang switch boxes are most commonly plastic, so begin by using a screwdriver or needle-nose pliers to remove its knockout(s). Feed cable (or cables) into the knockout(s) and staple it within 8 in. of the box. There's no need to insert cable clamps—two-gang and larger as well as some single-gang plastic boxes have an integral spring clamp inside the knockout to prevent cable from being yanked out. Leave about 8 in. to 10 in. of wire sticking out of the box.

If a single cable enters the switch box, you're looking at a "switch loop" (p. 52), in which an outlet or light fixture is closer to the power source. Code requires that new switch loops be served by 3-wire cable, because some electronic switches require a neutral wire. Historically, though, switch loops were also served by 2-wire cable and the white wire was used as a hot wire: See pp. 52–53 for the full story. In either case, remove the cable sheathing, and tuck the wires into the box.

If there are two cables entering the switch box, one is incoming power and the other is a switch leg. Remove the cable sheathing **1**, then twist the grounds together and add a grounding pigtail before splicing them with a wire connector **2**. Strip insulation from the ends of the neutral wires and splice them **3**. Fold the wires into the box **4**.

MAKING UP A MULTIGANG SWITCH BOX

The tricky part of making up a multigang switch box is keeping track of the wires. As you feed each cable into the box, use a felt-tipped marker to identify each cable's origin or destination. Write directly on the cable sheathing. Start by feeding the incoming cable into the box and marking it *hot*. This incoming cable will supply 120v from a panel or from an outlet upstream when the cable is connected later.

Next, nail a standoff to the side of the stud so you can secure each cable as you feed it into the switch box ❶. Before inserting a cable into a knockout, however, note which fixture or device the switch leg controls ❷. Be specific and use labels such as *sconce*, *can ctr* (center can), and *perim* (perimeter fixture).

As you pull each cable into the box, strip the sheathing and slide off the small section that has writing on it ❸. When all the cables have been stripped, separate and twist the bare ground wires clockwise. Leave one ground about 6 in. longer than the others for each device in the box, then feed it through the hole in the end of a special ground wire connector ❹. This longer ground wire will run to a ground screw on each switch.

Strip the insulation from the ends of the neutral wires; then use a wire connector to splice them together ❺. Fold both ground- and neutral-wire groups into the box.

Cut a hot-wire pigtail 8 in. to 9 in. long for each switch and splice all pigtails to the hot wire of the incoming cable—the one that was earlier marked *120v* ❻. Finally, pair a hot pigtail with each switch leg ❼. Fold the wire pairs into the box. When it's time to wire the switches later, you'll connect a hot pigtail to one screw terminal and a switch-leg wire to the other screw terminal.

If a cable serves a three-way or four-way switch, indicate whether a wire is a "traveler" or "common."

➜ **For more on three- and four-way switches, see "Receptacles and Switches," p. 36.**

1 Nail a standoff to secure three or more cables.

2 Before pulling each cable into the box, indicate which fixture it controls.

3 Score and remove the sheathing. Slide the label back on.

4 Feed the ground wire through the hole in the connector, and twist on the connector.

5 Twist on a wire connector to splice the neutral wire group.

6 Cut an 8-in. hot-wire pigtail for each switch in the box. Cap each pigtail.

7 When boxes contain multiple switches, indicate which fixture each switch leg controls.

⚠ **SAFETY ALERT**

If a box has more than one circuit in it, all the grounds must be spliced together, but the neutrals of the different circuits must be kept separate.

FLEXIBLE METAL CABLE

1 Flexible metal cable must be at least 1¼ in. from stud edges.

Staple AC or MC cable within 12 in. of the box and 4½ ft. between boxes. **2**

3 To cut AC or MC cable, bend the cable till the jacket splits, then snip.

or

When using a Roto-Split, follow manufacturer's instructions.

CABLE CONNECTORS

Quick lock for MC

Snap-Tite® for MC

Locknut connector for AC

In residences, MC and AC cable is most often used in short exposed runs—typically between a wall box and the junction box of an appliance. The cable's metal jacket protects the wiring inside, but you should still take pains to avoid puncturing MC or AC cable with a nail or a screw. For this reason, when flexible metal cable is run through stud walls, it's a good practice to run it through the center of the stud **1**. If several cables run through a stud, align holes vertically to avoid compromising the strength of the stud. Use nail-protection plates if a cable is closer than 1¼ in. to a stud edge.

→ **For more on nail-protection plates, see p. 199.**

Secure or support flexible metal cable within 12 in. of boxes **2** and at least every 4½ ft. along the span of the run—electricians typically staple it every 3 ft.

Flexible metal cable should also be secured to the underside of every joist it crosses or run through holes drilled through joists. Again, use nail-protection plates if the cable is less than 1¼ in. from a joist edge.

AC and MC cable require specialized connectors to secure them to boxes. You can use a hacksaw with a metal-cutting blade or diagonal cutters to cut through cable's metal jacket **3**, but a Roto-Split is the tool of choice. Whatever tool you use, cut through only one coil of the metal jacket to sever it. To prevent damaging the wire insulation within, cut no deeper than the thickness of the metal jacket. After cutting through the metal jacket, insert plastic anti-short bushings to protect the wire insulation from the sharp edges of the metal jacket.

CABLE, CONDUIT & MOISTURE

Moisture can short out electrical connections or, over time, degrade conductors and connectors. Thus it's important to use materials in appropriate locations.

■ Non metallic (NM) sheathed cable (one brand is Romex): Dry locations only.

■ Metal-clad (MC) or armored cable (AC): Dry locations; can be used in wet locations only if specifically listed for that use.

■ Underground-feeder (UF) cable: Can be buried; when used in interiors, same rules as for NM cable.

■ Electrical metallic tubing (EMT): Wet or dry locations; okay in wet locations if fittings (couplings and connectors) are listed for use in wet locations; may be in direct contact with earth, if suitable and approved by local code.

■ Rigid metal conduit (RMC): Same rules as for EMT; may be buried in earth or embedded in concrete.

■ PVC plastic conduit (schedule-40 PVC): Can be exposed if listed for direct sunlight or buried underground; fittings are inherently raintight, so can be installed outdoors and in damp crawlspaces.

INSTALLING AC CABLE

To install AC cable, start by marking the box heights onto the studs and installing the metal boxes flush to finish surfaces or flush to the stud edges. Remove a box knockout for each cable. Then drill the studs and run the AC cable through each hole. Staple it every 4½ ft. along the run and within 12 in. of each box.

Use a Roto-Split to cut through a single coil of the cable's metal jacket, then slide off the severed jacket section to expose the wires inside. Use diagonal cutters to snip off the kraft paper covering the wires ❶. Slide a plastic antishort bushing between the wires and the metal jacket ❷. Next, wrap the silver bonding wire around the outside of the jacket ❸. Wrapping this wire bonds the jacket and creates a continuous ground path.

Slide a setscrew connector over the end of the AC cable and tighten the setscrew to the metal jacket ❹. The screw compresses the cable jacket and the bonding wire, holding them fast and ensuring a continuous ground. Insert the threaded end of the connector into a box knockout. Then tighten the locknut that secures the connector ❺.

Attach a mud ring to the box to bring it flush to finish surfaces, which will be installed later, and fold the wires into the box ❻.

1 Pull and snip the kraft paper to expose the insulated wires and bare bonding tracer.

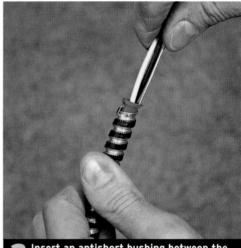

2 Insert an antishort bushing between the wires and the jacket to prevent shorts.

3 Wrap the bonding tracer around the outside of the metal jacket.

4 To ensure a solid ground path, tighten a setscrew connector over the cable end.

5 To secure the AC cable to the box, tighten a locknut onto the connector.

6 Attach a mud ring (here, a single-gang mud ring).

INSTALLING MC CABLE

MC cable is similar to AC cable, except that MC cable contains an insulated ground wire. Unlike AC cable, MC cable does not rely on its metal jacket to create a continuous ground for the circuit.

After using a hacksaw, diagonal cutters, or a Roto-Split to cut through the metal jacket of MC cable, slide on an antishort bushing to protect the wires inside from the sharp edges of the jacket. Remove the plastic wrapping ❶. Slide a quick-lock clamp over the end of the cable and snap the clamp into a box knockout. Then tighten the clamp screw to secure the MC cable to the box ❷.

To create a continuous ground, use wire strippers to strip the ends of the incoming ground wire ❸. Use a wire connector to splice the incoming ground, the ground-screw pigtail, and a grounding pigtail that attaches to the device ❹. Then fold the wires into the box and screw on a mud ring to bring the box flush to finish surfaces, which are installed later.

PRO TIP

If you're pulling conduit wires in a residence, you probably don't need to use pulling lubricant. Use lubricant when:

- Pulling long distances—more than 100 ft.
- Pulling wires through multiple 90-degree bends.
- Pulling "fat" wires, such as 10AWG or larger.
- Pulling the maximum number of wires a conduit can hold.

1 MC cable contains an insulated ground wire instead of a bonding wire (as AC cable does).

2 MC cable does not rely on its metallic jacket to create a ground path. Thus you can use a quick-lock clamp to attach MC cable.

3 Strip the end of the incoming ground wire.

4 Use a wire connector to splice all three ground wires.

WORKING WITH EMT STEEL CONDUIT (INTERIOR)

1 To steady the pipe as you cut it, brace it with your legs.

2 Use a reaming tool to remove burrs, which could nick insulation.

3 Use a setscrew coupling to join lengths of conduit. Tighten the screws snugly.

4 To secure pipe to a box, install a set-screw connector into a box knockout.

5 Use a strap to secure conduit pipe.

> **PRO TIP**
> Use a hacksaw to cut metal conduit. Do not use the tubing cutters often used to cut plumbing pipe because they create a razor-sharp burr inside the conduit that is almost impossible to remove with a reaming tool.

Because EMT conduit is easy to work with, it's the rigid conduit type most commonly used. The main difference between conduit and flexible metal cable is that conduit comes without wire inside. Fortunately, pulling wire into conduit is a straightforward operation.

Assembling conduit is also straightforward. After cutting conduit pipe to length and deburring it, insert pipe ends into setscrew couplings and tighten the screws to secure the pipes. Threaded male fittings connect the pipe to boxes and condulets—covered fittings that facilitate wire-pulling or enable changes in pipe direction. You can buy prebent fittings such as capped-elbows (two-piece elbows that you can access to

pull wires) and sweeps (single-piece elbows with a wide turning radius). Or you can rent a conduit bender to change pipe direction.

By code, EMT conduit must be strapped within 3 ft. of every junction box and at least every 10 ft. along runs. In actual practice, electricians strap pipe runs every 6 ft. to 8 ft. to prevent sagging.

Work from a layout sketch that indicates the power source, structural members, obstructions, existing outlets, and the locations of new outlets. Mount all the outlet boxes at the same height, and plumb a side of each one. Plumbed boxes look better and align better with conduit pipes.

Use a hacksaw with a metal-cutting blade to cut EMT pipe. EMT pipe typically comes in

10-ft. lengths **1**. After cutting the pipe, use a reaming tool to remove the burrs inside and out **2**.

To join EMT pipe, insert pipe ends into setscrew couplings **3**. To secure pipe to a box, use a setscrew connector on the box knockout **4**. In general, plumb vertical conduit sections before strapping them into place **5**. On the other hand, you may want pipe to follow an angled architectural element such as a brace, as shown in Photo 4 on the following page.

MAKING BENDS WITH METAL CONDUIT (INTERIOR)

To change directions in a metal conduit system, you can either bend the pipe or install directional fittings such as offset adaptors, elbows, or condulets. EMT pipe is rigid, but its walls are thin enough to bend easily with a conduit bender.

Pros bend conduit whenever possible. Bending pipe reduces the number of specialty fittings to buy and enables pipe to follow the contours of surfaces and structural elements. It's not necessary or desirable for conduit to follow every last jog or bulge in a wall; the simpler you can make an installation, the better it will look and the faster it will progress.

To bend pipe, use a felt-tipped marker to mark the beginning of the bend on the pipe. Slide the pipe into the bender ❶. Gently step on one side of the bender and simultaneously pull on the lever bar ❷. The raised marks on the outer curve of the bender indicate the angle you're creating in the pipe—typically, 15, 22½, 30, 45, or 60 degrees.

After bending the conduit—but before cutting it to final length—test-fit the piece to see if it lines up with the connector on the box ❸ or to a coupling that joins two pipe sections. With practice, you can also offset pipe ❹. Offsetting creates two bends in opposite directions so a length of conduit can move from one plane to another.

There are a couple of rules to keep in mind as you bend conduit. First, there's a minimum requirement bend-radius for conduit: 10× the diameter. For ½-in.-diameter conduit, for example, the minimum bend radius is 5 in.

Second, each turn makes it harder to pull wire. So between each pair of boxes, you can have no more than 360 degrees of bends. Splice wires only in a junction or outlet box.

1 Mark the start of the bend on the pipe; then position it in the bender.

2 Pull and simultaneously step on one side of the bender.

3 Test-fit the piece to see if it lines up with the pipe connector.

4 Conduit benders can also create multiple offset angles.

USING DIRECTIONAL FITTINGS

You can also use directional fittings to make turns. A T-condulet enables you to run wires in different directions and doubles as a pulling point when fishing wire. To attach pipe to a condulet, first screw a locknut onto the threaded shaft of a male adaptor. Turn the adaptor most of the way into the condulet hub and turn the locknut clockwise until it seats against the hub. Back-tightening the locknut in this manner ensures grounding continuity.

Use a T-condulet as a pulling point when fishing wires. Here, wires from the source diverge in two directions.

To attach pipe to a condulet, use an adapter and back-tighten the locknut until it lodges against the hub.

FISHING WIRE THROUGH CONDUIT

You can start fishing wire from either end of the circuit. If you're tapping into an existing outlet, it makes sense to fish from that outlet—after first turning off the power to the outlet and testing to make sure it's off.

In the installation shown here, a four-square extension box was mounted over an existing (recessed) box. Thus new wires can be pulled into the extension box and spliced to an existing cable to provide power for the circuit extension being added.

The fish tape can be fed easily into the conduit pipe ❶. At the other end of the conduit, tape wires to the fish tape ❷. To make wire pulling easier, leave the wire ends straight—do not bend them over the tape, but stagger them slightly so the bundled wires taper slightly. Wrap electrical tape tightly around the wire bundle so that wires stay together and won't snag as they're pulled. The pulling will also go easier if you pull stranded wire rather than solid wire, which is stiffer and less flexible.

Finally, use a wire caddy ❸, even if you have to build one out of scrap pipe and lumber. Using wire spools on a caddy helps minimize tangles.

TAPPING INTO AN EXISTING OUTLET

Tapping into an existing outlet is often a convenient way to supply power to a conduit extension. Remove the cover plate from the outlet, detach wires from the old receptacle, then use lineman's pliers to straighten the old wires so they'll be easier to splice to wires running to the new outlets.

Incoming cable (from power source) — **Box grounding screw** — **Wire connector** — **Pigtails to new receptacle** — **Four-square box extension** — **Existing recessed box** — **EMT conduit connector** — **Outgoing conduit and wires (to receptacles/ equipment downstream)**

1 Push the fish tape down into the conduit.

2 When the fish tape emerges from the conduit, attach the wires.

3 As you pull wires through the conduit, the spools on the wire caddy turn.

PREPPING RECEPTACLES FOR SURFACE METAL BOXES

1 Use diagonal cutters to snip the "plaster ears" off the receptacles so they'll fit into the industrial raised covers.

2 Attach solid pigtails to screw terminals.

3 Screw the covers to the receptacle's mounting tabs.

4 Screw the ground pigtail to the box.

To save time, professionals often divide receptacle wiring of a conduit system into several smaller tasks, each of which can be done with a single tool. Your conduit system may have slightly different materials, but these prep techniques should save you time.

Standard duplex receptacles come with plaster ears intended to seat against plaster or drywall surfaces. Consequently, the ears may not fit into metal boxes or behind the industrial raised covers often installed in conduit systems. Use diagonal cutters to snip off the ears **1** so they fit inside such covers.

To speed the assembly, precut all the pigtails that you'll attach to receptacles. To loop pigtail ends, strip 1/2 in. of insulation, insert the stripped ends into the little hole on the stripper jaw, and twist your wrist.

Use a screw gun to attach the looped ends to the receptacle screw terminals **2**. Remember to loop the pigtail ends clockwise so that when the screw tightens (clockwise), the loop stays on the screw.

Next, attach the prewired receptacles to the covers. Typically, there is a pair of machine screws (and nuts) that screw into the mounting tabs at top and bottom, and a single short screw for the center hole in the front of the receptacle **3**.

Finally, screw a ground pigtail to the box **4**. The threaded hole for the ground screw is raised slightly to facilitate surface mounting. If you surface-mounted a box on a concrete wall and the box didn't have this detail, the ground screw would hit concrete before it tightened all the way down—thus jeopardizing grounding continuity.

WIRING OUTLETS

1 Strip ½ in. of insulation from the ends of the stranded wire.

2 Splice the ground wires first, then neutral wires, then hot wires.

3 After splicing like-colored wire groups, fold them into place.

4 Then screw the receptacle cover to the box.

I f you've already attached pigtails to the receptacle screw terminals, the connections at outlet boxes on a conduit system will go quickly. *Note:* In the project shown here, the red wire is the hot conductor, the white wire is neutral, and green is the ground conductor. Code requires that green or bare wires are always the designated ground.

Use wire strippers to strip ½ in. of insulation from the wires pulled through the conduit **1**. Splice the receptacle pigtails to like-colored circuit wires pulled through the conduit. Typically, electricians splice the ground wires first, which means splicing three wires: the receptacle pigtail, the grounding pigtail to the box, and the circuit ground **2**. If the metal

conduit serves as the ground, there will be no circuit ground wire.

When splicing stranded wire to solid wire, strip the stranded wire slightly longer than the solid wire, so the stranded-wire end sticks out beyond the solid wire. By doing this, you force the stranded-wire end into the wire connector first, ensuring a solid connection. Use lineman's pliers to twist wires slightly before screwing on the connector.

Once you've spliced all wire groups, fold the wires into the box **3** and attach the cover. Hold the cover tight against the box and attach it with the cover screws **4**.

GROUNDING CABLE & CONDUIT SYSTEMS

Every newly installed circuit must have continuous grounding. Steel conduit acts as its own ground path. MC cable contains an insulated ground because its metal jacket does *not* serve as a ground path; it exists solely to protect the wires inside. AC cable's metal jacket, on the other hand, *does* serve as a ground path. To ensure a continuous ground in AC cable runs, wrap and secure the cable's thin silver bonding wire.

If code requires steel conduit, AC, or MC, you must use steel boxes. Steel boxes must be grounded as well. In addition to tightening the cable or conduit couplings to the box knockouts, screw a grounding pigtail into the threaded hole in the box. The box pigtail is then spliced to circuit grounds and pigtails that run to the device.

Alternatively, if you're using solid wire, you can use a grounding clip to ground a metal box. (Code prohibits using a grounding clip with stranded wire.) If the incoming ground wire is insulated, strip approximately 6 in. of the insulation and slide the grounding clip onto a section of bare wire. This will allow enough wire beyond the clip so you can splice the bare wire end to other grounds or attach it directly to the grounding screw on a device.

Premade grounding pigtails come with one end looped around a green ground screw. If your job is large, using premade grounds can save a lot of time.

Using a ground clip to ground a metal box is suitable for solid conductors only.

APPLIANCES

WIRING APPLIANCES, LIKE WIRING general-use circuits, is primarily a matter of solidly connecting conductors and following the requirements of the NEC and the manufacturer. Many appliances are big energy users, so it's particularly important to size circuit wires and breakers based on appliance loads. When your new appliances arrive, read—and save—the owner's manuals that come with them. Owner's manuals contain essential information on how to install the appliance, how to register the appliance and comply with its warranty, how to identify and order replacement parts, and other useful information. Increasingly, manufacturers offer owner's manuals online, so if your appliance lacks a manual, download a copy. Always turn off power—and test to be sure it's off—before wiring appliances.

BASICS

A quick look at kitchen appliances, p. 222

Preparing an unfinished appliance cord, p. 223

GARBAGE DISPOSERS

Installing a garbage disposer, p. 224

OVENS

Roughing in an oven outlet, p. 226

Wiring a drop-in oven, p. 227

HOUSEHOLD APPLIANCES

Wiring laundry setups, p. 228

Installing baseboard heaters, p. 230

Electric water heaters, p. 231

A QUICK LOOK AT KITCHEN APPLIANCES

There's a lot going on in a modern kitchen. Typically it contains a refrigerator, a dishwasher, a garbage disposer, a range hood, a slew of small countertop appliances, and, in many cases, an electric range, cooktop, or oven.

➤ For more on wiring range hoods, see p. 160.

Appliances have different wiring requirements. Smaller ones such as disposers, dishwashers, and range fans require 120v; other appliances require 240v; and others—such as electric ranges—require both 120v and 240v. Range burners and ovens use 240v, but a range's timer and clock use 120v.

Let's start with a handful of important concepts.

Covered junction boxes

All electrical connections must take place in a covered junction box–either an integral box inside the appliance or in a covered junction box secured to a framing member, such as a wall stud.

Equipment grounding

All appliances must have an equipment-grounding conductor that connects to both the appliance frame (or housing) and to the metal outlet box for the safe discharge of fault currents.

Accessible disconnect means

Appliances typically have an accessible "disconnect means" so you can cut the power.

(This is in addition to the fuse or breaker controlling the circuit.) For appliances that slide out–such as a dishwasher or a refrigerator–the disconnect means is typically a cord and a receptacle plug. Appliances that are *hard wired*, such as drop-in cooktops and wall ovens, must have an access panel near the junction box where incoming circuit wires connect to *appliance whips* made of flexible conduit.

Dedicated circuits

Code requires that every fixed appliance must be served by a separate, *dedicated* circuit–a circuit that serves only that appliance. This includes large energy users such as electric ranges, electric water heaters, and clothes dryers that require heavier wire and higher-rated breaker (or fuse) protection.

➤ For more on dedicated circuits, see p. 175.

COMMON ELECTRICAL APPLIANCE REQUIREMENTS

User	Typical Wire Size*	Fuse or Breaker
Small-appliance circuit	12AWG	20 amps
Refrigerator (120v)[†,‡]	12AWG	20 amps
Stand-alone freezer (120v)[†,‡]	12AWG	20 amps
Dishwasher (120v)[†,‡]	12AWG	20 amps
Disposer (120v)[†,‡]	12AWG	20 amps
Microwave (120v)[†,§]	12AWG	20 amps
Range (120/240v)[†,‡]	10AWG	30 amps
Range (120/240v)[†,‡]	8AWG	40 amps
Range (120/240v)[†,‡]	6AWG	50 amps
General utility/workshop	12AWG	20 amps
Laundry circuit (washer)[ᴰ]	12AWG	20 amps
Clothes dryer (120/240v)[†,‡]	10AWG	30 amps
Water heater (240v)[†,‡]	10AWG	30 amps
Baseboard heater (120v)[†,‡]	12AWG	20 amps (max. 1,500w on circuit)
Baseboard heater (240v)[†,‡]	10AWG	30 amps (max. 5,760w on circuit)
Whole-house fan[†]	12AWG	20 amps
Window air-conditioner (240v)[†,‡]	10AWG	20 amps

*Ratings given for copper (CU) wiring.
[†]Requirements vary; check rating on appliance nameplate and follow manufacturer's specifications.
[‡]Requires dedicated circuit.
[§]Microwaves are typically rated 15 amps but are installed on 20-amp kitchen circuits.
[ᴰ]Requires designated circuit.

PRO TIP

Don't use ground-fault circuit interrupter (GFCI) protection for a gas cooktop or a range with an electric igniter. When the igniter fires, it will cause the GFCI to trip unnecessarily.

PREPARING AN UNFINISHED APPLIANCE CORD

There are many different types of appliance cords. Some cords come with a molded plug and precrimped connectors that attach to terminals on the appliance. Other cords have a molded plug but an unfinished end that you must strip and splice to the lead wires of an appliance. In most cases, the splice is housed in an integral junction box inside an appliance.

The cord seen here is a typical 120v cord that you might attach to a smaller fixed appliance, such as a garbage disposer. It contains a hot wire, a neutral wire and—in the center—a sheathed ground wire. Look closely at the cord and you'll see that its sheathing has a ribbed side and a smooth side. The ribbed side contains a neutral wire that must be spliced to the neutral wire of the appliance; the smooth side contains a hot wire ❶.

Start by snipping and separating the three stranded wires within the cord ❷. Using a utility knife, carefully slice and peel back the cord's outer (gray) insulation from the middle wire. As you do so, you'll expose the ground wire's green insulation. Only the ground wire has this additional layer of insulation ❸. Next use a wire stripper to remove ½ in. of insulation from the ends of all three cord wires ❹. Now you're ready to splice those wires to the lead wires on the appliance.

1 The ribbed side of the cord contains the neutral wire.

2 Use diagonal cutters to cut the cord and separate the three wires.

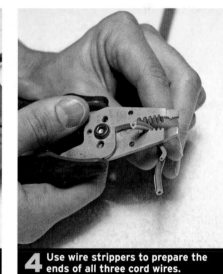

3 Peel back the gray insulation to expose the ground wire.

4 Use wire strippers to prepare the ends of all three cord wires.

PIGTAIL

For eons, how-to books had sections about replacing appliance plugs. Forget that. Today, you can easily find replacement cords—also called appliance pigtails—with molded plugs and precrimped connectors, which are far easier and safer to install. By the way, always grab the plug—not the cord—when unplugging an appliance.

Replacing the entire cord is often easier than replacing a broken plug.

The connectors on the appliance pigtail attach to terminals on the appliance.

INSTALLING A GARBAGE DISPOSER

1 The bundled yellow cables will supply the garbage disposer and dishwasher.

2 Remove the cover plate from the junction box and screw on a connector.

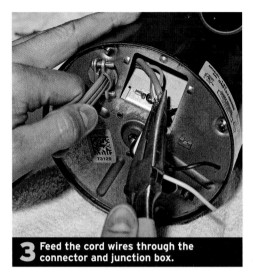

3 Feed the cord wires through the connector and junction box.

4 Tighten the cable connector to prevent stress on the wire connections.

5 Connect the appropriate wires with wire connectors.

6 Raise the disposer into place and turn it until the mounting rings lock into place.

Though installation of a disposer is largely the same from brand to brand, be sure to follow the instructions that come with your unit. Typically, plumbing supply and waste pipes are stubbed out, and 12AWG cable is roughed in before the finish walls and cabinets are installed **1**. After the base cabinet is in place, install a 20-amp duplex receptacle to supply power to the disposer and dishwasher. The receptacle for the disposer should be a switched receptacle.

➤ **For more on wiring a split-tab receptacle, see p. 47.**

Install the sink and attach the disposer mounting assembly in the sink outlet. Then route the dishwasher overflow pipe into the cabinet under the sink.

With these prep steps done, you're ready to attach the appliance cord. Remove the cover plate from the bottom of the unit and pull its wire leads. Then screw a cable connector into the knockout in the bottom of the unit **2**. Separate and strip cord wires and feed them through the cable connector. Use needle-nose pliers to pull the wires through the junction box **3** and then tighten the cable connector **4**.

Attach the green ground wire to the ground screw in the junction box. Then use wire connectors to splice like wires—neutral to neutral, hot to hot **5**. Fold all wires into the junction box and replace the cover plate. Lift the disposer until its mounting ring engages the mounting ring on the bottom of the sink. Turn the unit until the rings lock **6**.

Slide the tube from the dishwasher onto the dishwasher inlet stub and tighten its clamps **7**. Attach the P-trap to the discharge outlet on the disposer **8**. Plug the disposer plug into the switched half of the undersink receptacle. The second plug runs to the dishwasher.

7 Slide the dishwasher drain onto the inlet stub and tighten its clamp.

8 Attach the P-trap to the discharge outlet on the disposer.

DISPOSERS & DISHWASHERS

Disposers and dishwashers are often 120v, 15-amp appliances, so both are supplied by 12AWG cable. Most garbage disposers have a covered junction box on the bottom, to which a plugged cord attaches. You can also hard wire a disposer, but having a receptacle in the cabinet under the sink enables a homeowner to quickly unplug the unit should he or she need to repair or replace it. Typically, an undersink outlet is controlled by a switch above the counter, as shown in "Wiring a Garbage Disposer," at left.

A dishwasher and a disposer often plug into a split-tab receptacle located in the sink cabinet. A split-tab receptacle is a standard duplex receptacle whose middle tab has been removed to create a duplex receptacle fed by two circuits—that is, by two hot wires.

Because they slide out for installation and maintenance, dishwashers are also installed with a cord and plug. Most of the time, the dishwasher junction box is located in the front of the unit, just behind the kick panel. After attaching cord wires to wire leads in the junction box, run the cord in the channel behind the dishwasher to reach to an outlet.

WIRING A GARBAGE DISPOSER

BOTTOM OF DISPOSER, COVER REMOVED

Ground

Ground screw (green)

Neutral

Wire nut

Hot

Appliance cord

Ground screw (green)

Single-pole switch

Ground

Incoming power

Hot

Neutral

To disposer

Receptacle

Cord plug

⚠ SAFETY ALERT

The NEC specifies that you connect the two hot wires of a split-tab receptacle to a double-pole breaker. When you flip off the toggle for a double-pole breaker, you shut off both hot wires. If you instead connect the hot wires of a split-tab receptacle to separate, single-pole breakers and then flip off only one breaker, you might test the top half of the split-tab receptacle and conclude—mistakenly—that the bottom half was off, too. Attaching both hot wires to a double-pole breaker prevents such a potentially lethal mistake.

ROUGHING IN AN OVEN OUTLET

Roughing in an oven outlet is not that different from roughing in any other outlet. Remove the knockout from a four-square box, insert a plastic cable connector, and then feed in the 10/3 NM cable that will power the range. Staple the cable within 12 in. of the box; drive the staple just snug ❶.

Although an experienced electrician can use a utility knife to strip sheathing from any cable, using a cable ripper that can accommodate large-gauge wire makes sense for nonprofessionals ❷. Hold the ripper channel snug to the cable and pull it down the length of the cable to score the sheathing ❸.

Pull back the sheathing to expose wires inside. Then use diagonal cutters to cut the sheathing free. Leave 1/2 in. to 1 in. of sheathing inside the box ❹. Attach the ground wire to the box using a green ground screw in a threaded hole. Wrap the wire clockwise around the screw so it will stay in place as the screw tightens down on it ❺.

Fold the wires neatly into the box so they can be easily pulled out during the trim-out phase, when they'll be attached to a 30-amp receptacle or hard wired directly to a metal-clad appliance whip. Finally, attach a two-gang mud ring to the outlet box so it will be flush to the finish surface ❻.

1 10/3 NM cable is run to a four-square box.

2 Use a cable ripper that can accommodate larger-gauge wire.

4 With the wires exposed, use diagonal cutters to cut the sheathing loose.

5 Leave the ground wire long to be spliced to the ground in the appliance whip.

PRO TIP

Be sure to verify the ampacity of your range or cooktop. Many require 40A or 50A circuits, which will require larger-gauge cable.

ELECTRIC RANGES, OVENS, AND COOKTOPS

When discussing cooking appliances, you'll need to keep several terms straight: The enclosed cooking area in which you roast a turkey is an *oven*; you place pots and frying pans on *cooktop* burners. A *range* has both an oven and a cooktop.

In any case, the heating elements of ranges, ovens, and cooktops generally require 240v, but today's smart appliances come with a plethora of timers, clocks, sensors, buzzers, and other gizmos that use 120v. For this reason, many units require 120/240v wiring, with two hot wires, an insulated neutral, and an equipment ground wire.

As noted elsewhere, if the unit slides in and out for maintenance, it is usually installed with a plug inserted into a matched receptacle. The outlet box that contains that receptacle may be surface mounted or recessed (so that the receptacle can be flush mounted). If the unit drops in and stays put, it is typically hard wired to a junction box via an appliance whip.

3 Pull the ripper to score the sheathing.

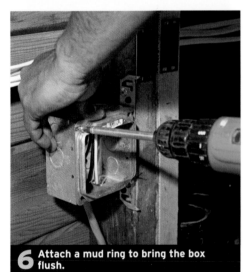

6 Attach a mud ring to bring the box flush.

WIRING A DROP-IN OVEN

Drop-in ovens and other stationary appliances must be hard wired. For the project shown here, an electric oven has been installed in a base cabinet, and the wires in its MC cable are ready to be connected to 10AWG wires, roughed into a four-square box. The edge of the box must be flush to the cabinet back, because plywood is flammable. If the box or its mud ring is below the cabinet back, add a four-square box extension to bring it flush **❶**.

Install a two-piece, right-angle cable connector (a flex-90) to the end of the cable whip. Slide the bottom of the connector onto the end of the whip and screw on the top of the cable connector **❷**. Remove the stamped knockout on the four-square cover; then feed the whip wires and the connector end through the knockout **❸**. Tighten a locknut onto the threaded connector end to lock the cable connector to the cover.

To ground the outlet box, loop the incoming ground wire under a green ground screw **❹**. Splice that ground wire to the appliance ground. Use wire strippers to remove ½ in. of insulation from the neutral and hot wires on the incoming cable **❺** (see p. 228); then use wire connectors to splice like-colored wires together **❻** (see p. 228): black to black, red to red, and white to white. To ensure that wire connectors grip the wires securely, use lineman's pliers. (There are two hot wires—red and black—because the oven requires 240v.)

Tuck them into the box. Then attach the cover to protect the connections within **❼** (see p. 228).

>> >> >>

1 A four-square box extension brings the outlet flush.

2 A right-angle cable connector is attached.

3 Remove a knockout and feed the wires through.

4 Wrap the incoming cable ground under a ground screw.

WIRING A DROP-IN OVEN (CONTINUED)

5 Remove ½ in. of insulation from the wires.

6 Fold the wires into the box.

7 Attach the cover to the box.

WIRING LAUNDRY SETUPS

In the photo sequence shown on the facing page, the metal conduit is the equipment ground. To bond each receptacle to the system, there is a green grounding pigtail that runs from each box's grounding screw to a receptacle ground screw. In this installation, wires are not yet attached to a power source, so they are safe to handle.

➡ **For more on installing metal conduit, see pp. 215–216.**

Start by fishing wire to the box nearest to the power source. Here, five insulated wires had to be fished: three 10AWG wires (hot-hot-neutral) to feed the 120/240v dryer receptacle; and two 12AWG wires (hot-neutral) to feed the 120v washer receptacle. Untape the fished-wire bundle and trim each set of wires to rough length so that at least 6 in. to 8 in. of wire sticks out of each box **❶**.

Attach a green grounding pigtail to each box and strip ½ in. of insulation off the ends of the incoming wires. If the point of a grounding screw hits the masonry wall, you may need to shorten the grounding screw so that it doesn't run into the masonry. The green pigtail grounds the device to the box; attach the pigtails first **❷** to the ground terminal on each receptacle. Next attach the neutral wires to each receptacle, then the hot wire(s) **❸**. Tighten each screw terminal, then gently tug each wire to be sure it's well attached.

The receptacle for the washer is a standard 20-amp receptacle. Use a wire stripper to create loops that you can attach to the screw terminals on the receptacle **❹**. Once both receptacles are wired, fold the wires into their respective boxes and attach the cover plates **❺**. If you install an industrial raised cover, secure the receptacle to the cover, then screw the cover to the box. Once you've installed the covers, attach circuit wires to breakers in the panel.

>> >> >>

MEASURING PIPE LENGTH

To determine the length of conduit pipe running between two outlet boxes, measure from the centerline of each box (A).

Subtract 2 in. from the centerline of each box (B).

Subtract the distance each adaptor sticks out of the box (C).

Add the distance that pipe ends fit into adaptor sockets (D).

Pipe length = A − 2B − 2C + 2D

Distance between centerlines of boxes

A

B (2 in.)

D

D

B

C

Pipe end fits into adaptor socket

C

Adaptor (pipe connector)

Outline of four-square box

1 Trim the wires running to each box so that 6 in. to 8 in. of wire sticks out of the box. Use grounding pigtails to bond receptacles to metal conduit.

WIRING REQUIREMENTS FOR LAUNDRY SETUPS

Clothes washers and dryers are often wired with two surface-mounted receptacles.

As with electric ranges, electric dryers typically require 120/240v wiring because, in addition to their 240v heating elements, dryers are also equipped with several elements that use 120v—such as drum motors, timers, and buzzers. So dryer circuits include two hot wires, a neutral wire, and an equipment ground wire.

Equipment grounds on washers and dryers connect to appliance housings to provide a safe route for fault current should a short circuit occur. Washer circuits are usually wired with 12AWG wire and protected by a 20-amp breaker or fuse; dryer circuits are wired with 10AWG wire and protected by a 30-amp breaker or fuse. But, as always, note the nameplate ratings on your appliances and wire them accordingly.

2 Screw the grounding pigtail into a specially machined screw hole in the outlet box. Such holes are typically located in a raised portion so the screw head can fully compress the wire.

3 The 120/240v dryer receptacle has screw terminals for two hot wires (red and black), a neutral wire (white), and a ground wire or pigtail (green).

4 The 120v washer receptacle is a standard 20-amp receptacle; strip and loop wire ends before attaching them to screw terminals.

5 Attach the cover plate to the receptacle, carefully fold the wires into the outlet box, and mount the cover to the box.

THE IMPORTANCE OF 4-POLE, 4-WIRE DRYER RECEPTACLES

In many older homes, 120/240v, 3-pole, 3-wire, nongrounded receptacles for appliances such as dryers and ranges are common. Older dryers were configured so that the neutral also served as the equipment ground; thus the circuit serving such a dryer had two hots and one neutral conductor.

The shift from nongrounding-type receptacles to grounded receptacles and appliances was made to improve safety and was required by the NEC in the early 1970s. Newer dryers had cords and plugs with 4 wires: hot, hot, neutral, ground.

Code allows a nongrounded receptacle to be replaced with another nongrounding receptacle, but code requires a grounded receptacle (120/240v, 4-pole 4-wire) if there is some way to bring an equipment-grounding conductor in the outlet box. Code also requires a grounded 4-pole, 4-wire receptacle for all new installations.

INSTALLING BASEBOARD HEATERS

Baseboard heaters are increasingly popular as a backup to a central heating system. Installing units with in-heater thermostats is a better choice than installing a central wall thermostat that controls all units. Baseboard units with in-heater thermostats are easier to install and more cost-effective to operate because they deliver heat to areas where it's needed most. Because most baseboard units are installed under windows, units with in-heater thermostats can respond faster to cold air as it enters.

Baseboard heaters are available in 120v and 240v models, but 240v models are generally more efficient. As a rule of thumb, you can connect several small heaters to one cable running from the main panel, as long as their combined continuous load doesn't exceed 80 percent of the cable's rating. In other words, if you run 12AWG cable with 20-amp protection, the continuous current should not exceed 16 amps. But because wattage varies from model to model, follow the installation instructions that come with your model.

Wiring an in-heater thermostat is pretty straightforward. Rough in wiring to each heater location, remove a cover plate on one end of each unit, feed the incoming cable through a cable connector, and splice the incoming circuit wires to the thermostat wires. Make sure to attach a grounding pigtail to the metal housing of the unit. Thermostats will be single-pole or double-pole switches. Double-pole thermostats are required by the NEC for 240v heaters, so that the thermostat, when off, cuts power to both legs of the unit, which is required for safety.

WIRING BASEBOARD IN-HEATER THERMOSTATS

SINGLE-POLE THERMOSTAT 110/120 VOLTS
- Hot
- Incoming power
- Ground screw (green)
- Ground
- Heating element
- Load side coming off thermostat
- Thermostat face

DOUBLE-POLE THERMOSTAT 220/240 VOLTS
- Tape white wire black to show it's hot.
- Hot
- Incoming power
- Ground screw (green)
- Ground
- Heating element
- Load side coming off thermostat
- Thermostat face

ELECTRIC WATER HEATERS

Replacing an electric water heater generally requires a permit, even if you attach the replacement to existing pipes. The reason is safety: Inspectors want to ensure that gas- and oil-fired units are properly vented and that electric heaters are correctly wired. Inspectors are particularly concerned that temperature and pressure relief (TPR) valves are correctly installed, because TPR valves keep water heaters from exploding in the event of a malfunction. For these reasons and for warranty issues, have a professional install your water heater. The drawing below is offered for information only.

──── WIRING A 240V WATER HEATER ────

Here's a look at a typical water heater installation. Three things to note: (1) The cutoff "switch" can be a circuit breaker or a fused switch rated for the load of the water heater, typically 30 amps. Place the disconnect (cutoff) switch close to the unit. You may use the circuit breaker in the service panel as the disconnect if it is within sight of the water heater and it is capable of being locked in the "OFF" position. (2) If you use 2-wire cable to wire the water heater, tape the white wire with red or black tape on both ends to indicate that it is being used as a hot conductor. (3) Use flexible metallic cable (rather than rigid conduit) between the cutoff switch and the water heater for extra safety in earthquake regions.

Incoming power

Connect the two appliance wires to a two-pole break.

Outlet (hot water)   Inlet (cold water)

Service panel

Junction box (cover removed)

Ground

Grounding screw (green)

Hot

White wire taped red to show it's hot

Metallic cable from the cutoff switch to the water heater

White wire taped red to show it's hot

OUTDOOR WIRING

ADDING AN OUTDOOR RECEPTACLE, a motion-sensor light, or low-voltage path lights can increase your security and safety and enable you to enjoy your property more fully. Because many outdoor devices are available as kits, they are usually easy to install and require few specialized tools. But before you start any project, review local building code requirements for outdoor installations. And remember: Before working on an existing outlet or fixture, be sure to turn off the power at the service panel or fuse box and test to be sure the power is off. Also, never operate power tools in damp or rainy conditions.

BEFORE YOU BEGIN

Planning your outdoor system, p. 234

Choosing outdoor lights, p. 235

Tools & materials, p. 236

OUTDOOR OUTLETS

Tapping into an existing outlet, p. 238

Mounting & wiring an exterior outlet, p. 240

OUTBUILDINGS

Running power to an outbuilding, p. 241

OUTDOOR PATH LIGHTS

Installing low-voltage path lights, p. 243

MOTION-SENSOR LIGHTS

Installing a motion-sensor light, p. 245

PLANNING YOUR OUTDOOR SYSTEM

Start by walking the property and noting where you'd like additional outlets, lights, and so on. Make a list. As you go, imagine activities that take place in different locations at night and day. Is there enough light along the path when you come home at night? Are there enough outlets to entertain or to do chores on the weekend? At this stage, think big and anticipate future uses, especially if you must dig up the lawn to install your present project. With a little advance planning, you can avoid digging up the lawn a second time, later.

If your wish list is extensive, next make a scale drawing of the house and yard on graph paper. Note sidewalks, paths, and important landscape elements such as trees and large bushes. Note electrical devices that you'd like to add and existing ones that need upgrading. The drawing will be especially useful when it's time to calculate the number of fixtures and amount of cable you'll need. If you intend to take power from an existing outlet, note where the nearest outlet is, even if it's inside the house.

Getting power

Once you know roughly where you want to add exterior outlets or light fixtures, figure out how to get power to them. This will depend, in part, on how many devices you're adding.

If you're adding just one exterior receptacle, for example, find the interior receptacle closest to the one you want to add outside. If you position the new receptacle in the same stud bay as the interior receptacle, you'll simplify the task immensely because you won't have to drill through any studs.

Before cutting holes in anything, however, calculate the load on the circuit. Add up the wattage of all the lights and appliances presently in use and the wattage of the new outlet or light you want to add. If the total load on a 15-amp circuit exceeds 1,440w, run a new grounded circuit from the panel to the exterior device instead. Likewise, if you are running power to an outbuilding, run a new grounded circuit from the panel.

Install a 20-amp circuit if your plans call for electrical usage that exceeds the load limits of an existing circuit, includes a large number of receptacles, or contains three or more large flood lamps or other large lighting fixtures rated more than 300w each. If you will be using large, stationary tools in a workshop or heating the area with electricity, you may need to add several 120v and 240v circuits. Again, calculate the loads involved.

Two important points: First, the NEC allows you to tap into a general-use or lighting circuit only. You may not tap into circuits feeding kitchen-countertop receptacles or bathroom receptacles or into any dedicated circuits that supply power to air-conditioners, clothes washers or dryers, or other power-hungry appliances. Second, if you discover that the circuit you'd like to tap into is wired with nongrounded NM cable, BX armored cable, or knob-and-tube—don't tap into that circuit. The new extension may not be properly protected. Instead, run a new grounded circuit from the panel. In addition, don't forget weatherproof housings or covers and GFCI protection.

Finally, take your plans for new circuits or extensions to existing line-voltage circuits to the local building department and have them sign off before you start.

Outdoor safety: Checking codes and utilities

Outdoor outlets and fixtures are exposed to weather; because moisture greatly increases the chance of electrical shocks, local codes are strict about what materials you can use and how they must be installed. In general, you don't need a permit to install low-voltage lights because the chance of shock is low, but if you want to add an outdoor receptacle or a light fixture that uses line voltage (120v or 240v), you'll need a permit.

If you'll be running cable underground, check with local utilities before you dig. Call 811 (or visit www.call811.com). There may be water pipes, gas lines, telephone or cable lines, or electrical cables buried in the yard. Often, utilities will send out a technician to show you where such lines are located. If your lawn has a sprinkler system, note where sprinkler heads are and try to avoid the water pipes that feed them. Remember that only a licensed electrician should install hot tubs and swimming pools and the like because such installations require special grounding methods.

CHOOSING OUTDOOR LIGHTS

There are a wide variety of light fixtures to choose from. For starters, choose line-voltage lights (120v) if you want to deter intruders, accent an architectural feature, or illuminate a work area such as an outdoor grill. To light up a walkway or add accent lights to the landscaping, however, low-voltage lights (12v or 24v) are usually a more economical choice and are generally easier to install. There are also lo-vo solar units (no wiring needed) that charge during the day and glow softly all night.

In general, don't install more light than you need to serve the function for a given area. Outdoor lights that are too bright waste energy and will be too glaring for intimate dining or entertaining at night. Your neighbors will also thank you for not spot-lighting their house when they're trying to relax or sleep.

In addition to overhead lights, side-mounted lights, step-riser lights, in-ground fixtures, post-mounted lights, and stake-mounted lights, there are many switching options. You can control lights with standard on-off switches, timers, motion detectors, and photocells that turn lights on when the sun goes down. Most home centers and lighting stores have a dazzling array to choose from.

Outdoor lights are available **in an array of styles. Here,** Mission-style lights brighten a stone stairway.

ILLUMINATING OUTDOOR LIGHTS

As for your own safety, remember that intruders dislike being in the limelight. Install a security light, and they'll probably go elsewhere. A few tips to make your lights more effective:

- Install motion-sensor lights. Because they are dark until triggered by motion, motion-sensor lights startle intruders. Better-quality sensors can be calibrated so they are activated only when someone nears the house—not by every dog walker on the block.

- Put security lights high on a porch or under the eaves. Lights that can be reached without a ladder can be easily unscrewed. Most security lights have dual sockets so that if one bulb burns out, there's still one shining.

- Light walks and doors. It's easier for you to quickly approach and enter your house if sidewalks and entry doors are lit. Groping for your house keys in the dark is especially ill-advised if you live alone or along a dimly lit street.

- There are also security light kits that turn on lights inside the house if someone approaches or touches a window. And if you're leaving the house for an extended period, put lamps on timers to confuse would-be intruders.

Motion-sensor lights **not only welcome you home but also help keep** intruders away.

TOOLS & MATERIALS

A Use a square-nosed shovel to create shallow slots so you can tuck lo-vo cable into the ground.

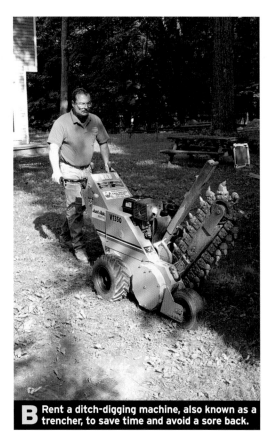

B Rent a ditch-digging machine, also known as a trencher, to save time and avoid a sore back.

The tools you need to install outdoor wiring are pretty much the same ones needed to wire a house interior. The big exceptions, obviously, are digging and earth-moving tools. A *square-nosed shovel* or *spade* is the most useful tool when you're making a shallow slot for low-voltage cable **A**. If you're actually digging a trench, use a trenching shovel with a pointed nose and a reinforced shoulder that you can stamp on with a boot to drive it deep.

Digging trenches is hard work, however; so when the pros have to dig a long or deep one, they rent a gas-powered ditch-digging machine, also known as a *trencher* **B**. A trencher looks like a cross between a pow-ered garden tiller and a chainsaw and typi-cally cuts a trench 4 in. to 6 in. wide, and as

deep as 24 in. Spread sheet plastic on either side of the trench so you can place the dirt from the trench nearby—which makes refill-ing the trench easier. Wear heavy boots, heavy gloves, safety glasses, and ear plugs when operating a trencher.

Materials

The NEC requires that all exterior outlets and circuits have GFCI protection. This pro-tection includes the following:

- A GFCI receptacle installed in a weather-proof box.
- A standard receptacle installed in a weatherproof box protected by a GFCI receptacle installed *upstream* (toward the power source).
- A circuit protected by a GFCI breaker.

Exterior light fixtures do not need GFCI protection. If the box is surface mounted, it needs to be raintight. If the box is recessed in the wall, it does not. The fixture must be listed for *damp locations* if under eaves and listed for *wet locations* if directly exposed to weather.

There are two common types of weather-proof covers (also called raintight covers) (see top photo on the facing page). A *weatherproof while-in-use cover* has a plastic cover that shuts over an electrical cord, such as that used for holiday lights. A *weathertight cover* is a gasketed cover that shuts tight over the receptacles when not in use. For any receptacle exposed to rain or splash, the NEC requires covers to be the "weather-proof in-use" type, per NEC 406.9(B). For receptacles in damp locations but not subject to beating rain or water runoff, a simple weathertight cover is required, but an in-use cover is not required, 406.9(B). Also, all exterior receptacles are required to be of the "weather-resistant" type.

Aboveground, electrical cable must be housed in conduit with raintight fittings (see bottom photo at right). You can use polyvinyl chloride (PVC), thin-walled electrical metallic tubing (EMT) conduit, threaded intermediate metal conduit (IMC), or rigid steel conduit (RSC). PVC fittings are glued together to achieve a raintight fit; EMT conduit uses compression fittings; and IMC and RSC use threaded fittings or compression fittings. *Note:* Common EMT conduit fittings (both setscrew and compression type) are intended for interior use, are not raintight, and therefore are not suitable for exterior use. Look for compression fittings that are identified as raintight.

Belowground, you can run flexible underground feeder (UF) cable at a depth acceptable to local codes—typically, 18 in. deep. Some codes allow you to dig a shallower trench if the cable runs in steel conduit, but because threading steel conduit requires special equipment and advanced skills, it's not a reasonable option for most nonprofessionals.

SAFETY ALERT

Avoid plugging or unplugging devices into exterior receptacles—or using corded power tools outside—when it's raining or snowing.

Raintight (weatherproof) covers include a weatherproof while-in-use receptacle cover with adapter plates (left) and a weatherproof box with gasketed cover (right). Plastic adapter plates enable you to use the cover with a duplex or GFCI receptacle. The weatherproof box gasket is precut, so it accepts either a duplex or GFCI receptacle.

Overview of exterior conduit types, fittings, and boxes: A, 1/2-in. PVC pipe; B, PVC elbow; C, PVC box with unthreaded openings (for slip-in fittings); D, male adapter (MA) PVC fitting, which can be used with a threaded box or conduit; E, RSC pipe; F, RSC elbow; G, LB condulet; H, RSC coupling; I, EMT pipe; J, EMT elbow; K, bell box with three threaded holes; L, threaded EMT compression fitting; M, EMT compression coupling. Note: The LB conduit and bell box accept any 1/2-in. (trade size) threaded fitting—whether PVC adapter, EMT, or RSC.

TAPPING INTO AN EXISTING OUTLET

1 Turn off the power, remove the cover plate, and unscrew the receptacle.

2 Pull the receptacle out of the box and remove the wires attached to its terminals.

3 Use a screwdriver to pry out a knockout.

7 Pull the new cable through and attach a cable clamp.

8 Leaving one ground wire long, use a green grounding nut to splice.

When adding a single outdoor receptacle, it's usually easiest to tap into an interior outlet within the same stud bay. In the installation shown here, the electrician solved the box-capacity problem by replacing the old receptacle with a commercial-grade duplex receptacle. Instead of splicing new and old wires and using pigtails—which would have required twist-on wire connectors and thus a larger box—he joined incoming and outgoing wires by inserting them into terminal holes in the back of the receptacle and then tightened down the terminal screws. *Note*: Wiring a commercial-grade receptacle in this manner is not the same as back-wiring a standard receptacle because standard receptacles have inferior spring clamps that are unreliable.

➡️ **For information about backwiring, see p. 41.**

Start by turning off the power to the receptacle at the panel or fuse box; then use a noncontact tester to make sure the power is off. Remove the cover plate and unscrew the mounting screws securing the receptacle to the outlet box **1**.

Pull the receptacle out of the box, being careful not to touch the screw terminals; then test them again to make sure they're not energized **2**.

Detach the wires from the terminals, fold them out of the way, and look for a knockout in the box to remove. Typically, a pair of knockouts will be hidden beneath an integral cable connector—unscrew it. Then remove a knockout from the outlet box **3**. Drill through the exterior wall and into the same stud bay as the interior receptacle **4**. Then, inside the house, push fish tape through the knockout hole and into the stud bay **5**. Outside, a helper can catch the tape, pull it out of the hole you just drilled, and attach the new cable to it **6**.

Inside, pull the fish tape and the attached cable into the box. Pull about 1 ft. of new cable out of the box and then replace the integral cable clamp **7** to secure the cable. Strip the cable sheathing and splice like wires together, starting with the ground

wires. Use a special green grounding nut to splice the grounds **8**. Use wire strippers to remove 1/2 in. of the insulation from the ends of the hot and neutral wires **9**.

To save space in the old box, insert the stripped wire ends into terminal holes in the back of the commercial-grade receptacle **10**. Because commercial-grade receptacles solidly clamp wire ends, this connection is as solid as any splice. Fold the wires into the box as you push the receptacle into place until it is fully seated in the box—do not use mounting screws to pull the receptacle into the box because this could strip the screw threads. Then replace the cover and screw it into place.

➡️ **See "Mounting & Wiring an Exterior Outlet," on p. 240.**

4 Outside, have a helper drill through the siding.

5 Push the fish tape through the knockout hole, into the stud bay.

6 Outside, retrieve the fish tape and attach the new cable.

9 Use wire strippers to remove 1/2 in. of insulation off wire ends.

10 Connect all wires; gently push receptacle into box.

PRO TIP

To power holiday lights safely, plug them into a GFCI receptacle housed in a water-proof while-in-use box cover. But before installing the lights, calculate the total wattage of all the bulbs so you don't overload the circuit.

ADDING AN OUTDOOR RECEPTACLE

If you tap into an existing receptacle at the end of a circuit, there should be enough room inside the box to bring a cable to feed the new outdoor receptacle. However, if there are already two cables in the box—incoming and outgoing—you may need to replace the existing box with a larger one.

Existing interior receptacle

Incoming cable (from power source)

Weather-proof cover

Pigtails ensure continuous power down-stream.

Gasket

GFCI receptacle

New cable to outdoor receptacle

MOUNTING & WIRING AN EXTERIOR OUTLET

1 Feed the cable through the connector in the box and secure it to the building.

2 Loop the bare ground wire around the green grounding screw.

3 Attach the long ground wire to the green ground screw on the receptacle.

4 Insert wires into terminals: brass screw for hot wire; silver screw for neutral wire.

5 Fold and tuck the wires into the box. Then secure the receptacle to the box.

6 Fit the gasket around the receptacle and screw on the weatherproof cover.

Once the new cable is spliced to the cable in an existing receptacle, feed the cable through the cable connector in the back of the exterior box and mount the box. (The hole drilled in the exterior wall must be wide enough for the cable connector or the box won't sit flat to the wall.) To mount the box, use mounting ears or the small holes in the back. Apply siliconized caulking to the hole before attaching the box. Plumb the box and screw it to the outside of the building **1**.

Strip sheathing from the cable and ground the box by looping the bare ground wire around the green grounding screw. Leave this ground wire long **2**. Use a wire stripper to remove ½ in. of the insulation from the ends of the neutral and hot wires. Next loop and attach the long ground wire to the green ground screw on the GFCI receptacle **3**. Then connect the hot and neutral wires in their respective screw-terminal holes **4**.

If the GFCI receptacle has plaster ears, use diagonal cutters to remove them; otherwise, the receptacle may not fit into the box. Fold the wires and push the receptacle into the box; then screw down the mounting screws that secure the receptacle to the box **5**. A weatherproof gasket is used to keep water away from the wires—set it in place around the receptacle before you attach the cover **6**.

PRO TIP

GFCI receptacles are larger than standard duplex receptacles, so there will not be enough room in a single-gang box if you also need to splice an outgoing cable to feed another outdoor outlet downstream. In that case, install a deep box or install an extension to the single-gang box.

RUNNING POWER TO AN OUTBUILDING

The first step to wiring an outbuilding is to figure out how many lights and outlets you need. If your needs are modest, you may be able to tap into an existing outlet in the main house and extend the circuit from it. Calculate the total loads for the existing circuit and the extension to see if the circuit has enough capacity. Otherwise, run a new circuit from the panel to the outbuilding.

If the outbuilding isn't more than 50 ft. from the house and has a few lights and outlets, it usually can be supplied by a 120v, 20-amp circuit and 12/2 w/grd UF cable. But check with local building authorities before you start. Get the necessary permit, code requirements, and inspection schedules.

The hardest part of the job is usually digging the trench, because local codes typically require it to be 18 in. deep. Fortunately, you can rent a gas-powered trencher, to do the digging for you. After removing the dirt from the trench, pick out any rocks or debris that could damage the cable. Then lay the UF cable in the trench, flattening it as you go **❶**.

>> >> >>

1 As you walk along the trench, unwind the cable. Ideally, it should lay flat in the bottom of the trench.

RUNNING POWER TO AN OUTBUILDING

GETTING POWER FROM THE HOUSE

AT THE OUTBUILDING

LB conduit or weatherproof outlet box

Weatherproof outlet box with cover or LB condulet

Junction box

Adapter

Male adapter (threaded)

³/4-in. PVC conduit

Incoming cable

Coupling

Elbow (sweep)

18 in. min., required by code

Female adapter

Bushing

UF cable 12/2 w/grd

RUNNING POWER TO AN OUTBUILDING (CONTINUED)

Use electrical-grade PVC conduit, couplings, and adapters to protect the UF cable between the bottom of the trench and the outdoor boxes in which connections will be made. At the house, UF cable is typically spliced to an interior wire in a covered single-gang, weathertight box ❷. On the other end, the cable typically passes through an LB condulet and a short length of PVC pipe before terminating in a junction box inside the outbuilding ❸.

2 A PVC stub protects UF cable as it emerges from the ground.

3 Strap rigid PVC pipe (with LB condulet) to the outbuilding.

WORKING WITH PVC CONDUIT

PVC conduit can be heated and bent, allowing you to change pipe direction with far less cutting and fewer fittings than you would need for rigid pipe. PVC conduit is intended to be used outside: It is flexible, durable, and waterproof; but its assemblies are not as protective as metal pipe or cable. Be sure to use only the gray PVC conduit rated for electrical work (also called schedule-40 PVC conduit). White PVC plumbing pipe is unsuitable as electrical conduit; moreover, heating it can release noxious fumes. Wear work gloves to avoid burns when heating gray PVC pipe.

It's best to use a hacksaw with a metal-cutting blade to cut PVC pipe, though any fine-tooth saw will work. Make the cut as square as possible. Use a pocket knife or curved file to remove burrs from the pipe end, then wipe it with a rag. Apply an even coat of PVC cement to the outside of the pipe and the inside of the fitting. If you're bending pipe, screw the threaded adaptor into the outdoor box or conduit first, then glue the bent pipe to the adapter.

To bend PVC pipe, heat it with a MAP-gas torch; one common brand is the Bernz-Omatic. You can also use a hot box or a

PVC heating blanket (Greenlee). Keep the torch point moving constantly, rotate the pipe periodically, and tape the pipe ends to contain the heat and speed up the process. When the pipe droops, it's ready to shape. Place it against an irregular wall or foundation and it will conform to that contour. Strap the pipe close to the outdoor box and the foundation. To secure straps to the foundation, first predrill with a masonry bit. Then insert expandable plastic anchors into the holes and drive strap screws into the anchors.

To bend PVC pipe, heat it with a handheld MAP-gas torch. Rotate the pipe and keep the torch moving to heat the pipe evenly.

When the heated PVC pipe begins to droop, you know it's ready to bend. Shape it to fit the side of the building or foundation.

Use straps to secure the pipe to exterior walls and foundations.

INSTALLING LOW-VOLTAGE PATH LIGHTS

Low-voltage lights make nighttime paths and walkways safer, are easy to install, and pose almost no shock threat. But turn power off to be sure. Always follow the installation instructions that come with your low-voltage kit. Kits usually include light assembles, lo-vo cable, posts, ground stakes, and a timer-transformer power pack whose transformer reduces house current from 120v to 12v.

In the installation shown here, the power pack was mounted inside the garage, so PVC conduit was installed to protect the lo-vo cable as it traveled up the exterior wall into the garage. If you install the power pack outside, you probably won't need conduit. If you do install conduit, start by inserting a fish tape down the conduit ❶. Separate the two wires in the lo-vo cable, snip one, loop and tape the remaining wire to the fish tape, and pull the lo-vo cable through the conduit.

Place the lights where they'll best illuminate a walkway or highlight a landscape feature, then run the lo-vo cable to them ❷. Run cable along the ground and cover it with a few inches of mulch, or use a square-nosed shovel to create a shallow slot for the cable. Stomp on the shovel so it goes down 4 in., then rock the shovel from side to side to create a V-shaped slot ❸. Press the cable into the slot ❹; then stamp your feet to close the soil over the cable.

>> >> >>

Lo-vo light kits typically contain **screw-together parts: lamps, shades, riser posts, and ground stakes.** At right: a coil of lo-vo cable and a power pack–a combination timer and transformer to step down voltage to 12v.

1 After installing PVC conduit, insert a fish tape down the conduit and pull the wires through.

2 Place the lights and run the conduit to each of them.

3 Use a square-nosed shovel to create a small slot to bury the cable.

4 Press the lo-vo cable into the slot, making sure that it's fully covered.

INSTALLING LOW-VOLTAGE PATH LIGHTS (CONTINUED)

Each light fixture has two wire leads that terminate in sharp-pointed cable connectors. When snapped together, the connectors pierce the insulation of the lo-vo wires and supply each light with 12v current **5**. To power the system, attach lo-vo cable wires to the terminals on the power pack **6**. Mount the power pack securely to the wall and plug it into the outlet. Power packs are equipped with timers so that the lights come on and turn off whenever you like—whether you're home or away **7**.

5 Connectors are used to join the cable in the ground to each light.

6 Attach the wires of the lo-vo cable to transformer terminals. (Power is off.)

7 Once hung, plug the power pack into a nearby outlet and set the timer.

LOW-VOLTAGE LIGHT PARTS

Shade

Bulb

DETAIL

Prongs pierce cable.

Post (riser post)

Wire leads to fixture.

Low-voltage cable

Ground stake

Wire leads

RUNNING LO-VO CABLE UNDER A SIDEWALK

The easiest way to run lo-vo cable under a sidewalk is to cut a piece of EMT pipe about 1 ft. longer than the sidewalk is wide. Hammer one end of the EMT shut so it creates a point, then use a hand sledge to drive the EMT under the sidewalk. To prevent closing the end of the pipe you hammer on, hold a scrap of 2×4 against the pipe end as you hit it. When the pointed end emerges from the other side of the walk, use a hacksaw to cut it off. Then feed the lo-vo cable through the EMT pipe.

Scrap lumber prevents damage to open end of conduit.

CLOSE-UP

EMT conduit hammered into a point

Push-on plastic bushing to protect wire insulation

When point emerges, cut off crimped end.

INSTALLING A MOTION-SENSOR LIGHT

Motion-sensor lights require 120v, so they must be mounted on boxes rated for outdoor use. The fixture must be listed for damp locations if installed under eaves or must be listed for wet locations if directly exposed to weather. If you are replacing an existing light with a motion-sensor light, don't assume that the old box is raintight—examine it. Exterior boxes should have flexible gaskets between the box and the fixture base and threaded openings with closure plugs. If the box has only standard knockouts, it's not raintight.

Turn off power to the fixture and test to be sure it is off. Then unscrew the mounting screws securing it to the box. Holding the fixture in one hand, touch a noncontact tester to the wire splices to be sure they are not energized. Disconnect the wire splices; if the existing box is damaged or inappropriate, remove it. The new box must be raintight ❶.

Feed the incoming wires through the cable connector in the back of the box and then attach the box to the wall ❷. Mounting screws should sink into sheathing or into a block screwed to the sheathing. Attach the mounting bar to the box and attach a ground wire to the ground screw on the box ❸ or mounting bar. Splice the ground wires from the box and the incoming cable ❹.

Fit a weatherproof gasket over the cable wires; then splice them to fixture leads: hot to hot, neutral to neutral ❺. Tuck the wires into the box and attach the fixture ❻. Before screwing the bulbs into the sockets, slide waterproof washers onto them ❼. Adjust the motion sensor so that it is triggered by people approaching the house—not by passing cars, dog walkers, and the like.

1 A code-approved outdoor box must be used.

2 Feed incoming wires through the back of the box; then attach the box.

3 The green ground screw ensures a continuous ground path to the box.

4 Splice all ground wires.

5 Slide a weatherproof gasket over the incoming cable wires.

6 Fold all of the wires back into the box; attach the fixture.

7 Waterproof washers around each bulb prevent water from getting into the sockets.

PANELS & SUBPANELS

THIS CHAPTER RECAPS THE BASICS of electrical service; then shows how to create a neat, well-organized panel; install a one-pole breaker (for general-use, lighting, and small-appliance circuits); install a two-pole breaker (for large-appliance circuits); install AFCI and GFCI breakers; and set up a subpanel.

Caution: Only a licensed electrician should work inside an electrical panel. There are several reasons for this caution:

- In service panels, there is an area above the main breaker that stays energized even after that breaker is set to an OFF position (p. 248).
- There is no easy way for a nonprofessional to be sure that an existing system is correctly grounded. In some cases, just removing a panel cover is risky (p. 11).
- Local building codes may specify that any upgrade requiring a permit be done by a licensed electrician.
- Work not done by a licensed electrician may nullify appliance or equipment warranties or even void your homeowner's insurance should a mishap occur.

UNDERSTANDING PANELS

Understanding service panels & subpanels, p. 248

Power to the panel, p. 251

Grounding the system, p. 252

Sizing for the load, p. 253

Organizing a panel box, p. 253

ADDING A CIRCUIT

Adding a circuit, p. 257

Wiring a standard one-pole breaker, p. 258

Testing a new circuit for shorts, p. 259

Installing a two-pole breaker, p. 260

Installing an AFCI breaker, p. 261

INSTALLING A SUBPANEL

Installing a subpanel, p. 262

UNDERSTANDING SERVICE PANELS & SUBPANELS

PERSONAL PROTECTION EQUIPMENT

A qualified person testing or working in a potentially energized electrical panel must wear personal protection equipment (PPE) as specified in NFPA 70E® PPE Hazard Level 1, Table 130.7 (C) (16). "The PPE requirements of 130.7 are intended to protect a person from arc flash and shock hazards." This protective equipment includes the following:

- Hard hat
- Arc-rated long-sleeve shirt and pants or arc-rated coverall
- Arc-rated face shield or arc flash suit hood
- Safety glasses or safety goggles
- Hearing protection (ear canal inserts)
- Heavy-duty leather gloves (over) rubber insulating gloves
- Leather work shoes

Reproduced with permission from NFPA70E-2012, *Electrical Safety in the Workplace*, Copyright© 2011, National Fire Protection Association. This reprinted material is not the complete and official position of the NFPA on the referenced subject, which is represented only by the standard in its entirety.

SAFETY WARNING

In service panels, a small area around the main breaker stays hot even after the breaker is set to the off position. The only way to cut *all* power in a service panel is to pull the meter–which we don't recommend–and which is illegal in many jurisdictions. Typically, only the utility company can cut a meter seal or pull a meter.

Avoid touching the service conductors that attach to the main breaker–they stay hot even when the main breaker is turned off.

LOCK 'EM OUT!

Once you've shut off power in a service panel, tape the panel shut and post a warning sign of work in progress. Pros prefer to use a *panel lockout*, however, which limits panel access to the person holding the key; electrical suppliers and home centers sell them.

P ower from the utility company is typically delivered through three large conductors, which may enter the house overhead or underground. Overhead service wires are called a *service drop*. The drop runs to a *weatherhead* atop a length of rigid conduit. When fed underground, service conductors are installed in buried conduit or run as underground service-entrance (USE) cable.

Whether it arrives overhead or underground, 3-wire service consists of a service neutral and two energized (hot) service conductors–which are also called *Service Phase A* and *Service Phase B*–two phases of alternating current (AC). Three-wire service delivers 120v relative to ground, and 240v between the energized conductors.

>> >> >>

⚠ SAFETY ALERT

If you are at all uncertain whether a panel is energized, do not remove its cover. Call a licensed electrician. Many jurisdictions forbid panel work by nonlicensed electricians.

TESTING: THE KEY TO WORKING SAFELY

Always turn off the power before working on an electrical system. If you are working in a subpanel, turn off the subpanel disconnect in the service panel.

First test the noncontact tester on a receptacle or device that you know is hot. Here, the tester indicates that subpanel breakers are energized.

Test breakers after power to the subpanel has been shut off.

Carefully remove the subpanel cover and touch the tester to the insulated portion of a hot feed or to a main lug.

Use a multimeter, a more sensitive tester, to verify earlier readings. First touch tester probes to Phase A lug (hot) and to the neutral bus.

Test Phase B lug (hot) and the neutral bus.

Test Phase A lug and Phase B lug. If the tester shows no voltage on any of these tests, the subpanel is de-energized and safe to work in.

Cut power inside a service panel by switching off the main breaker, or by removing the main fuse in a fuse box. This de-energizes the hot buses. *Note:* Incoming hot service conductors—and the lugs where they terminate—will still be energized—as shown on the facing page. Unscrew the panel cover and set it aside.

To cut power to a subpanel, flip off the subpanel breaker in the service panel—and lock the service panel so no one can turn the subpanel breaker back on. That should de-energize the subpanel so it can be safely opened and worked in.

But *always test, never guess*. As shown above, we recommend using two testers.

TESTING WITH A NONCONTACT TESTER

Start with a noncontact tester, which can detect voltage through wire insulation. First test the tester to make sure it is working correctly.

Before removing the subpanel cover, touch the tester to several breakers in the ON position. If the tester tip doesn't glow, the panel is probably dead. But keep testing to be sure: Remove the cover and test again inside the panel. Touch the tester to insulated portions of the two main feeds, and to the main lugs.

TESTING WITH A MULTIMETER

Test lugs with a multimeter. Be careful not to touch the bare-metal probes of this tool. Set your multimeter on AC VOLTAGE and touch its probes to hot and neutral *bus lugs* in this sequence:

- Phase A lug (hot) to neutral lug
- Phase B lug (hot) to neutral lug
- Phase A (hot) to Phase B (hot)

If all of these tests do not detect voltage, you can work safely in the subpanel.

UNDERSTANDING SERVICE PANELS & SUBPANELS (CONTINUED)

THREE-WIRE SERVICE DROP

Aluminum/steel "messenger wire"

Service neutral

Service phase-B (hot)

Service phase-A (hot)

A typical 3-wire service drop **consists of two insulated hot conductors wrapped around a stranded bare aluminum wire with an internal steel messenger cable—the bare aluminum wire also serves as a neutral.**

SERVICE ENTRANCES

Older homes may have overhead service, but underground service is increasingly common. The utility's responsibility ends where the service-drop cables are spliced to the service conductors running to the meter. In some areas, Code requires that underground conductors be housed in conduit.

AERIAL SERVICE ENTRANCE

Hot primary

Service drop (3-wire)

Splice point

Weatherhead

Neutral primary

12 ft. min. over driveway

Ground wire

Meter panel

BURIED SERVICE ENTRANCE

Neutral primary

Hot primary

Conduit to bottom of pole

Ground wire

Meter panel

Service laterals (three insulated conductors) buried 4 ft. underground

SERVICE ENTRANCE TO THE EAVES SIDE

When the service drop approaches over eaves, the service riser is sent up through the eaves and the point at which the riser emerges from the roof jack is caulked.

Hot   Weatherhead

Neutral

2 ft. to 3 ft.

Service drop

Service riser

Support braces

Roof jack

Point of attachment 18 in. min. above roof

4 ft. max.

Clamp every 3 ft.

2-in. threaded galvanized steel conduit

Threaded hub

Meter panel

POWER TO THE PANEL

PANELS, SUBPANELS & CONDUCTORS

Inside a meter-main combination panel, before the meter has been installed.

If there's no room left in the main panel, adding a subpanel is a good option.

Hot service conductors

Rigid conduit and service riser

Hot service conductors

Meter base

Neutral/ ground bus (service panel only)

Neutral feed to subpanel

Hot feeds to subpanel

Neutral service conductor

Main breaker

Subpanel breaker

Hot feeds to subpanel

Hot buses

Grounding wire to ground rod

Protective plastic bushing

Ground feed to subpanel

Hot bus lugs

Neutral feed

Hot buses

Ground bus

Neutral bus

Neutral bus

Hot Feeds

Equipment ground conductor

S ervice conductors run to a meter base, where they attach to lug-screws (lugs) on the *line side* of the meter. When a meter is inserted into the base, power flows to the *load-side* meter lugs, and then on to a main disconnect (main breaker) in the *service panel*. As it straddles the two sets of terminals on its base, the meter measures the wattage of electricity as it is consumed.

At the service panel, the two hot service conductors from the meter base attach to lugs on the main breaker. The service neutral attaches to the main lug of a neutral/ ground bus. *Important*: In service panels, neutral and ground wires terminate at a shared neutral/ground bus (or buses). However, *in subpanels and all other outlets downstream* from the service panel, ground and neutral components must be electrically isolated from each other. Thus, in a subpanel, neutral wires attach to a neutral bus and ground wires attach to a ground bus– that is, the buses are separate and electrically isolated.

The two hot feeds (Phase A and Phase B) to a panel energize the *hot buses* that run down the middle and distribute power to various branch circuits when breakers are snapped on to the buses, and circuit wires are attached to the breakers. The two hot buses, electrically separated by a plastic insulator running between them, are named for the hot feeds that energize them: hence, Phase A bus and a Phase B bus. (We will say more about A and B phases in "Installing a Two-Pole Breaker," p. 260.)

GROUNDING THE SYSTEM

A GROUNDING BUSHING

A grounding bushing can be a very important detail. Usually the teeth of a conduit locknut bite into the metal panel enclosure and establish an effective ground. However, where there are concentric or eccentric knockouts (metal punch-outs held by small welds, as seen in this photo), a good ground often cannot be established. So a grounding bushing is used to ensure a good mechanical ground between the conduit and the enclosure. The ground wire that loops through the grounding bushing terminates at the pane's ground bus.

Narrow contact points

Concentric knockout pulling away from panel box

Grounding lug

Grounding bushing

Ground feed from conduit

Ground wire terminates to ground bus

As explained at length in "Working with Electricity" (p. 4), electricity moves in a circuit, eventually returning to its source unless its path is interrupted. The return path is through the white neutral wires that bring current back to the main panel. Ground wires provide the current with an alternative low-resistance path.

Ground wires (more accurately called *equipment grounding conductors*) connect to every part of the electrical system that could possibly become energized—metal boxes, receptacles, switches, fixtures—and, through three-pronged plugs, the metallic covers and frames of tools and appliances. Ground conductors, usually bare copper or green insulated wire, create an effec-

tive path back to the service panel in case the equipment becomes energized. When a breaker detects the excessive flow of a fault current, the breaker trips and shuts off all power to the circuit.

The neutral/ground bus

In the service panel, the ground wires attach to a neutral/ground bus bar, which is bonded to the metal panel housing via a *main bonding jumper*. If there's a ground fault in the house, the main bonding jumper ensures the current can be safely directed to the ground—away from the house and the people inside. It is probably the single most important connection in the entire electrical system.

Some grounding protects buildings

Attached to the neutral/ground bus in the service panel is a large, usually bare, copper ground wire—the grounding electrode conductor (GEC)—that clamps to either a *ground rod* driven into the earth, or an *Ufer grounding electrode* in the footing of a concrete foundation. The primary function of the grounding electrode system (GES) is to divert lightning and other outside high voltages to earth before they can damage the building's electrical system. The GES has almost nothing to do with reducing hazards from wiring problems *inside* the house. That's the role of the equipment grounding conductors.

SIZING FOR THE LOAD

Sizing a service panel is covered in "Planning" (p. 166). Typically, electricians calculate total household loads (ampacity), then add 20 percent to 25 percent for future needs. For a family in a 2,000-sq.-ft. house, a 125-amp service panel is probably adequate, but a 200-amp panel is often recommended for an "average" household in a 3,000-sq.-ft. house that is not heated with electricity. The NEC allows a maximum of 42 breaker spaces in a single panel. If your system still has capacity but you've used up the available panel spaces, add a subpanel. If your needs exceed system capacity, upgrade the service.

→ **For more on calculating household needs, see p. 171.**

Similarly, all conductors—whether they feed a service panel or energize wall outlets—must be sized according to the loads they carry. A home with a 200-amp service panel, for example, should be fed by three 2/0 copper THHN/THWN conductors. Whereas a 15-amp general-use household circuit must be fed with at least a #14AWG cable. If you'd like more information on sizing conductors, get the most recent National Electrical Code or a copy of *Code Check: Electrical* (Taunton Press), which does a good job of summarizing NEC tables. For a thorough discussion of electrical safety, visit the OSHA/ NIOSH website on electrical safety: www.cdc.gov/niosh/docs/2009-113.

ORGANIZING A PANEL BOX

A neat, well-organized subpanel bundles wires to conserve space and improve access. Ideally, wire groups are installed in layers and wires are bent at right angles to buses or breakers. Label short sheathing sections (slugs) to indicate which circuits wires serve.

A neat, well-organized service panel or subpanel is easier and safer to work in; it will also be an easier panel in which to add circuits later on. To create an orderly panel, plan where everything will go and then methodically execute that plan.

Label circuits

In "Rough-in Wiring," we emphasize labeling cables at outlets so that when it comes time to attach wires to devices, you'll always know which switch controls which circuit. Labeling is equally important—perhaps more important—to identify the many cables converging on a panel box. Before you run each cable to the panel, use a permanent marker to write—right on the end of the Romex sheathing—which circuit the cable feeds: "Kitch A," "Bath B," "2d Flr Lights," and so on.

Remove knockouts, insert connectors

Typically, most cables will approach and enter the panel from one direction—from above, if the panel is in the basement. Remove knockouts for the cables, starting with the largest cables, which take up more room and, being stiffer, are more difficult to muscle into place. Insert a cable connector (clamp) into each knockout you remove. Large feeder cables (#4AWG or larger) require insulated fittings (bushings) to protect wire insulation from sharp conduit edges. Most Romex cable,

>> >> >>

ORGANIZING A PANEL BOX (CONTINUED)

however, doesn't require bushings—just appropriately sized cable connectors. Larger circuit cable (#10AWG and #8AWG) fits one per connector, but most household circuit cable (#12AWG or #14AWG) can fit two to a connector—but never more than two. (Cable connectors' capacity is marked on the box or the instruction sheet.)

Strip sheathing, identify hots

Once you have pulled cables into the box and tightened cable connectors, strip Romex cable sheathing, leaving at least ¼ in. of sheathing extending into the panel box. *Note:* As you remove each cable's sheathing, cut off the labeled end and slip that short piece of sheathing (called a "slug") over the end of the cable's hot wire. Bend the wire to keep the slug on. If cable feeds a 240v circuit, slip the slug over both of the cable's hot wires. If a cable hot wire attaches to an AFCI or a GFCI breaker, slide the slug over its neutral, too; the neutral must attach to the AFCI or GFCI breaker, as explained below.

As you strip sheathing, the panel quickly fills up with the "spaghetti" of individual wires; many electricians drive a nail to one side of the box and loosely drape wires over the nail as they strip them, to get them out of the way. Once all the cable sheathing has been stripped, you can loosely group like-wire groups—grounds, neutrals, and hots—in advance of terminating them (attaching wires to lugs) inside the panel. As is customary in all phases of house wiring, terminate the ground wires first.

Snap breakers onto buses

There is no one right sequence for installing panel elements, but many pros prefer to snap in all the breakers to the busing at this point—before terminating any wires. Placing breakers onto the buses gives you an overview of where everything will go and ensures that larger two-pole breakers will be located where they can be wired most easily—and positioned correctly in relation to hot-bus phasing. (More about that in a second.)

Electricians typically put two-pole breakers near the main lugs—in most panels, at the top of the hot buses. Here's why:

1. Two-pole breakers serving 120v/240v or 240v circuits must be correctly *phased*. That is, the top jaws of a 2-pole breaker must clip

PRO TIP
Wiring a panel is complicated, so many electricians divide the task into steps—cutting wires to length, stripping wire ends, bending wires toward a bus, tightening bus screws—and perform each step on all wires before going on to the next step. This greatly speeds a task because each step typically requires only one tool.

ACCORDING TO CODE
By definition, a 120v/240v receptacle will have two hots, one neutral, and a ground. Large appliances such as dryers require 120v/240v wiring because they need 120v to operate their electronic switches or timers. A 240v circuit will have only two hots and a ground—no neutral—because there is no need to derive 120v from a 240v circuit.

PRO TIP
Adding a circuit is easy in a well-organized panel because like-wire groups tend to be installed in layers. Ground wires, installed first, are the bottom layer; then neutrals. Hot wires attach to breakers last, so they are typically the top layer. An electrician in a de-energized panel can carefully slide his hand under the hot-wire layer and lift it *en masse* to gain access to buses or wires underneath, then fold the hots down flat when he's done.

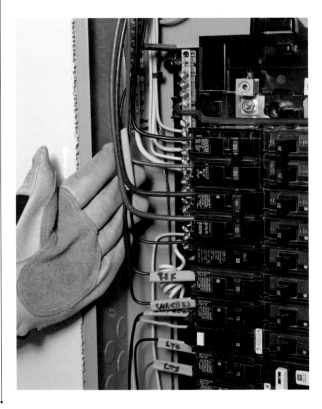

THE IMPORTANCE OF CORRECT PHASING

The two large hot conductors in a service panel or subpanel connect to the two hot buses that distribute power to house circuits. Those two hot wires (and their buses) are called Phase A and Phase B because they are two phases of the alternating current (AC) that are 180° of rotation apart. These phases feed into the house from utility lines. (See the photo on p. 250.)

To balance electrical loads between phases in the panel, bus *blades* (the parts that stick up and breakers snap on to) alternate between Phase A and Phase B as you move up or down a panel. It must be noted, however, that the two buses are electrically isolated from each other by a plastic insulator weaving between them. (The photo at right shows this clearly.)

Wiring a panel can be a straightforward matter if you have an understanding of alternating current and phases; this is another reason why only a licensed electrician should work in a panel. There are certain instances where if you get phasing wrong, you can create hazardous conditions.

A HAZARDOUS EXAMPLE!
Let's say that an amateur electrician runs a 12/3 cable to feed two different 120v circuits. In other words, each of the cable's two hot wires will feed a different circuit, while the circuits share the cable neutral (or "common neutral"). This setup is appropriate only if the two hot wires are connected to different phases (e.g., one hot wire on Phase A and one on Phase B). If the circuit(s) is built correctly, the common neutral will carry the unbalanced return load back to the panel.

If the circuit is built incorrectly and the two hot wires are connected to the same phase, the common neutral will carry the sum of the return loads back to the panel. For example, in a proper installation, if one hot wire in a 12/3 cable is connected to Phase A and carries 15 amps and the other hot wire connected to Phase B carries 18 amps, the common neutral will carry 3 amps (or the unbalanced return load) back to the panel.

However, if both hot wires are connected to Phase A, then the neutral in the same example will carry 33 amps back to the panel (or the sum of the return loads). In this instance, since #12 wire is rated for 20 amps, the neutral would be carrying 165% of its rated capacity—a very hazardous condition.

Moreover, the breakers that the hot wires are attached to *won't* snap off because standard breakers monitor only outgoing current in the hot wires. The 33 amps of combined return current would look normal to the breakers. So current will continue to flow.

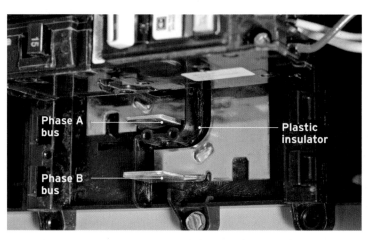

Hot buses are electrically isolated **from each other by a plastic insulator between them.**

Correct:

One wire (black) on Phase A (15A)

One wire (red) on Phase B (18A)

Common neutral carries (3A)

Incorrect:

One wire (black) on Phase A (15A)

One wire (red) also on Phase A (18A)

Common neutral carries (33A): HAZARDOUS!!

---

onto an A-phase bus and the bottom jaws onto a B-phase bus. If you install a bunch of one-pole breakers at the top, two-pole breakers lower down may not land on correct phase-positions on the buses. (The perils of ignoring phasing is discussed above.)

2. If you put larger breakers at the top, you will need shorter runs of large-gauge wire to reach those breakers. No. 10AWG and No. 8AWG wire, for example, are stiff, hard to work with, and take up

space. If you wire large breakers first—when the panel is relatively empty—you will have more room to wrestle stiff wire into place.

3. Snap AFCI and GFCI breakers to buses next, after 120v/240v and 240v breakers are in place. Here, the issue is not the size of wires but the number of them. As you'll see on p. 261, you must attach neutral wires directly to AFCI and GFCI breakers rather than to neutral buses—which means running neutrals slightly longer distances.

>> >> >>

ORGANIZING A PANEL BOX (CONTINUED)

Various breakers. From upper left, clockwise: one-pole 15A, one-pole 20A, one-pole 20A GFCI, one-pole 20A AFCI, two-pole 30A (for 240v loads).

Terminate wires

Your panel layout will determine in part where you attach the wires. In other words, terminate wires on the side they come in, if possible. That's just common sense. Wires making long loops to get to a bus on the other side take up space. Thus, if you have wires coming down from both sides, it makes most sense to divide wire groups. To facilitate this, panels typically have neutral and ground bus bars on both sides.

Attach grounds first. As noted earlier, it's customary to first separate out ground wires and terminate them to a ground bus. So if most of your cables enter at the top of a panel, it's most logical to start at the top of a ground bus bar and work down as you terminate individual wires. In this manner, subsequent wires can come in right over the top of those installed earlier, creating a relatively flat layer.

Bundle wire groups loosely to conserve space but stop strapping bundles just above a bus so you have room to turn wires towards the bus. Take a pair of pliers and turn the first wire toward the bus, noting how long its "leg" must be to reach the bus. Maintain that same length as you terminate subsequent wires, so that all turns are consistent. (Snip excess wire as you go.) That's just a personal preference: The important detail is tightening down bus screws so that each wire is tightly held.

Attach neutrals to buses, except for neutrals that feed AFCI or GFCI breakers. *In a service panel*, attach neutrals to a common ground/neutral bus; *in a subpanel*, attach neutrals to a separate neutral bus. As with grounds, if panel cables come in from the top, start at the top of the neutral bus and work down methodically so subsequent wires will lie flat.

AFCI and GFCI breakers, on the other hand, have factory-attached neutral coils. Attach those coils to a neutral bus, as shown in photo 1 on p. 261. Then terminate circuit-cable neutrals to designated lugs on AFCI or GFCI breakers, as shown in photo 2 on p. 261.

Terminate hots to breakers. As with grounds and neutral wires, move in one direction as you attach hot wires to breakers—typically from top to bottom, if panel feeds enter at the top of the panel. (This will create a flat layer of hot wires with a neat, workmanlike look.) As you did with grounds and neutrals, loosely bundle hot wires till you are ready to start bending them towards breaker lugs. A sweeping bend looks best, so try to maintain that angle for all hot wires as you attach them to breakers on both sides of the panel. Strip $3/8$ in. to $1/2$ in. of insulation from the ends of hot wires before inserting them into breaker lugs. This will ensure that breaker screws will tighten down on bare wire.

If you placed larger two-pole breakers at the top of the hot buses, you will attach larger-gauge wires first. The labeled slugs you slipped on the hot wires will tell you which hot wire attaches to which breaker. Correctly matching wire gauge to breaker amps is essential because both will be rated for the loads that circuit will carry. When attaching the two hot wires served by two-pole breakers, electricians typically maintain the A-B phasing established earlier, to match the Phase-A (black) and Phase-B (red) feeds.

As with all electrical connections, screw breaker lugs tightly on hot wires so there is a solid mechanical connection. This will ensure a good electrical connection.

ADDING A CIRCUIT

A Remove a knockout from the existing panel.

B Insert the threaded shaft of the cable connector (clamp) into the knockout.

C Score Romex cable sheathing lightly to avoid damaging the wire insulation inside.

*O*nly a licensed electrician should work inside a panel. When adding a circuit to an existing panel, first cut the power to the panel and test to be sure it's off. If working in a subpanel, turn off the subpanel breaker in the service panel, where feeds to the subpanel originate. If working in a service panel, the area about the main lugs will always be hot (p. 248)—even when the main breaker is off—so take care to avoid that area and wear appropriate safety equipment (p. 248).

(*Note:* The sequences that follow differ slightly from "Organizing a Panel Box," on pp. 253-256, because they show circuits being added to a subpanel this is already wired.)

After disconnecting power to the panel, remove its cover, determine where the new circuit cable will enter the panel, and use a sturdy pair of needle-nose pliers or a screwdriver to jab out a knockout **A**. Into the knockout, install the appropriate cable connector (clamp) for the cable you're using—in our sequence, NM cable (Romex). Pull the cable through the connector, and tighten the connector to prevent strain on electrical connections **B**. To avoid stressing connections, staple incoming cable within 12 in. of the panel.

Score the cable sheathing by making two diagonal passes and sliding the sheathing off. Or score the sheathing lightly down the middle **C**, peel back the sheathing, and use diagonal cutters to snip it off. Leave at least 1/4 in. of sheathing sticking into the panel. Snap the breaker onto an open space on the bus bar, then rough-cut cable wires so they will be long enough to reach that breaker—you can trim off excess later. Separate the ground, neutral, and hot wire(s) and strip about 3/8 in. to 1/2 in. of insulation off the ends of insulated wires. Torque all bus and breaker lug connections as specified by manufacturer.

WIRING A STANDARD ONE-POLE BREAKER

Typically, 15-amp or 20-amp one-pole breakers control general-use, lighting, or small-appliance circuits; they might also run a furnace, a pool pump, or a garbage disposer. In the photo sequence shown here, a single-pole breaker is being installed in a subpanel whose power has been turned off.

Terminate the ground wire first ❶. In a subpanel, the ground will attach to a separate ground bus bonded to the metal panel. Insert only one ground wire beneath a lug screw. Note the consistent angle of all grounds in which they bend toward the bus. Look closely and you will also see that both ground and neutral wires are bundled with plastic ties to keep the box orderly.

Next strip insulation from the neutral wire and connect it to the neutral bus ❷. Because this is a subpanel, the neutral bus sits atop a black plastic bracket that electrically isolates the neutral bus from the metal panel box.

Snap the one-pole breaker onto a hot bus ❸. The heel of the breaker seats on a plastic cleat and then pivots so that its jaws engage a metal bus sticking up. Press down to seat the breaker securely. Strip 3/8 in. to 1/2 in. of insulation from the end of the hot wire, then connect it to the lug screw on the end of the breaker ❹. *Note:* Before attaching the hot wire, slip on the labeled slug of sheathing that identifies the circuit it feeds. Tighten the breaker lug to secure the hot wire.

Before flipping on the breaker, use a multimeter to test the new circuit for dead shorts as described in "Trade Secret" on the facing page. Once you are certain that the circuit has no shorts, remove a breaker-knockout from the subpanel cover, replace the cover, energize the subpanel, and flip on the new breaker.

1 Connect the ground wire to the ground bus of the subpanel.

2 Connect the neutral wire to the neutral bus.

3 Snap the breaker to a hot bus.

4 Insert the hot wire into the breaker lug and tighten it down.

TESTING A NEW CIRCUIT FOR SHORTS

After terminating (attaching) all circuit wires—but before re-energizing the panel or plugging devices into the circuit—use a multimeter to test the circuit for dead shorts. Set the meter to the resistance setting (ohms).

Touch multimeter probes to the breaker lug (where hot wires terminate) and to the ground bus. Next touch tester probes to the breaker lug and the neutral bus. In other words, hot to ground, then hot to neutral. If the multimeter indicates no dead shorts, the circuit is correctly wired. Remove breaker knockout(s) from the panel dead-front, replace the cover on the panel, and energize the panel. Then flip the breaker on.

Amateur electricians mistakenly think you can use the breaker to test for dead shorts: Don't do it. That's not what a breaker is designed to do. Use a multimeter to test, with the power off. It's the right tool and a safer procedure.

120v twin breaker If your electrical system has unused capacity, but you've run out of breaker spaces, you may be able to replace a standard 12-amp one-pole breaker with a 20-amp twin *(pancake)* breaker. A twin is two slim, one-pole breakers that fit into a standard one-pole breaker space. *Note:* The panel must be designed and listed for the use of such breakers. The number of twin breakers allowed varies—some panels allow none, some allow use of twin breakers in some spaces, some allow their use in every space. It is important to know which spaces in a panel can take twin breakers, because putting in too many circuits can lead to overheating of the panel and the breakers.

TRADE SECRET

After installing a circuit breaker—but before energizing the panel and flipping on the breaker—use a multimeter set to test resistance (ohms). First make sure there are no loads on the circuit (e.g., light fixtures or appliances turned on). Touch the tool's probes to (1) breaker lug and ground bus, then (2) breaker and neutral bus. You are looking for *dead shorts*—a reading of no resistance (0 ohms). If you get a 0 ohms reading DO NOT turn on the new breaker until you correct the problem. Dead shorts are commonly caused by drywall screws or nails driven through a cable, improperly wired devices, or connections in an outlet box that have come apart.

Before re-energizing the panel, test the circuit for shorts. Touch the tester probes to the breaker lug and ground bus, then touch the probes to the breaker lug and neutral bus.

INSTALLING A TWO-POLE BREAKER

In residences, two-pole breakers typically control ovens, dryers, ranges, AC condensers, and other big energy users. The photo sequence at right shows a 30-amp, two-pole breaker being installed in a subpanel. As 120v/240v wiring tends to be appliance-specific, this circuit feeds a dryer receptacle. As the dryer's electronic components need 120v, this 30-amp circuit was wired with 10/3 w grd Romex cable: In addition to two hot wires, the cable contains a neutral wire and a ground.

After calculating that the electrical system had sufficient capacity to add a 30-amp circuit and that there was room in the subpanel for a double breaker ❶, the electrician turned off the subpanel breaker in the service panel and then tested the subpanel to be sure the power was off. That done, he removed the panel cover, removed a knockout in the panel box, installed a cable connector and fed 10/3 w grd cable through it, tightened the cable connector, and removed the cable's protective sheathing.

He terminated the cable's bare ground wire at the subpanel's ground bus, stripped insulation from the end of the neutral wire, and terminated it at the neutral bus. Before snapping a two-pole breaker onto hot buses ❷, he made sure that it would land on a correct A-B bus position, that is, that the top jaws of the two-pole breaker would connect to a Phase A bus and the bottom jaws to a Phase-B bus.

After slipping a labeled slug onto the cable's black hot wire, the electrician terminated it to the breaker's upper lug, then terminated the red hot wire to the breaker's lower lug ❸. He tightened both screws to ensure solid connections, then used a multimeter to test the circuit for *dead shorts*, as described on p. 259. Finding no dead shorts, he removed two breaker knockouts (two-pole breaker) from the subpanel cover, replaced the cover, energized the subpanel, and flipped on the new breaker.

1 Two-pole breakers clamp onto two hot buses. At left, you can see the plastic cleats that receive the heel of the breaker; at right, two hot-bus blades.

2 Place the heel side of the breaker on the plastic cleats, then pivot the breaker so its jaws snap onto hot-bus blades.

3 Attach the circuit ground wire to the ground bus, neutral wire to neutral bus, then two hot wires to two-pole breaker lugs.

INSTALLING AN AFCI BREAKER

Installing a one-pole, 15-amp AFCI (arc-fault circuit interrupter) breaker is exactly the same as installing a one-pole GFCI (ground-fault circuit interrupter) breaker. But before we see how to install one, here is a quick refresher about how each of these code-required devices protects you.

AFCI breakers are designed to detect arcing patterns of current in very short time intervals—such as when there is a loose connection on a receptacle and electricity arcs (jumps) between conductors. Drywall nails or screws puncturing a cable are other common causes of arc faults. When an AFCI breaker detects such patterns, it shuts off power to protect you from house fires.

GFCI breakers are designed to sense an imbalance between the amount of current flowing from the hot wire and returning on the neutral wire, which suggests a ground-fault current is leaking to ground somewhere (see p. 12). GFCIs can detect minuscule (5 milliamp) current leaks and shut off power almost instantaneously—typically within $1/40$ second—to protect people from potentially fatal shocks.

Always turn off power to a panel and test to be sure it's off. After pulling the new circuit cable into the subpanel, the electrician secured it with a cable connector and stripped its sheathing, as described above. As is customary, he first terminated the cable's bare ground wire to the ground bus.

Every AFCI (and every GFCI) breaker has a coiled neutral conductor that is molded into the breaker at the factory. After snapping the AFCI breaker onto a hot bus, the electrician attached that coiled neutral to the neutral bus ❶. The electrician then stripped $3/8$ in. to $1/2$ in. of insulation from the end of the circuit-cable neutral and terminated it to the AFCI breaker-lug, designated by a small white dot next to it ❷. *Note:* Most circuit neutral wires terminate to a neutral bus. But here the circuit neutral attaches to the *breaker* so it can sense fluctuations in current throughout the circuit.

Finally, the electrician stripped insulation from the end of the circuit hot wire and attached it to the remaining breaker lug ❸. He used a multimeter to test for a dead short in the circuit. Finding nothing out of the ordinary, he removed a breaker knockout from the subpanel cover, replaced the cover, and energized the subpanel. Then he flipped the AFCI breaker on and pressed the white TEST button on the face of the breaker. The TEST button should snap off immediately; if it doesn't, the breaker is probably defective and should be replaced immediately. Inspectors are very serious about AFCI protection, so always test AFCI breakers after installing them—even if they are right out of the box.

>> >> >>

INSTALLING AN AFCI BREAKER ————————

1 Terminate the circuit ground wire. Then terminate the coiled, factory-attached white wire of the AFCI breaker to the neutral bus.

2 Next terminate the circuit neutral to the neutral lug on the AFCI breaker. A small white dot on the breaker indicates the neutral lug.

3 Terminate the circuit hot wire to the hot lug on the AFCI breaker.

INSTALLING AN AFCI BREAKER (CONTINUED)

TWO-POLE AFCI BREAKERS

Since the 2008 NEC, AFCI protection is required for branch circuits in all areas inside the house except bathrooms, kitchen, garage, and unfinished basements and attics.

AFCI breakers are wired somewhat differently from conventional breakers, with an integral coiled neutral attaching to the neutral bus, and the circuit neutral attaching to an AFCI breaker neutral-lug. The circuit hot then attaches to the AFCI breaker hot-lug.

This configuration allows an AFCI breaker to monitor current flow throughout the circuit, but it sometimes leads to problems when inexpert installers use 3-wire cable to serve two circuits—one of which must be AFCI-protected and the other is not. Their mistaken solution is to attach one hot wire of the 3-wire cable to an AFCI breaker and the other hot to a regular (non-AFCI) breaker. They then find that the AFCI breaker doesn't work—it keeps flipping off.

The solution: If you want to use 3-wire cable to provide AFCI protection to at least one of the circuits, you must install a two-pole AFCI breaker and attach both hot wires to it. The cable's neutral attaches to the breaker's neutral lug, as described above. In this manner, the AFCI can monitor current flow in both circuits.

If you run 3-wire cable to serve two circuits and at least one of the new circuits must be AFCI-protected, you must terminate *both* cable hot wires to a two-pole AFCI breaker.

PRO TIP

GFCI *breakers* are relatively uncommon because GFCI receptacles are a cheaper way to get protection and easier to access and reset when they trip. A 30-amp GFCI breaker, however, is standard protection for hot tubs.

INSTALLING A SUBPANEL

There are many reasons to install a subpanel:

- Increasingly, main service panels are installed outside so firefighters can disconnect power before going into the house—in this case, a subpanel inside contains all the branch circuits.
- When a system has unused capacity but the service panel has no available slots for more circuit breakers, a subpanel allows for expansion.
- A subpanel distributes power to a separate building.
- A subpanel can offset voltage drops on circuits that are too distant (70 ft. or 80 ft.) from the service panel. In this case, the larger-gauge wires that feed subpanels suffer less voltage drop than the smaller-gauge wires of branch circuits.

Size subpanels based on anticipated loads. If you're adding a subpanel in the same building as the main panel so you can add lighting and general-use circuits, install a 60-amp subpanel with at least 12 breaker slots. If the subpanel is distributing power to a distant building, install a 100-amp or 150-amp subpanel.

People frequently add subpanels when planning a major kitchen remodel, because kitchens have a lot of appliances. Locate the subpanel as close as possible to the kitchen.

When adding a subpanel to an existing system, an electrician first shuts off power at the service panel and tests to be sure the power is off.

If studs are spaced 16 in. on-center, install a standard, $14\frac{1}{2}$-in.-wide panel. Use at least four $1\frac{1}{4}$-in. by 10 screws to mount the panel ❶; screws should embed at least 1 in. into studs. Install the panel at a comfortable height, so it will be easy to wire and access—and make sure that there is room for mandatory clearances about it (see "Locating a Subpanel," on the facing page). Remove a concentric knockout in the panel and install a connector appropriate to the cable or conduit that feeds the panel. Also install a protective cable bushing. Here, the feed is a #2 Romex cable. Pull 3 ft. of cable into the panel, tighten the connector, and strip the cable sheathing ❷. (Note the cross-brace between the studs, just below the panel.)

Code requires that you secure the cable within 12 in. of the panel, but 2/0 cable is stiff. Strapping cable to a stud would force it to enter the panel at a sharp angle, which could stress the knockout. It is far easier to strap the cable to a brace in the middle of the stud bay and run the cable straight into the panel.

Secure the ground wire to the main lug of the subpanel ground bus ❸. Cut the three insulated feed wires, allowing enough extra to loop them gently. Avoid sharp bends, which can damage wire. Strip 1 in. of insulation from the feed ends. Use an Allen wrench or torque wrench to connect the feed wires to their respective lugs ❹. Loop the hot feeds around the perimeter of the panel, distancing them from the neutral feed so there will be an open area through which to run smaller circuit wires ❺. Looping the wire generously also ensures that there will be enough extra cable in case you need to strip and reconnect feed ends later ❻.

1 Use at least four screws when installing a subpanel between 16-in. O.C. studs.

2 Pull the feeder cable into the subpanel; strap the cable to a cross-brace.

3 First connect the ground wire from the feeder cable to the ground-bus lug.

4 Connect the neutral wire to the neutral bus lug.

5 Strip the hot feed ends and attach them to hot-bus lugs.

6 In the completed subpanel, all feeds terminate into lugs.

LOCATING A SUBPANEL

Any panel—whether a main or a subpanel—must have sufficient clearance around it. NEC minimums require 78 in. of headroom, 36 in. free space in front of the panel, and 30 in. across the face of the panel. The panel should be installed at a comfortable height, meaning that no breaker handle may be higher than 72 in.

The area must be dry and easily accessed. Do not install a subpanel in a bathroom, kitchen, or clothes closet. If you install a panel in a fire wall (typically the wall between an attached garage and the living area), you will need to check your local codes for measures required to maintain the wall's fire rating. If you place the panel in an interior wall, a typical subpanel will fit between studs that are 16 in. on-center.

78 in.

30 in.   36 in.

GLOSSARY

ACCESSIBLE Not permanently concealed by the structure or finishes. Able to be accessed without damaging the building.

AMPACITY (AMPS) The amount of current a circuit or conductor can safely carry (conduct). Measured in amperes (amps).

AMPS The measure of the number of electrons flowing through a system (current).

ARC FAULT CIRCUIT INTERRUPTER (AFCI) A circuit breaker designed to de-energize a circuit within a period of time if it senses arcing. An arc is a spark between conductors or connections.

BONDING JUMPER (MAIN) Conductor connecting the neutral conductor to the grounding electrode conductor in a service panel.

CABLE An assembly of several conductors. Most often refers to plastic- or metal-sheathed cable that contains several individual wires.

CFL Compact fluorescent lightbulb

CIRCUIT (BRANCH) Circuit originating at a circuit breaker or fuse in an electrical panel and feeding utilization equipment (lights, switches, receptacles, appliances).

CIRCUIT BREAKER A device intended to de-energize a circuit if current exceeds specified parameters.

CONDULET A conduit body with a cover designed to act as a pulling point in a conduit run, to change conduit direction, or as an intersecting point of multiple conduit runs.

CONDUCTOR Technically, anything that conducts electricity. Most often, it denotes a wire.

CURRENT The flow of electrons in a system. Current is measured in amperes (amps). There are two types of current: DC (direct current) and AC (alternating current). Typically, AC is found in homes and buildings.

ENERGIZED Live. The presence of voltage in a circuit or conductor.

FEEDERS Large conductors that supply a service panel, subpanel, or other high current piece of equipment.

FIXTURE A light fixture (table lamp, sconce, chandelier, recessed can, etc.).

FUSE BOX A metal box designed to house fuses installed for circuit protection.

GROUND A connection to earth (the ground). To make such a connection.

GROUND BUS A piece of metal designed to connect multiple wires to a grounding electrode conductor.

GROUNDING CONDUCTOR A wire in an electrical system designed to bond metal parts of the electrical system to the earth (ground).

GROUNDING ELECTRODE CONDUCTOR A wire of a gauge determined by the ampacity of a service panel that connects the service panel (and ground bus) to a grounding electrode (ground rod or equivalent).

GROUND FAULT A fault situation in which an energized conductor or piece of equipment comes in contact with grounded metal parts.

GROUND FAULT CIRCUIT INTERRUPTER (GFCI) A special receptacle or circuit breaker intended to protect people by de-energizing a circuit within a specific period of time if current to ground exceeds specified parameters.

GROUND SCREW A green-colored screw used to connect ground conductors to boxes and devices.

LED Light-emitting diode.

LINE SIDE The direction from which power enters; also referred to as "upstream." The direction from the device toward the circuit breaker or fuse.

LISTED Equipment and materials included on a list published by an organization, acceptable to the authority having jurisdiction, that states that the equipment or materials meet specific design criteria or are suitable for the use intended. Most commonly UL (Underwriter's Laboratory) listed.

LOAD SIDE The direction toward which power is consumed; also referred to as "downstream." The direction from the device away from the circuit breaker or fuse.

LOCATION, DAMP Protected from weather and not subject to saturation (under eves, canopies, etc.).

LOCATION, DRY Not subject to moisture (interior, protected from weather).

LOCATION, WET Underground; exposed to weather; subject to saturation.

LUG A screw-terminal used to clamp down a bare-wire end. Lugs come in a range of sizes. Main lugs secure incoming feeders; breaker lugs secure circuit wires that terminate in circuit breakers.

MAIN CIRCUIT BREAKER A large-ampacity circuit breaker that protects and acts as a means to de-energize a service panel or subpanel.

MC Metal clad cable

NEMA National Electrical Manufacturers Association.

NEUTRAL The neutral or grounded conductor (not ground conductor) is the return path for current in an electrical system; designated by a white or light (or natural) gray color. The neutral is bonded to ground at the service panel.

NEUTRAL BUS A piece of metal designed to connect multiple wires to the neutral conductor.

OHMS The measure of resistance to the flow of electrons (current).

OVERLOAD A situation in which the current flowing through a circuit or circuit conductor exceeds the safe operating ampacity of the conductor.

PLUG The device at the end of an appliance or light fixture cord (cord cap) that is designed to connect the appliance or fixture to a receptacle. (The plug on your lamp fits into the receptacle in the wall.)

RECEPTACLE Device designed for the connection of a plug.

ROMEX Type of NM cable, sheathed with nonmetallic material.

SERVICE PANEL (MAIN PANEL) The primary electrical panel located immediately after the meter socket and housing the main circuit breaker or main fuses and/or other devices designed to de-energize and protect circuits.

SERVICE DROP Conductors from the utility pole to the point of connection (weather head).

SERVICE-ENTRANCE CONDUCTORS (OVERHEAD) Conductors between the point of connection (meter lugs) and a point outside (weather head) connected to the service drop.

SERVICE-ENTRANCE CONDUCTORS (UNDERGROUND) The conductors between the point of connection (meter socket) and the utility transformer or secondary pull box (service lateral).

SCREW SHELL The metal conductive interior body of a light socket or fuse holder with large threads (or ridges) that allow a bulb or fuse to be screwed in.

SPLICES The point at which two wires or conductors are joined or connected together. For branch circuits, splices are commonly made with pressure connectors (wire nuts).

SUBPANEL An electrical panel that is supplied from a service panel and is installed either to provide additional circuit breakers or to distribute branch circuits at a distance from the service panel.

SWITCH A device that opens and closes a circuit, controlling the operation of a light fixture, fan, other equipment, or appliances.

VOLTAGE, NOMINAL (VOLTS) A value assigned to a circuit or system to designate its class. Modern single family residences in the U.S. typically have 120/240v systems.

VOLTAGE TO GROUND (VOLTS) The difference in potential (voltage) between a single energized conductor and ground (neutral or equipment ground).

WATERTIGHT Enclosures built to prevent the intrusion of moisture.

WATTAGE (WATTS) A measure of power consumed.

WEATHERPROOF Equipment or enclosures built so that weather will not interfere with their operation.

WIRE A generic term for an individual conductor, most often used when specifying its size, such as # 12 AWG (Average Wire Gauge).

PHOTO CREDITS

Unless noted below, all photos appearing in *Wiring Complete* are by Michael W. Litchfield.

Chapter 1

p. 10: Photo by Brian Pontolilo, courtesy of *Fine Homebuilding*

Chapter 2

p. 19, 20 (right), 21, 22 (top left and middle), 34: Photos by Sandor Nagyszalanczy

p. 23 (bottom left), 31 (bottom right), 33 (bottom right): Photos by Andy Engel, courtesy of *Fine Homebuilding*

p. 28 (right), 31 (top): Photos by Brian Pontolilo, courtesy of *Fine Homebuilding*

p. 29 (top): Photo by Scott Phillips, courtesy of *Fine Homebuilding*

p. 31 (bottom left): Photo by Charles Bickford, courtesy of *Fine Homebuilding*

Chapter 6

p. 137 (left), 138, 139: Photos by Justin Fink, courtesy of Fine Homebuilding

p. 137 (right): Photo courtesy of www.mountsmadesimple.com

Chapter 7

p. 149: Photo by Charles Miller, courtesy of *Fine Homebuilding*

p. 151 (top): Photo by David Edrington

p. 155 (right top and bottom): Photos © Ken Gutmaker

p. 156 (top): Photo by Brian Pontolilo, courtesy of *Fine Homebuilding*

p. 158 (bottom): Photo by Jason McConathy

p. 161: Photos courtesy of Casablanca Fan Company (www.casablancafanco.com)

p. 163, 164: Photos by Tom O'Brien, courtesy of *Fine Homebuilding*

Chapter 8

p. 168 (right), 169 (both top), 170: Photos courtesy of Roger Robinson, Star Inspection Group

p. 174: Photo by Brian Pontolilo, courtesy of *Fine Homebuilding*

p. 179: Photos by Muffy Kibbey

Chapter 9

p. 204 (top): Photos by Ken Gutmaker

Chapter 11

p. 241 (top), 242 (both top): Photos by Chris Green, courtesy of *Fine Homebuilding*

INDEX

A

AFCIs (arc-fault circuit interrupters), 174, 254, 255-56, 261-62
Aluminum wiring, 170
Amps, volts, and watts, 6, 171
Analyzers, 19, 22
Appliances, 220-31
  about: overview of wiring, 220
  baseboard heaters, 230
  basics of, 222-23
  common, requirements, 222
  dishwashers, 225
  garbage disposers, 224-25
  laundry setups, 228-29
  oven outlets/connections, 226-28
  small, circuits, 172, 175
  unfinished cords (preparing), 223
  water heaters, 231
Audio systems. See Multimedia

B

Backstab devices, 41
Back-wired devices, 41
Baseboard heaters, 230
Bathroom circuits/lighting, 172, 175
Bathroom fans, 151-57
Boxes
  capacity of, 23
  ceiling, 79, 93, 197, 205
  for ceiling fans, 162-63
  choosing, 23-24
  code requirements, 173
  connectors and clamps, 24, 30
  covering all connections, 54, 173
  cut-in, 24
  cutting holes for, 204
  fill worksheet, 23
  getting edges flush, 49
  grounding, 173
  installing, 25, 79, 93, 162-63,
    196-97, 204-05
  locating, 25, 49, 194, 195, 196-97
  metal vs. plastic, 23-24
  mounting between joists, 27, 192
  old, new devices with, 62
  removing knockouts, 26
  retrofitting, 205, 207
  sizing devices to match, 62
  surface, metal, 218-19
  symbols for, 178
  wall, 25, 196
Building codes, 173-74. See also
    Inspections
  boxes, 173, 193
  cable, 173, 193
  checking, 3, 4, 176, 234
  circuit breakers, 193
  circuit wiring, 173
  code requirements, 193
  general wiring guidelines, 173
  general-use circuit requirements,
    174
  GFCIs, 39, 46
  grounding, 173, 193
  homeowner work allowed?, 176
  outdoor wiring, 234

  receptacles, 25, 174
  rough-in, 193
  wire connections, 173, 193

C

Cable rippers, 19, 20, 32
Cables. See also Multimedia
  AC, installing, 213
  armored, stripping, 20
  code requirements, 173, 193
  connectors. See Connectors, wire/
    cable
  corner feeds, 200
  drilling for, 198
  evaluating condition of, 170
  fishing, 201-03, 217, 238, 239
  flexible metal (installing), 212-14
  home run, marking, 199
  isolating low- from line voltage,
    139
  low-voltage. See Low-voltage (Lo
    Vo or LV) fixtures
  MC, installing, 214
  nail plates protecting, 199, 207
  nonmetallic sheathed (NM or
    Romex), 28
  ordering, 193
  pulling, 199, 207
  reading codes on, 29
  securing to framing, 31, 199
  service panel attachment, 10
  standoffs/clips for, 31, 199
  stapling, 31, 199
  stripping, 32-33
  supporting, requirements, 193
  12/3, 12/2, 14/3, and 14/2, 28, 29
  types of, 28, 29
  from utility service, 8, 99, 171, 250
Ceiling fans, 161-65, 178
Ceiling fixtures. See Lighting
Chandeliers, 80-81
Circuit analyzers, plug-in, 19, 22
Circuit breakers. See also Service
    panels
  AFCI, 174, 254, 255-56, 261-62
  amp ratings, 10
  code requirements, 193
  cutting power at, 15
  GFCI, 254, 255-56, 261, 262
  lockouts, 189, 248
  one-pole, 258
  repeated tripping of, 171
  snapping into buses, 254-55
  testing, 259
  twin, 259
  two-pole, 260
Circuits
  adding, 172, 257-62
  bathroom and kitchen, 172, 175
  capacities, 171
  code requirements, 173, 174
  dedicated, 172, 175, 222
  load calculation, 172
  overloaded, 171
  requirements by room, 175
  wiring requirements, 173
Clamps and clips, 24, 30, 192

Compact fluorescents (CFLs), 68,
    69, 71
Conduit, 215-19
  about, 28
  bending, 216
  directional fittings, 216
  EMT (electrical metallic tubing),
    212, 215, 237, 244
  fishing wire through, 217
  fittings, 216, 237
  flexible, 29
  grounding, 28, 219
  illustrated, 29
  laundry setups with, 228-29
  measuring pipe length, 228
  moisture and, 212
  PVC, 29, 212, 237, 242
  receptacles, metal boxes and, 218
  running power to outbuilding,
    241-42
  under sidewalks, 244
  tapping into existing outlet, 217
  types of, 28, 29, 237
  underground, 237, 241
  wiring outlets and, 219
  working with, 215-17, 228-29, 242
Connectors, wire/cable, 30, 34, 35,
    192, 212
Connectors/jacks, multimedia, 116,
    128-32
Continuity testers, 22, 106
Cordless power tools, 19, 21
Current, defined, 6
Cut-in boxes, 24
Cutters and pliers, 19, 20

D

Dedicated circuits, 172, 175, 222
Diagonal cutters, 19, 20
Dishwashers, 225
Doorbells, 106-11
Drill bits, 21, 191
Drill extension, 191
Drilling for cable, 198
Drills, 21, 190, 191
Drywall saws, 20
Dust masks, 7, 190

E

Electrical notation (systems), 178
Electrical systems. See also Planning
    new work; Rough-in wiring
  components, illustrated, 8-9 (see
    also specific components)
  inspecting/evaluating, 168-72
  service drops/entrances, 8, 9, 171,
    250
  sizing of, 171-72
Electricity, understanding, 6

F

Fans, 148-65
  about: overview of wiring, 148
  bathroom, 151-57
  integral junction boxes in, 150
  range hoods, 158-60
  remote inline, 151
  roof vents for, 153-54
  wiring schematics, 150
Fish tape, 19, 21, 191
Fishing cable, 201-03, 217, 238, 239
Floor plan, developing, 176-77
Fluorescent fixtures, 86-87. See also
    Compact fluorescents (CFLs)
Fuse boxes, 11, 15, 168-69, 171-72
Fuses
  amp ratings, 10
  blown, 11, 171
  "pennying," 168
  types of, 11

G

Garbage disposers, 224-25
GFCI breakers, 254, 255-56, 261, 262
GFCIs (ground-fault circuit interrupt-
    ers)
  boxes for, 23, 62, 240
  code requirements, 39, 46
  for exterior outlets, 236, 237, 239
  functions of, 8, 14, 44, 174
  gas cooktop use precaution, 222
  multiple-location protection, 181
  in old boxes, 62
  single-location protection, 181
  sizes (amps), 39
  symbol for, 178
  wiring, 45-46, 239
Grounding. See also GFCIs (ground-
    fault circuit interrupters)
  basics of, 12-14
  bushings, 252
  cable and conduit systems, 28, 219
  code requirements, 173, 193
  equipment, 222
  service panels, 12-14, 168-69, 173,
    252
  subpanels, 10, 251, 252
  ungrounded outlets, 44, 170

H

Halogen bulbs, 69, 70, 73, 103
Hammers, 20
Hand tools, 19, 20, 190
Headlamps, 20
Holes, cutting, 190-91, 204, 205

I

IC-rated, 68, 76
Incandescent bulbs, 69
Incandescent fixtures, LED retrofit, 78

Inspections, 3, 177, 188–89. *See also* Building codes
Inspectors, reviewing plans, 177

K

Kitchen circuits/lighting, 172, 174, 175. *See also* Lighting
Knob-and-tube wiring, 28, 170

L

Lamps, defined, 68
Lasers, 190, 194, 195
Laundry setups, 228–29
Leads, defined, 68
LEDs, 68, 69, 72–74, 87
Levels, 20, 190
Light box, defined, 68. *See also* Boxes
Lighting, 66–103. *See also* Switches, wiring
    basics, 68
    bathroom, 175
    bulb types and technologies, 69
    ceiling box for, 79, 93
    ceiling fixture elements, 75
    chandeliers, 80–81
    disconnecting ceiling fixtures, 80
    for electrical work, 20
    fan-light combinations, 165
    general, 174
    installing ceiling fixtures, 81–85
    kitchen, 174, 175
    LED fixture conversion, 74
    "listing" requirements, 76
    load calculation, 172
    low-voltage. *See* Low-voltage (Lo Vo or LV) fixtures
    mounting fixtures, 75–76
    outdoor. *See* Outdoor wiring
    recessed, 82–85, 209
    removing fixtures, 77
    safety precautions, 76, 77
    sample plan, 178–79
    symbols for fixtures, 178
    task, 174
    terms, 68
    undercabinet fluorescent, 86–87
    wall sconces, 77–78
Line voltage, defined, 68
Lineman's pliers, 19, 20
Load calculation, 172
Load ratings, 39
Low-voltage (Lo Vo or LV) fixtures, 68, 88–103. *See also* Transformers
    attaching feed rods and fixtures, 96
    canopies, 89, 92, 95
    installing cable lighting system, 89–96
    installing light fixtures, 103
    installing monorail track lighting, 97–103

keeping line-voltage cables separate, 139
    mounting box for, 93
    outdoor path lights, 243–44
    running and tensioning cables, 90–91
    schematics, 89, 97
    standoffs, 89–90, 98
    systems overview, 88
Low-voltage controls, 104–13
    about: overview of repairing/ replacing, 104
    doorbells, 106–11
    thermostats, 112–13
Lumens, defined, 68

M

Main breaker, 10–11
Media distribution panels, 122–26
Meter-mains, 11
Meters, 8, 9
Motion detector, wiring, 64
Motion-sensor lights, 235, 245
Multimedia, 114–47
    about: overview of wiring, 114
    basic wireless controls, 143
    cable, 116–17
    cable isolation for, 139
    connecting cables at panel, 126
    connectors and jacks, 116, 128–32
    faceplate connections and options, 131–32
    installing cable connectors, 128
    installing wall-hung TV, 137–39
    integrating whole-house systems, 142–43
    media distribution panels, 122–26
    multi-room audio systems, 145–46
    outlets, locating/installing, 127
    phone lines and jacks, 118–21
    signal strength, 116
    speaker retrofit, 133–34
    stripping cable, 116–17
    twisted wires, 117
    USB charger/receptacle combo, 135–36
    whole-house control systems, 140–44
Multimeters, 22
Multi-tools, oscillating, 21, 191

N

National Electric Code® (NEC), 3, 173
Needle-nose pliers, 19, 20
Neon voltage testers, 16, 22
Nipple, defined, 68
Non-contact testers, 16–17, 19, 22, 42
Nonmetallic sheathed (NM or Romex) cable, 28
Notation, electrical, 178
Nut-driver bits, 190, 191
Nuts, push-in, 63

O

Ohms, defined, 6
Oscillating multi-tools, 21, 191
Outdoor wiring, 232–45
    about: overview of, 232
    adding receptacles, 239
    choosing lights, 235
    getting power, 234
    holiday lights, 239
    low-voltage path lights, 243–44
    motion-sensor lights, 235, 245
    outlets, 240
    planning, 234
    power to outbuilding, 241–42
    running cable under sidewalk, 244
    safety precautions, 234
    tapping into existing outlet, 238–39
    tools and materials, 236–37
    weatherproof covers, 236–37
Outlets. *See* Receptacles
Oven outlets/connections, 226–28

P

Panels. *See* Service panels
Phasing importance, 255
Phone lines and jacks, 118–21
Pigtails, 223
Planning new work, 166–85. *See also* Building codes
    about: overview of, 166
    adding outlets and circuits, 172
    assessing wiring condition, 170
    developing floor plan, 176–77
    electrical notation (symbols) for, 178
    electrical system overview, 8–9
    getting feedback, 177
    inspecting fuse box/breaker panel, 168–69
    load calculation, 172
    materials lists, 176, 177
    on-site inspections, 177
    pro's take on rewiring, 170
    remodeling kitchens, 172
    requirements by room, 175
    reviewing plans with inspector, 177
    sample plans (lighting/switches, and power), 178–79
    sizing system, 171–72
    wiring schematics, 180–85 (*see also* Receptacles, wiring; Switches, wiring)
Pliers and strippers, 19, 20
Plug-in circuit analyzers, 19, 22
Plumb laser, 194
Polarized receptacles, 38, 39, 44
Power, defined, 6
Power tools, 21, 190–91
Primary wires, defined, 68
Programmable thermostats, 113
Pulling grips. *See* Swivel kellum grips
Push-in nuts, 63

R

Range hoods, 158–60
Receptacles, 38–49. *See also* GFCIs (ground-fault circuit interrupters); Receptacles, wiring
    about: overview of, 36
    adding, 172, 239
    amp ratings, 39
    attaching wires to, 41
    backstab, 41
    back-wired, 41
    choosing, 38–40
    circuit capacities, 171
    code requirements, 174
    4-pole, 4-wire, 229
    grounding, 44, 170, 173
    high-quality hybrid, 41
    load calculation, 172
    locating, 25, 48, 194, 195, 196
    making flush to drywall, 48–49
    matching load ratings, 40
    neutral wires attached to, 42
    120/240, 185, 229, 254
    outdoor, 240
    polarized, 38, 39, 44
    screw terminals, 41
    spacers (caterpillars) building up, 48
    surface metal boxes for, 218–19
    symbols for, 178
    tapping into existing, 238–39
    testing, 16–17, 42
    three-prong, 8
    two-slot ungrounded, 44, 170
    USB charger combo, 135–36
Receptacles, wiring, 208
    controlled by switch, 184–85
    duplex receptacles, 43–44, 180–81
    at end of circuit, 180
    ganged receptacles, 181
    GFCIs, 44, 45–46, 62, 181
    in mid-circuit, 43, 180
    options, 180–81, 184–85
    split-tab receptacles, 47, 184–85, 225
Recessed lighting, 82–85, 209
Reciprocating saws, 21
Repeaters, 141–42, 144, 146
Romex (nonmetallic sheathed cable), 28
Roof vents, 153–54
Rotary cutters, 21
Rough-in wiring, 186–203
    about: overview of, 186
    box locations, 194, 195, 196–97
    code requirements, 193 (*see also* Building codes)
    conduit systems, 215–19
    corner cable runs, 200
    creating wiring trench, 206
    cutting box holes, 204, 205
    drilling for cable, 198
    fishing cable, 201–03, 217
    inspection, 188–89
    installing boxes, 196–97
    laying out job, 194–95
    materials for, 192–93
    metal cable, 212–14

ordering materials, 193
outlet box, 208
pulling cable, 199, 207
recessed light can, 209
retrofitting boxes, 205, 207
starting and organizing, 188
switch boxes, 210-11
tools for, 190-91

S

Safety. *See also* Grounding
    avoiding shocks, 12
    evaluating system, 168-72
    gear, 7, 190
    general guidelines, 7
    lighting fixtures, 77
    respecting power, 4, 7
    service panels, 7, 11, 189, 248
    wiring in orderly way, 44
Safety glasses, 7
Saws, 20, 21, 191
Sconces, 77-78
Screwdrivers, 19, 20, 190
Secondary wires, defined, 68
Service conductors, 8, 9
Service drops/entrances, 8, 9, 171, 250
Service panels, 10-11, 246-63. *See also* Circuit breakers; Subpanels
    about: overview of, 246
    cable attachments, 10
    components, illustrated, 10, 11, 251
    cutting power at, 15
    grounding, 12-14, 168-69, 173, 252
    how it fits into system, 9
    inspecting/evaluating, 168-69
    internal workings, 10-11
    knockouts and connectors, 253-54
    labeling circuits, 253
    main breaker, 10-11
    meter-mains, 11
    neutral/ground bus, 10, 13-14, 185, 251, 252, 256, 259
    organizing, 253-56
    phasing importance, 255
    power to, 251
    safety precautions, 7, 11, 189, 248
    sizing, 171-72, 253
    terminating wires, 256
    testing, 249, 259
    understanding, 248-56
7-in-1 tool, 20
Smart grids, 140
Solenoid voltage testers, 22
Source (supply) wires, 68
Speaker retrofit, 133-34
Splicing wires, 35, 63, 64, 190, 193
Staples, 31, 199
Stepladders, 20, 190
Strippers and pliers, 19, 20
Stripping cable, 32-33, 116-17
Subpanels. *See also* Service panels
    about: overview of, 246
    connection between panels and, 29, 189

cutting power to, 249
grounding, 10, 251, 252
installing, 262-63
meter-mains and, 11
phasing importance, 255
safety precautions, 169
testing, 249
understanding, 248-56
Switches, 38-42. *See also* Switches, wiring
    about: overview of, 36
    attaching wires to, 41
    backstab, 41
    back-wired, 41
    choosing, 38-40
    code requirements, 174
    dimmer, 56-57
    four-way, 50, 62
    high-quality hybrid, 41
    locating, 194, 195, 196
    matching load ratings, 40
    motion detector, 64
    neutral wires attached to, 42
    replacing (single-pole), 54-55
    roughing in (three-way), 59
    sample plan, 178-79
    screw terminals, 41
    single-pole, 50-55
    symbols for, 178
    testing, 42, 49
    three-way, 50, 59-61, 182-84
    timer, 65
    vacancy/occupancy sensors, 64
    wireless, 58
Switches, wiring, 50-65, 210-11
    with back-fed wiring, 52, 61, 165
    controlling receptacles, 184-85
    with fixture at end of cable run, 182
    four-way, 62
    ganged switches, 182, 211
    loops, 52-53, 61
    options, 182-85
    single-pole, 50-51, 210
    slide dimmers, 56-57
    specialty switches, 63
    three-way, 59-61, 182-84
    timers, 65
    vacancy/occupancy sensors and motion detectors, 64
    wireless switches, 58
Swivel kellum grips, 21, 202
Symbols, common, 178

T

Tape measures, 20, 190
Television, wall-hung installation, 137-39
Testing
    receptacles, 16-17, 42
    service panels/circuit breakers, 249, 259
    switches, 42, 49
    testers for, 19, 22
    testing, 7
    transformers, 104, 106, 107-08

Thermostats, 112-13
Timer switches, 65
Tool belts, 20, 191
Tools, 18-22, 190-91, 236. *See also* *specific tools*
Transformers
    doorbell, 106-08
    functions of, 68, 78
    installing, 89, 93-94, 97, 99-100
    testing/troubleshooting, 104, 106, 107-08
    types of, 88
Trench, wiring, 206

U

Undercabinet fixtures, 86-87
USB charger/receptacle combo, 135-36
Utility knife, 19, 33

V

Vents, roof, 153-54
Volts, amps, and watts, 6, 171

W

Water heaters, 231
Watts, volts, and amps, 6, 171
Whole-house control systems, 140-44
Wire
    aluminum, 170
    choosing, 34
    splicing, 35
    strippers/crimpers, 19
    types of, 34
Wire connector driver, 190
Wire connectors, 34, 35, 192
Wire reels, 20, 190, 191
Wireless audio systems, 145
Wireless controls, 143
Wireless switches, 58
Wiring. *See also* Receptacles, wiring; Switches, wiring; *specific components*
    assessing condition of, 170
    code requirements, 173
    new work. *See* Planning new work; Rough-in wiring
    push-in nuts for, 63
    safety precaution, 44